Alternative Voices in Muslim Southeast Asia

The ISEAS – Yusof Ishak Institute (formerly Institute of Southeast Asian Studies) is an autonomous organization established in 1968. It is a regional centre dedicated to the study of socio-political, security, and economic trends and developments in Southeast Asia and its wider geostrategic and economic environment. The Institute's research programmes are grouped under Regional Economic Studies (RES), Regional Strategic and Political Studies (RSPS), and Regional Social and Cultural Studies (RSCS). The Institute is also home to the ASEAN Studies Centre (ASC), the Singapore APEC Study Centre, and the Temasek History Research Centre (THRC).

ISEAS Publishing, an established academic press, has issued more than 2,000 books and journals. It is the largest scholarly publisher of research about Southeast Asia from within the region. ISEAS Publishing works with many other academic and trade publishers and distributors to disseminate important research and analyses from and about Southeast Asia to the rest of the world.

Alternative Voices in Muslim Southeast Asia

Discourse and Struggles

EDITED BY
NORSHAHRIL SAAT • AZHAR IBRAHIM

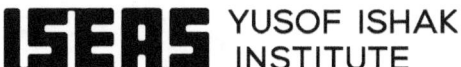
YUSOF ISHAK INSTITUTE

First published in Singapore in 2020 by
ISEAS Publishing
30 Heng Mui Keng Terrace
Singapore 119614

Email: publish@iseas.edu.sg
Website: bookshop.iseas.edu.sg

All rights reserved. No part of this publication may be reproduced, stored in a retrieval system, or transmitted in any form or by any means, electronic, mechanical, photocopying, recording or otherwise, without the prior permission of the ISEAS – Yusof Ishak Institute.

© 2020 ISEAS – Yusof Ishak Institute, Singapore

The responsibility for facts and opinions in this publication rests exclusively with the authors and their interpretations do not necessarily reflect the views or the policy of the publisher or its supporters.

ISEAS Library Cataloguing-in-Publication Data

Name: Norshahril Saat, editor. | Azhar Ibrahim, editor.
Title: Alternative voices in Muslim Southeast Asia : discourse & struggles / edited by Norshahril Saat & Azhar Ibrahim.
Description: Singapore : ISEAS – Yusof Ishak Institute, 2020.
Identifiers: ISBN 9789814843805 (paperback) | ISBN 9789814843812 (pdf) | ISBN 9789814843829 (epub)
Subjects: LCSH: Islamic modernism—Southeast Asia. | Islamic renewal—Southeast Asia. | Islam—21st century—Southeast Asia. | Islam and politics—Southeast Asia. | Islam and state—Southeast Asia. | Islamic sociology—Southeast Asia. | Muslims—Southeast Asia.
Classification: LCC BP173.25 A46

Typeset by International Typesetters Pte Ltd

Contents

Preface	vii
About the Contributors	xi

Overview-Opinion Pieces

1. The Politics of Islamic Discourse in Malaysia   1
   Norshahril Saat

2. Civil Society–State Engagements on Religion in Malaysia   9
   Dina Zaman

3. Religious Orientations in Contemporary Indonesia   17
   Pradana Boy

4. Inhibited Reformist Voices: The Challenge of Developing Critical Islamic Discourse in Singapore   22
   Azhar Ibrahim

Progressive Islam As Alternative Voices

5. Religious Resurgence amongst the Malays and Its Impact: The Case of Singapore   33
   Noor Aisha Abdul Rahman

6. The Trials of the Progressive: Malay Literary and Cultural Expressions in Singapore   67
   Azhar Ibrahim

7.	The Meaning and Objectives of Progressive Islam *Syed Farid Alatas*	89
8.	Mainstreaming Alternative Islamic Voices in Malaysia *Norshahril Saat*	118

Challenges Facing Alternative Voices

9.	Democracy and the "Conservative Turn" in Indonesia *Zainal Abidin Bagir and Azis Anwar Fachrudin*	139
10.	Sunni-Shia Reconciliation in Malaysia *Mohd Faizal Musa*	156
11.	Contemporary Human Rights Issues in Indonesia *Ahmad Suaedy*	183
12.	Ahmadiyah and Islamic Revivalism in Twentieth-Century Java, Indonesia: A Neglected Contribution *Ahmad Najib Burhani*	199

Index   221

Preface

In the past, Southeast Asia has been regarded as the bastion of "moderate Islam". Some argue it is the "smiling face of Islam" compared to Muslim societies in the Middle East, where Islam originated 1400 years ago. Southeast Asian Muslims have always shown respect for local beliefs, traditions and cultures while remaining committed to their faith. The ulama or religious elites of the past did not consider respecting local traditions as compromising their religion. However, events in the 1970s, known as the Islamic revivalist period, led to Muslims in Southeast Asia embracing more conservative interpretations of Islam. Malaysia, Indonesia and Singapore have shown an "Islamist turn", some say. Muslim religious elites are promoting traditionalist discourses that are holding the community back from progress and modernity.

Recent episodes in the three countries feed this narrative. Chief among them was the 2016 mass rallies in Indonesia that sought to challenge Chinese-Christian governor Basuki Tjahaja Purnama, also known as Ahok. He was campaigning for re-election to the Jakarta governorship in 2017 when one of the speeches he gave was interpreted as constituting blasphemy. Ahok later lost the Jakarta election and was sentenced to jail. The mass protests were led by ultra and firebrand conservative Habib Rizieq Shihab. Indonesian president Joko Widodo was also banking on the rising conservatism to stay in power. In the April 2019 presidential election, in which he sought re-election, he chose the conservative Ma'ruf Amin as his running mate, despite the latter's controversial position towards minority Shias, Ahmadis and liberals. Jokowi won the election, which means Ma'ruf will serve as his vice-president between 2019 and 2024. In 2005, Ma'ruf endorsed the SIPILIS fatwa—anti-secularism, pluralism and liberalism—when he was head of the MUI (Ulama Council of Indonesia) fatwa committee. Ma'ruf has also concurrently been the chairman of MUI and Nahdlatul Ulama (NU) since 2015, making him the leader of the largest Muslim organization in the country. This book presents chapters on Indonesia that deal with issues pertaining to minority rights under the first Jokowi government. In the same vein, one chapter discusses the contribution of the Ahmadiyah to modernist Islamic discourse in the country, despite the group being seen as a deviant sect today. Another chapter addresses the debates surrounding the "conservative turn" in Indonesia and questions whether this is really taking place.

The situation in Malaysia underwent a significant change after the May 2018 general election, which saw an end to the sixty-one-year rule of the Barisan Nasional government. The Pakatan Harapan government was swept into power, led by its leader, ninety-two-year-old Mahathir Mohamad. Some of the chapters in this book examine the policies undertaken by the Barisan Nasional government towards minorities, such as liberals and Shias, and address the question of whether there will be any significant change under the new regime. These chapters also examine whether progressives have the space to voice their views in a revivalist environment. To be sure, some people who were activists during the Islamic revivalist period of the 1970s held key positions in the previous Barisan Nasional government, and the same case applies for the current Pakatan Harapan government. Some of them have become mentors to young politicians and officials in government. On the other hand, the book also tackles engagements civil society has had with the government, under both the Barisan Nasional and Pakatan Harapan.

Singapore, too, has experienced changes on the Malay-Muslim leadership front. First, Masagos Zulkifli replaced Dr Yaacob Ibrahim as the Minister-in-charge of Muslim Affairs in 2018. In the same year, the Islamic religious council of Singapore (Muis) also celebrated its fiftieth anniversary. While issues beleaguering the Malay-Muslim community—which constitutes 13 per cent of the five million population—normally centre on radicalism, especially reports of individuals supporting radical groups such as ISIS or Jemaah Islamiah (JI), less attention has been given to minority groups such as Shias, Ahmadis and the so-called liberals. Muslims in Singapore are predominantly Sunnis, while the Shiites represent a tiny minority. Due to the majority of Muslims in Singapore being predominantly of Malay ethnic descent, the issues members of this ethnic group in the country face are invariably intertwined with Muslim/Islamic issues, and vice-versa. Any Islamic issues that are brought to attention in the public sphere obviously focus on the Malay community. As a minority group, and with its socio-economic position being at the lowest rung in the country, the Malay Muslim community is facing a tremendous challenge to attain a decent level of socio-economic progress. It is also not uncommon for the fact of Malays in Singapore lagging behind in various dimensions of development to be linked to the cultural deficit, alongside Islam's purported conservatism and fatalism. An important question is how are progressive Islamic ideas articulated in the public sphere dominated by individuals from the same stream? Or, could progressive ideas be articulated by the religious elites themselves? The book examines some of the controversial ideas promoted in Singapore and how progressive views are being silenced. Yet, progressivism does not necessarily come from the religious elites, but also includes articulations from members of the Malay literati.

Who are the alternative voices? Despite the growing conservative views among the religious elites, there are groups promoting alternative ideas to those promoted by the religious establishment. These groups not only call for Islam to be practised according to context, they also agree that multiculturalism and secularism are the only way forward for harmonious living in diverse societies such as Singapore, Malaysia and Indonesia. They believe in respecting the tenets spelt out in the constitutions of their respective countries that guarantee freedom of religion. This book hopes to showcase the challenges and struggles faced by the champions of alternative discourses in the face of a growing conservative climate. It examines how state and quasi-state institutions and ordinary citizens police groups or individuals promoting alternative ideas. It also explores the avenues utilized by the progressives in championing their vision.

This book features articles by scholars, activists and observers. We have kept the authors' preferred writing styles as far as possible to bring out the key messages of their works. Some of the writers themselves have been victims of repression and discrimination by both quasi-state and non-state actors, and we want to ensure their voices of struggle are represented. Most of the pieces here are academic in nature, while others are shorter think pieces in the form of opinion editorials. These shorter pieces provide an overview of the case studies and concepts discussed in the later chapters.

The editors would like to express our gratitude to Director of the ISEAS – Yusof Ishak Institute Mr Choi Shing Kwok and Director of Konrad Adenauer Stiftung (KAS) Mr Christian Echle for supporting the publication of this book. We wish to record our special thanks to our partners from KAS and the Department of Malay Studies at the National University of Singapore (NUS) for making this publication possible. We wish to thank ISEAS Publishing for their professional help, especially Mr Ng Kok Kiong, Head of ISEAS Publishing, and Mr Stephen Logan. Special thanks also goes to Ms Aninda Kurnia Dewayanti for her editorial assistance.

Norshahril Saat
Azhar Ibrahim

About the Contributors

Ahmad Suaedy is currently an Ombudsman of the Republic of Indonesia 2016–21 and Dean of the Faculty of Islamic Archipelago (Islam Nusantara Faculty) for undergraduate, master's and doctoral programmes at Nahdlatul Ulama University of Indonesia (UNUSIA), Jakarta. He received his doctoral degree on Islamic Studies from the State Islamic University Sunan Kalijaga Yogyakarta. Suaedy is a Founder and former Executive Director (2003–12) of the Wahid Institute; Founder and former Director (2013–16) of the Abdurrahman Wahid Center at the University of Indonesia; and Founder and Director (2014–present) of the Institute of Southeast Asian Islam (ISAIs) UIN Sunan Kalijaga Yogyakarta. He is interested in several research themes, including minority rights, Islamic politics, social inclusion, conflict and reconciliation, social movements, and separatism movements. Suaedy has written and edited several books, including *Gus Dur, Islamic Archipelago and Multicultural Citizenship/Gus Dur, Islam Nusantara dan Kewarganegaraan Bineka* (2018); *Islam, Minorities and Identity in Southeast Asia* (2018); and *Intolerance, Revitalization of Traditions and Challenges of Indonesian Diversity/Intoleransi, Revitalisasi Tradisi dan Tantangan Kebinekaan Indonesia* (2017). Together with Ota Atsushi and Okamoto Masaaki, he edited *Islam in Contention: Rethinking Islam and the State in Indonesia* (2010). He also writes for various national and international journals. He is a member of the International Editorial Board of *Walisongo* Journal, issued by Universitas Islam Indonesia (UIN) Walisongo, Semarang, Jawa Tengah, and is a reviewer for Jurnal *Masyarakat*, of Departemen Sosiologi Universitas Indonesia (UI). Private library: www.suaedy-library.net.

Ahmad Najib Burhani is Senior Researcher at the Indonesian Institute of Sciences (LIPI), Jakarta. He received his doctorate in Religious Studies from the University of California–Santa Barbara in 2013. During the last year of his study he won the Professor Charles Wendell Memorial Award from UCSB for academic achievement in the field of Islamic and Middle Eastern Studies. He received his master's degrees from the University of Manchester, United Kingdom (MSc in Social Research Methods & Statistics) and Universiteit Leiden, the Netherlands (MA in Islamic Studies). Najib Burhani was selected as a member of the elite group of Indonesian Young Scientists of the Indonesian Academy of Sciences (AIPI). He has been active in publishing articles in academic journals such as the *Asian Journal of Social Science, Indonesia and the Malay World, Islam and Christian-Muslim Relations, SOJOURN: Journal of Social Issues in Southeast Asia, Contemporary Islam,* and *Asian Politics & Policy.* He has also contributed articles for edited volumes published by Palgrave Macmillan Press, Amsterdam University Press and ISEAS. His books include *Sufisme Kota* (2001), *Islam Dinamis* (2001), *Tarekat Tanpa Tarekat* (2002), *Muhammadiyah Jawa* (2010), *Muhammadiyah Berkemajuan* (2016), and *Menemani Minoritas* (2019). Najib Burhani currently serves as the editor-in-chief of the journal *Masyarakat dan Budaya* and is on the editorial board of the journal of *Contemporary Islam* and the *International Journal of Islamic Thought* of the National University of Malaysia (UKM).

Azhar Ibrahim is Lecturer at the Department of Malay Studies, National University of Singapore (NUS). He obtained his doctorate and master's from the same department. His doctoral dissertation focuses on humanism and intellectualism among the Malay literary intelligentsia, while his MA thesis deals with the study of religious orientations as reflected in feudal Malay society and its continuities in the present. He majored in both Malay Studies and Southeast Asian Studies at NUS. He teaches Malay-Indonesian literature and ideologies of development. His research interests include the sociology of religion, the sociology of literature and critical literacy, and Malay-Indonesian intellectual development. Among his published books are *Emancipated Education* (2019), *Historical Imagination and Cultural Responses to Colonialism and Nationalism: A Critical Malay(sian) Perspective* (2017), *Menyanggah Belenggu*

About the Contributors   xiii

Kerancuan Fikiran Masakini (2016), *Contemporary Islamic Discourse in the Malay-Indonesia World: Critical Perspectives* (2014), and *Narrating Presence: Awakening from Cultural Amnesia* (2014).

Azis Anwar Fachrudin currently works as a researcher at the Center for Religious and Cross-cultural Studies (CRCS), Gadjah Mada University, Yogyakarta. He completed his bachelor's degree in Arabic Literature in 2013 and obtained his master's from CRCS in 2016 following his graduate student fellowship at the Asia Research Institute (ARI), National University of Singapore. His latest publications include *Linguistik Arab: Pengantar Sejarah dan Mazhabnya* (2017) and *Polemik Tafsir Pancasila* (2018). He has penned many opinion columns for the *Jakarta Post* and Indonesian newspapers since 2014, mostly on the topic of Islam in Indonesia. During Indonesia's 2019 elections he was an Indonesia Correspondent Fellow for *New Mandala* (an academic blog based at the Australian National University's Coral Bell School of Asia and Pacific Affairs), specifically covering issues on Islam and social change.

Dina Zaman is a former columnist who wrote about Muslim life in Malaysia. She wrote for Malaysiakini.com, the *Malaysian Insider* and the *Malay Mail Online*. In 2007 she wrote a book, *I AM Muslim*. In 2017, her latest book, *Holy Men Holy Women* was published. With friends, she founded IMAN Research in 2015. The main focus of IMAN's work is on countering violent extremism and on deradicalization. IMAN Research has worked on violent extremism among urban and rural youths, on refugees and radicalization, voluntary repatriation in Sabah, and young peoples' perceptions of Malaysia's regime change. She is a former British High Commissioner Chevening scholar and a Senior API Fellow.

Mohd Faizal Musa (also known as Faisal Tehrani) is a Research Fellow at the Institute of the Malay World and Civilization (ATMA), National University of Malaysia (UKM). The *Jakarta Post* (28 August 2017) called him "Malaysia's Rebel Author". Andrew Fowler, famous Australian journalist and author of *The Most Dangerous Man in the World*, stated that Faisal's translated works into English, *The Nurse* (*Misi*) and *Crises* (*Kegawatan*), were "great narratives on the battle for ideas and freedom in Malaysia". Seven of Faisal's literary works were banned by the previous Malaysian government. His best remembered novels are *1515* and *Profesor*, which has been translated into English by Brigitte Bresson as *The Professor*. Among his key academic publications are "The Malaysian Shi'a: A Preliminary Study of Their History, Oppression, and Denied Rights" (*Journal of Shi'a Islamic Studies*, 2013); "The Axiology of Pilgrimage: The Malaysian Shi'ites Ziyarat to Iran and Iraq" (*International Journal of Philosophy of Culture and Axiology*, 2013); "Religious Freedom in Malaysia: The Reading of the Qur'an 2:256" (*The Qur'an in the Malay-Indonesian World*, Routledge Studies in the Qur'an, 2016); and "State-backed Discrimination against Shia Muslims in Malaysia" (*Critical Asian Studies*, 2016). He is now an Associate of the Global Shi'a Diaspora at the Project on Shi'ism and Global Affairs at the Weatherhead Centre for International Affairs, Harvard University.

Noor Aisha Abdul Rahman is currently an Associate Professor at the Department of Malay Studies, Faculty of Arts and Social Science, National University of Singapore (NUS). Her research and teaching areas include Malay legal history, Muslim law and its administration in Southeast Asia, Muslim marriage and family and the sociology of religion, with a focus on Islam and Malay religious orientations. She has authored and edited books and articles on Islamic religious elites, the sharia legal system in Singapore, Muslim marriage and divorce, madrasah education and Muslim women and development.

Norshahril Saat is Fellow at the ISEAS – Yusof Ishak Institute. In June 2015 he was awarded his doctorate in International, Political and Strategic Studies by the Australian National University (ANU). His research interests are mainly on Southeast Asian politics and contemporary Islamic thought. In 2018 he published three books: *The State, Ulama, and Islam in Malaysia and Indonesia*; *Tradition and Islamic Learning: Singapore Students in the Al-Azhar University*; and *Islam in Southeast Asia: Negotiating Modernity*. His earlier books include *Faith, Authority and the Malays: The Ulama in Contemporary Singapore*; *Majulah! 50 Years of Malay/Muslim Community in Singapore* (co-edited with Zainul Abidin Rasheed); and *Yusof Ishak: Singapore's First President*. His articles have been published in journals such as the *Asian Journal of Social Science*,

Contemporary Islam: Dynamics of Muslim Life, *Review of Indonesian and Malaysian Affairs*, and *Studia Islamika*. He has also published numerous opinion and think pieces, including those in local newspapers such as the *Straits Times*, *Berita Harian* and *Today*; and international newspapers such as the *Canberra Times*, *Bangkok Post* and the *Jakarta Post*.

Pradana Boy is a lecturer in Islamic Studies at the Faculty of Islamic Studies, University of Muhammadiyah Malang, Indonesia. From 2015 to 2018 he led the Center for the Study of Islam and Philosophy (Pusat Studi Islam dan Filsafat) at the same university. He was trained as an Islamic legal scholar at the University of Muhammadiyah Malang, where he received his degree in Islamic Legal Studies (2000). In 2007 he obtained his Master of Arts in Asian Studies from the Australian National University (ANU). He pursued his doctorate at the Department of Malay Studies, National University of Singapore and completed his studies in 2015. His publications include *Fatwa in Indonesia: An Analysis of Dominant Legal Ideas and Modes of Thought of Fatwa-Making Agencies and Their Implications in the Post-New Order Period* (2018). Pradana is currently serving the Indonesian Government as Assistant to Presidential Staff for International Religious Affairs.

Syed Farid Alatas is Professor of Sociology at the National University of Singapore. He has a joint appointment with the Malay Studies Department at the university. His areas of interest are historical sociology, the study of epistemicide, the sociology of religion, and inter-religious dialogue. His books include *Alternative Discourse in Asian Social Science: Responses to Eurocentrism* (2006), *Ibn Khaldun* (2013), *Applying Ibn Khaldun* (2014), and *Sociological Theory beyond the Canon* (co-authored with Vineeta Sinha, 2017).

Zainal Abidin Bagir teaches at the Center for Religious and Cross-cultural Studies, Graduate School of Gadjah Mada University, Indonesia. He is also a board member of the Indonesian Consortium for Inter-religious Studies, Yogyakarta. He was a visiting lecturer at the Department of Religious Studies, Victoria University of Wellington, New Zealand (2013–14). In 2008–13 he was the Indonesian Regional Coordinator for the Pluralism Knowledge Programme, a collaboration between four academic centres in the Netherlands, India, Indonesia and Uganda. His two main research interests are the democratic management of religious diversity, and religion and science, with an increasingly greater focus on ecology. His recent publications include a report on Indonesia's defamation of religion law (2018), a chapter on governance of religions in the *Routledge Handbook of Contemporary Indonesia* (2018) and a contribution on Islam and ecology in the *Routledge Handbook of Religion and Ecology* (2017).

Overview-Opinion Pieces

1

The Politics of Islamic Discourse in Malaysia

Norshahril Saat

In 1987, academic and political observer Chandra Muzaffar published a seminal work, *Islamic Resurgence in Malaysia*, analysing the rise of religiosity in Malaysian society and its impact on Malaysian social, economic and political life. The community's outlook was undergoing change: more urban dwellers wanted to be in touch with religious values, and this meant embracing conservative teachings. Chandra defined Islamic resurgence to mean "the endeavour to establish Islamic values, Islamic practices, Islamic institutions, Islamic laws, indeed Islam in its entirety, in the lives of Muslims everywhere. It is an attempt to re-create an Islamic ethos, an Islamic social order, at the vortex of which is the Islamic human being, guided by the Quran and Sunnah."[1] The causes were multifold. Malaysia was undergoing political and economic changes with Mahathir Mohamad taking over as the country's prime minister in 1981. The country was also undergoing rapid urbanization and industrialization, and those from the working class sought to strengthen their religious values so that they could have some form of spirituality to fall back on. Second, international events that seemingly oppressed the Islamic world—such as Arab wars, the Palestinian issue and the Soviet invasion of Afghanistan in 1979—led to Malaysian Muslims wanting to be part of the global *ummah* and to stand up against imperialists. Islamist literature is used to strengthen anti-colonial sentiments. The Iranian revolution of 1979 was also significant because it inspired many Muslims to believe the leadership of the ulama (Islamic religious elites) could generate social change. The Iranian revolution sparked interest in many Islamic societies, including Malaysia, because they saw Islam as a force to unite fragmented societies against the West and oppression. This also meant the ulama could lead a revolution and provide the necessary leadership to mitigate their hardships.

In the 1980s and 1990s, Islamic institutions were built and expanded. While the Malaysian government intended to out-Islamize PAS (Islamic Party of Malaysia)—which was also undergoing reforms after infighting in the 1970s—some of these institutions supported Mahathir's pro-capitalistic, industrialization and development models. It was during this period that the state began to support Islamic finance, banking and the halal economy.

The discourse promoted by the Muslim resurgence glosses over past cleavages between the traditionalists and modernists. For centuries the two camps have not been able to settle differences over rituals. The traditionalists, broadly, are close to the Malay courts and practise rituals such as mass prayers for the dead, celebration of the prophet Muhammad's birthday (*maulid*), visitations to graves of pious Muslims (*ziarah*), and special supplications during morning prayers (*qunut*). The modernists frown upon these practices. While such contestations still exist, even between the religious officials and ulama (mufti), both camps agree on the need for the public dominance of Islam. They however cannot agree how to operationalize the vision of an Islamic state and society.

Malaysia is undergoing an era of post-Islamic revivalism today. The promotion of sharia-based ideas, instruments and institutions is no longer a struggle, but has been integrated into the social psyche of the masses. In fact, society has become so overzealous in guarding Islamic institutions and revivalist ideas that it is no longer possible to argue against them. For example, there have been instances of Muslims not wanting to consume food without halal labels, even though this is permissible on religious grounds. Interestingly, even bottled water is produced with halal labels. Malaysian Muslims are becoming overly sensitive to the issue of food and halal labelling. In 2016 the media covered a controversy over Auntie Anne's "pretzel dogs" snack. Jakim (Malaysia's Federal Department of Islamic Development), which oversees halal certification, initially refused to issue the certificate because the name of the sausage contains the word "dog".[2] To be sure, halal certificates did not exist prior to the 1970s, and the idea is still foreign to many Islamic societies in the Middle East.

At the discursive level, Malaysia has gone down the route of Islamizing knowledge. Malaysian Islamic universities (or Islamic faculties or departments) have adopted this approach in their curricula. The idea may have originated with Ismail Faruqi, but in Malaysia it was popularized by Syed Muhammad Naquib Al-Attas through his book *Islam and Secularism*. Modules on Islamization of modern sciences were offered in Malaysia, and students have been taught to integrate the sciences with theology. These ideas have then been exported to neighbouring Indonesia and Singapore. The promoters of the idea, which began in ISTAC (International Institute of Islamic Thought and Civilization), based in IIUM (International Islamic University Malaysia), have now moved to the Centre for Advanced Studies on Islam, Science, and Civilisation (CASIS) of the Malaysian Technological University (UTM). CASIS offers such courses as the Islamic philosophy of science and the Islamization of contemporary knowledge.

State Responses to Islamization

Past Malaysian prime ministers have portrayed the country as practising moderate Islam. Mahathir, for example, in 2001, during his first term as prime minister (1981–2003), pointed out that Malaysia is an Islamic state. His vision to amalgamate Islam and development earned him significant respect from the international community. US president George W. Bush hailed him as a moderate Islamic leader in the aftermath of the 9/11 attacks.[3] The Abdullah Badawi government (2003–9) invested heavily in promoting civilizational Islam, called Islam Hadhari, which highlighted ten principles, including piety and faith in Allah, a just and trustworthy government, mastery of knowledge, cultural and moral integrity, and protecting the environment. Islam Hadhari however remained at the discursive level and had only a minimal impact on the masses. Under Pak Lah's leadership (what Abdullah Badawi is affectionately called), there were complaints by minority groups of their rights being disrespected. A major complaint against his government was the neglect of minority Indian communities, leading the Hindu Rights Action Force (HINDRAF) to garner support, as well as a failure to clamp down on conservatives.

After coming to power in 2009, Prime Minister Najib Razak introduced the 1Malaysia concept to emphasize the country's multicultural outlook. On Islam, the prime minister hailed Malaysia as promoting Islam Wasattiyah (or moderate Islam). Najib's attempts at promoting an image of moderation, and for that matter progressive Islam, was no different from those of his predecessors Abdullah Badawi and Mahathir Mohamed (1981–2003). The two earlier leaders had also played the foreign policy card for domestic gains—by portraying Malaysia as the voice of moderation in the international community—in order to out-Islamize the opposition party PAS. Nevertheless, it was under Najib's government that book banning was common. Several of Dr Faisal Tehrani's novels were banned. Also banned was a compilation of articles by a group of academics and retired bureaucrats calling themselves G25. As will be discussed in the chapters in this section, progressive voices were restricted under Najib's watch.

Academics and activists in the county may have a counter view about the country's moderate image, and their contention not only centres on security issues. On the one hand, the threat of radicalization is real. There have been reports of Malaysians sympathizing with the cause of the international terrorist group ISIS (Islamic State in Iraq and Syria), including some in the civil service and the army. The Malaysian police have been keeping a close watch on some members of the armed forces after it detected some security personnel sympathizing with the radical group.[4] The government is wary of youths being attracted to ISIS ideology. So far the Malaysian police have arrested more than 150 people suspected of having ties to ISIS.[5]

Besides security threats and radicalization, scholars have painted a generally gloomy picture of moderate Islamic thought in Malaysia. Some have expressed their disappointment that Malaysia is undergoing a conservative turn. Others have mentioned that Malaysia is undergoing Arabization, meant in a negative light, that the Malays are neglecting the essence of their culture and mimicking Arabs. Leading the charge that Malays are becoming Arabized—particularly with reference to the rise of Wahhabi/Salafi ideology—have been activists and the Sultan of Johor Ibrahim Iskandar. Comments made by the Sultan of Johor should not be taken lightly, given that in Malaysia the Malay Rulers are the custodians of Islam and Malay culture. However, the growing assertiveness of the federal religious bureaucracy—namely, JAKIM—has eclipsed the authority of the rulers on religious matters. Under the Najib Razak administration, the institution's budget was reported to be as high as a billion ringgit, surpassing what is necessary, given its role. Ultimately, the strength of this federal bureaucracy resulted from the Islamization agenda that began under the first Mahathir government in response to the Islamic resurgence movement.[6]

Given the alleged rise of puritan ideas in Malaysia and the strengthening of the authority of federal religious institutions, there are doubts whether alternative discourses can flourish in the country. In general, groups and individuals presenting counter viewpoints have been targeted by the religious authorities. According to the Malaysian constitution, Islam is the religion of the federation, and other religions have the right to exist in the country. However, recent incidents, such as the ruling against the use of the term "Allah" by non-Muslims; the debates on ACT 355, which is intended to increase the maximum punishments for sharia laws; and the right to convert minors to Islam after one of their parents has converted to the religion seem contrary to the religious freedom accorded by the constitution. In fact, in 2018, Malay-Muslims staged a huge protest against Pakatan Harapan's plans to ratify the International Convention on the Elimination of All Forms of Racial Discrimination (ICERD). Non-Muslim groups are not the only ones targeted by the religious elites; Muslims who hold different viewpoints are also penalized. Overall, only those who adhere to the Sunni school of thought are allowed to preach in states. Groups holding views the religious authorities define as liberal or feminist are also targeted and harassed by the religious elites.

Resurgence ideas and thought, and the support given to these by the previous governments, have resulted in it being a challenge for progressive ideas to penetrate society. If they remain uncurbed, these ideas may penetrate key institutions further. Much hope rests on the current Pakatan Harapan government to reverse these trends and for subsequent governments to follow up to ensure that the multicultural and multi-religious space of Malaysia can be preserved.

Notes

1. Chandra Muzaffar, *Islamic Resurgence in Malaysia* (Petaling Jaya: Fajar Bakti Sdn Bhd, 1987), p. 2.
2. Norshahril Saat, "The Key Forces underlying the 'Pretzel Dogs' Controversy", *Straits Times*, 25 October 2016.
3. The first Mahathir government co-opted key Islamic figures into the government and developed Islamic institutions and think-tanks to promote the government's Islamic agenda.
4. "Malaysia Police Keep Tab on Armed Forces after Detecting ISIS Sympathisers: Report", *Straits Times*, 6 December 2014.
5. Mohd Azizuddin Mohd Sani, "ISIS Recruitment of Malaysian Youth: Challenge and Response", 3 May 2016, Middle East Institute, https://www.mei.edu/content/map/isis-recruitment-malaysian-youth-challenge-and-response (accessed 11 September 2017).
6. Chandra Muzaffar, *Islamic Resurgence*.

2

Civil Society–State Engagements on Religion in Malaysia

Dina Zaman

Malaysia has an estimated population of 31.7 million, of which 28.4 million are citizens. While the country is seen as multi-ethnic, the dominant ethnic group is made up of Malays/Bumiputras (68.6 per cent) who are predominantly Sunni Muslims and considered the original settlers of the land. Malaysia is composed of thirteen states and operates within a constitutional monarchy under a Westminster-style parliamentary system. The Federal government controls most policies and decision-making, with religion and some limited matters left to the state level. The respective ruler—the sultan—heads all religious matters for each state, assisted by the state religious department.

Malaysia has always been viewed as one of the more stable countries in Southeast Asia, having had uninterrupted democratic elections since independence. The country is relatively secular and has experienced positive economic growth. In 1958 more than 60 per cent of Malaysians lived in poverty, a stark difference from the situation in 2016, when only 0.6 per cent lived below the poverty line. Today, Malaysia is a highly open upper-middle-income country, providing universal access to twelve years of basic education and to healthcare. In terms of gender equality, Malaysia is doing relatively well, with women accounting for the majority of students in public universities, and with nearly 32.3 per cent of decision-making positions in public service held by women.[1]

However, despite the country's economic successes, media reports, both national and international, have constantly published news, articles and opinion pieces on how racism has become rampant in Malaysia. IMAN—a Malaysian independent research centre that looks at how society, beliefs and perceptions impact and influence a nation and the region—has reviewed statements made by leaders and commenters as reported in the conservative Malay newspaper *Utusan Melayu* over the Selangor state's decision in 2010 to allow the building of an Indian temple in a Malay-majority neighbourhood of Shah Alam. Conservatives have used the decision to play up racial sentiments, claiming that Islam is "under attack" and that the Selangor chief minister was trying to deny Islam its position as the official state religion. They also consider the move an attempt at making all religions equal and to disrupt racial harmony.[2] The rising tempers culminated in a demonstration outside the Selangor State Administrative Building, where demonstrators stepped on the severed head of a cow in front of the building's gate. The actions of the protesters received wide condemnation. Two of the men involved ended up pleading guilty to charges of sedition and being fined 3,000 ringgit each, while twelve others pleaded guilty to illegal assembly and were fined 1,000 ringgit each.[3]

A shift is also taking place at the personal level. A survey conducted by Merdeka Centre in 2015 revealed that 60 per cent of Malaysian Malay-Muslims identified themselves as Muslims first. A 2013 Pew Survey on global Muslim attitudes found that 86 per cent of Malaysian Muslims believed that sharia should be the official law of the country. These findings concur with another Merdeka Centre survey on attitudes towards *hudud* (punitive Islamic laws, which include punishments such as stoning, lashing and amputation) among Malaysian Muslims, where 71 per cent of Malays polled said that they supported *hudud* laws. However, only 30 per cent of those surveyed said that Malaysia was ready for it to be implemented. Meanwhile, in response to another question in Pew's 2013 survey, 39 per cent of Malaysian Muslims were of the view that violence can be justified against "enemies of Islam". A 2015 Pew survey reported that 11 per cent of Malaysian Muslims have a favourable opinion of ISIS, while 25 per cent claimed that they were unsure. In comparison, 79 per cent of Indonesian Muslims had an unfavourable opinion of ISIS, with 18 per cent unsure.

If we are to consider the outcomes of these surveys, the experience of increased religiosity among Muslims in Malaysia is not without its nuances. While overwhelming support is voiced for ideas that conform to orthodox Muslim beliefs (such as Qur'anic criminal penalties), there is a great deal of disagreement when it comes to actual implementation. However, the idea of a struggle against "enemies of Islam" has some appeal, as we can see from the Pew survey results.

CSO Challenges and Successes

While we acknowledge that conservatism in Malaysia is on the rise, one should not discount the work of CSOs (civil society organizations) in countering it. CSOs in Malaysia can be categorized as faith-based, human rights oriented, and ethnocentric. Examples of their activities include interfaith dialogues, interracial forums, and work against hate crimes. The CSOs detailed below were selected because they work on issues pertaining to faith and religious extremism.

Projek Dialog

Projek Dialog was established between 2011 and 2012. Its evolution saw many different manifestations, as it was the umbrella banner for a number of activities funded by Internews, including Islamic Renaissance Front (IRF), Kota Kita, and Sisters in Islam (SIS). The project began to grow in 2012–13. The idea was to bring different facets of civil society organizations to work together to promote greater intercultural multifaith awareness through various initiatives. Hence the mapping project of Malacca by Kota Kita and the videogame on Muslim women's rights by SIS. The goal has been to promote interfaith dialogue and multicultural understanding. Around 2011 and 2012, election fever took centre stage (the election was held in March 2013), and Projek Dialog began organizing forums that tackled many current issues.

The first project to come out of Projek Dialog was one organizing walking tours of houses of worship. The tours were captured on video and uploaded to YouTube. They received a lot of attention and developed a following. Other projects have also been successful, including Pesta Filem KITA, Pesta Puisi Kota, and two art exhibitions—Khabar & Angin and Merata Suara. Pesta Filem KITA 2 was scheduled for March 2019. The organization has also been collaborating with social media influencers and YouTubers to produce viral videos.

Prior to Projek Dialog, religious or interfaith discourse was not mainstream, so the aim of the project was to bring it to the mainstream. Many different groups and individuals had been pushing for this agenda, but they had not been talking to each other. Seeing this gap, Projek Dialog sought to bring everyone together. Whenever there was discord, Projek Dialog would feature it in a forum or article.

The activities of the group had very little to do with the state because many of the issues they dealt with were less about criticizing the establishment (this was during the Barisan Nasional government) and more about creating religious awareness. The steady growth they saw at the time was very encouraging and demonstrated that Malaysians were ready to deal with serious issues. They wanted new ideas about how to understand interfaith situations and about how to navigate multicultural situations.

IKRAM

IKRAM (IKRAM Foundation Malaysia) is a faith-based non-governmental organization that was established in October 2009. It formed as a result of the split within JIM—Pertubuhan Jamaah Islah Malaysia (Malaysia reform society organization)—when the right-wing members moved on to found ISMA (Malaysian Muslim Solidarity) and the progressive Muslim members left to found IKRAM. It is a missionary organization that is socially oriented. It focuses on multiculturalism within an Islamic framework. IKRAM aims to present the progressive voice of Islam to the Malaysian public, as the religion of *rahmah* (compassion), which has more to offer than is usually perceived. IKRAM aspires to work in line with the advocacy of Prophet Muhammad (PBUH) whereby he proclaimed all the citizens of Madinah as one ummah.

IKRAM was among the first Islamic organizations to come up with a statement on the International Convention on the Elimination of All Forms of Racial Discrimination (ICERD), where it sought rather than to ratify ICERD to instead seek solutions for the unique multiracial context of Malaysia. This stance was initially met with misgivings, but other CSOs are now coming to see IKRAM's point of view.

IKRAM is part of the Southeast Asian Network of Civil Society Organisations (SEAN-CSO) set up by Professor Greg Barton of Deakin University. Dr Badlishah Sham bin Baharin, chair of IKRAM's Civil Society Committee, explained how IKRAM has been active in many events promoting multiculturalism based on Islamic principles. These activities have the support of the Malaysian government, such as from the Ministry of Education. According to Dr Badlishah, the public programmes conducted by IKRAM include the celebration of Chinese New Year and cross-cultural programmes between national schools and vernacular Chinese schools. It has co-organized International Mother Language Day with other CSOs, and it has been involved in organizing GBM (Gabungan Bertindak Malaysia) Unity and Harmony programmes, tours of the places of worship of other faiths, and in engaging in dialogues with Christian, Buddhist and Hindu groups.

Has it met with resistance? Yes. But less from the state and more from ultra-Malay groups like ISMA and JMM. "They call us liberals. But our standing among CSOs is quite high. We are normally known as the progressive voice of Islamic organizations", Dr Badlishah said. Some of IKRAM's programmes have been funded by the state. Since IKRAM effectively represents a continuation of the work of previous organizations such as JIM and other units, public engagement has continued as before but under the new name. Some programmes have been handled solely by IKRAM and some in collaboration with the state.

Under the previous administration, IKRAM, like IMAN, did not have much luck engaging with the government and the authorities over matters of CVE (countering violent extremism). Today, however, they are actively engaging with the state (as is IMAN). IKRAM's community work and its observations of radicalization and of sentiments on the ground are being relayed to state actors.

Kairos Dialogue Network

Kairos Dialogue Network (KDN) was established in 2012 to address the lack of interfaith initiatives, particularly relating to Christian-Muslim relations. Since GE14 (9 May 2018), and with the change of political atmosphere and the government, KDN has found more people engaging in inter-religious dialogues and initiatives. At the time it was established, KDN had no interest in dealing with the state. This was under the old Barisan Nasional regime. Any state-led initiative then was formal and customary. KDN focused more on building concrete relationships and mutual understanding on sensitive matters.

KDN began engaging the public and interested parties in such matters—irrespective of race or religion—through forums and seminars aimed at creating better understanding of each other and of each other's faiths. Their first programme was a forum to explain their objectives: a platform for both Christian and Muslim professionals and leaders to discuss contentious issues involving religion and to explore how Christian-Muslim relations in Malaysia could be strengthened at the grass-roots level. KDN's approach is encapsulated in their vision statement, which is to use "our Christian social vision and call upon fellow-Malaysians of goodwill to come together for rational discourse and open dialogue. Our hope is that with commitment, we will succeed in building consensus, regardless of our colour, creed or confession and work together to build a harmonious, peaceful and progressive society." Forums conducted in Kuala Lumpur, Penang and Sarawak have been reasonably well received and people have been excited about them, "though there were some who were puzzled and cautious because of Islam", said Eugene Yapp, a spokesperson for the group and GBM's programme consultant on unity in diversity initiatives.

In the opinion of KDN, pre-emptive measures for CVE are needed in order to address issues of racial-religious harmony, as well as changes to policy and legislation for religious freedom. Yapp surmised that under the previous government the state was rather "indifferent". KDN would prefer that established channels such as the JKMPKA (Committee to Promote Inter-faith Understanding and Harmony) or the MCCBCHST (Malaysian Consultative Council of Buddhism, Christianity, Hinduism, Sikhism and Taosim) address the situation. "But these mechanisms had their limitations. Nothing beyond the cursory. The situation changed much as we move towards GE14 and particularly after GE14." KDN feels that Malaysians cannot place too much hope on the new Pakatan Harapan government. The new government has its own limitations, as exemplified by the ICERD issue. CSOs now have a greater role to play. Yapp indicated that this would be the next challenge.

Conclusion

The Pakatan Harapan government has no choice but to face the rising challenges of conservatism and security. The issue of Islam and Malay rights will dominate the discourses of both the opposition and ruling coalitions. The main challenge for the new government will be to address the trust deficit it has with the public. Further politicization of Islam is expected; Tun Dr Mahathir Mohamed is not well liked among conservative Muslims. A compromise therefore between UMNO and PAS on the tabling of the Hudud Bill (ACT 355), allowing for its implementation in the state of Kelantan, currently governed by PAS, is a significant possibility. This would embolden conservative groups (including PAS), as it would be hailed as a major milestone in the implementation of their mission of "Islamic" governance. On the other hand, if a compromise is not reached, then the narrative that Islam is under attack by non-Muslims will strengthen.

The youth will turn even more to Islam. The leadership vacuum in the opposition will exacerbate this. The Internet, particularly social media, will continue to be the dominant platform for the youth. However, if extremist narratives are left unchallenged, the youth will continue to be vulnerable to extremist and conservative propaganda. The rise in popularity of Zakir Naik among youths is an example of this, and the continued support afforded him by government agencies is aggravating the situation. Pro-ISIS narratives will also continue to dominate social media platforms, and there is a great need to challenge this. There are simply not enough positive alternative narratives, particularly those using the local language and with local nuances. If Malaysia does not address the lack of social cohesion, the situation will only deteriorate further. As non-Muslims lose even more trust in the government, Malaysia may become even more insular. For many religious bodies, the inability to address the rising conservative tide has more to do with the inability to engage with the public, especially the youth. In conclusion, while there has been a rise in extremism in

Malaysia, there is still a large middle ground that can yet be swayed to not go further to the right. The window in which to address this, however, is closing.

Notes

1. "Continue Hiring Women", *The Star* (Malaysia), 7 October 2016, http://www.thestar.com.my/news/nation/2016/10/07/continue-hiring-womenurges-wee/ (accessed 29 August 2018).
2. "Rakyat Selangor dapat 'hadiah' lagi", *Utusan Malaysia* (Malaysia), 10 June 2008, http://ww1.utusan.com.my/utusan/info.asp?y=2008&dt=0610&pub=Utusan_Malaysia&se c=Dalam_Negeri&pg=dn_18.htm (accessed 29 August 2018).
3. "Two Men in Infamous 'Cow Head' Incident Pay RM 3,000", Asiaone News (Singapore), 28 July 2010, http://news.asiaone.com/News/AsiaOne%2BNews/Malaysia/Story/A1Story20100728-22 9169.html (accessed 29 August 2018).

3

Religious Orientations in Contemporary Indonesia

Pradana Boy

In the 1960s, Peter L. Berger argued that religion would face serious challenges dealing with modernity. He believed that when confronted with the wave of modernity, religion would steadily but surely decline and be marginalized from public life. He also maintained that the more rational human beings became, the narrower and smaller would be the roles that religion would play in the public sphere.

However, Berger's projection is not in line with contemporary trends. Religion has moved in the opposite direction. There has been a vociferous resurgence of religion in the public sphere. Religious resurgence has emerged in various dimensions and manifestations in many parts of the world. Diana L. Eck observed this phenomenon in the context of the United States. In Europe, religious resurgence not only saw the rise of the Christian right but also of Islamophobia—anti-Muslim sentiments. Geertz Wilders, a former Dutch member of parliament, produced a film, *Fitna*, that offended many Muslims. Wilders' movie can be read as part of the anxiety over the Islamic religious resurgence emerging in the Netherlands.

In the same vein, Tariq Ramadan depicted Muslim dynamics in Europe and projected the future of Islam in that continent.[1] His primary concerns were what it means to be a Muslim in Europe and how do European Muslims play their part within the continent's social and political context. He also noted, amongst others, the dynamics of religious resurgence that have implications on Muslim public life.

In short, religious resurgence has become a global phenomenon, and Indonesia has also been feeling its impact. The wave of resurgence and rising religious consciousness has become more visible in recent years. Religious consciousness has come to colour the lives of Indonesians more so than in the past. It is interesting however to see the impact of this rising religious consciousness, especially in the context of political contestation and identity assertion. Generally, this chapter argues that the direction of Muslims' religious consciousness in Indonesia will manifest and affect the political, economic, ideological and civilizational orientation of the masses.

Political Orientation

When religious resurgence in Muslim circles gets stronger, it becomes more politically appealing. Accordingly, it invites certain political agencies to attempt to utilize religion as a political tool. In this context, politics operates in the name of religion that is a condition of faith. Following this logic, those who do not meet this condition can be judged as being faithless. Obvious evidence of this phenomenon is the series of "Aksi Bela Islam" (the Action of Defending Islam) protests that took place in 2016 and 2017, which have coloured politics and religious life in Indonesia today. Although the perpetrators have identified themselves as defenders of Islam, they have failed to conceal their political motivation. The agenda surrounding the protests has shifted significantly. Is not the main agenda of the movement to sentence and imprison a man guilty of blasphemy? Certainly, politics underpins the movement. The groups involved in the protests are fragmented: they have different views and interests.

Political consciousness has resided in the minds of Indonesia's religious elites. They can mobilize the masses by controlling various media channels. Meanwhile, at the grass-roots level, the masses participating in the protests have been motivated purely by the spirit of wanting to defend religion. Thus, there is a gap between the consciousness of the elites and that of the masses. At the level of the elite, religious consciousness can be an instrument for gaining political goals. Yet, at the level of the masses, it is genuine religious consciousness. A Muslim activist from Batu, East Java shared his experience of joining one of the protests. He went to Jakarta by train and was amazed to find that many other passengers shared similar objectives to his; namely, to defend Islam. Perhaps because of his curiosity, he asked some of the more elderly persons how they funded their trip. Interestingly, almost all claimed that it was from their own pockets—money from cashing in goods, or savings accumulated from working in agriculture.

Some agreed to take part in the protest because they wanted to defend Islam and the sanctity of the Qur'an. Unfortunately, some groups with political interests have capitalized on and manipulated the good intentions of the people, by arrogantly claiming to be representatives of the Islamic *ummah* (community). In this context, it can be understood that the Ulama Council of Indonesia (MUI) objected to the use of its name to justify the action. Considering what has happened in Indonesia with regard to issues of religion and politics, the politicization of religion is likely to become even stronger. The main reason is because religion will be used as an essential source of legitimation to achieve the political interests of certain groups.

Economic Orientation

Besides political interests, the rise of religiosity also has an economic dimension. Businesses carrying religious labels have intensified. The fashion, food, cosmetics and property sectors have all used Islamic labels and symbols. On the one hand the phenomenon can be seen in a positive light. It means the Islamic *ummah* has a greater opportunity to develop its critical consciousness and rationality, which are essential when facing religious dilemmas. At the very least, for matters of consumption the people can identify what is *halal* (allowed) or *haram* (forbidden). In addition, groups can campaign against certain practices that are seen as contradicting Islamic principles, for instance to avoid *riba* (usury) in economic transaction.

On the other hand there has been a monopoly of interpretation over certain religious concepts by groups claiming to be authorities and having the capacity to do so. Unwittingly, there have been identifications or claims that products bearing religious labels contain certain religious qualities. Yet, it can be found that when an individual wears an outfit having a religious connotation, for example, the person feels he is more pious or is in tune with religious principles (*syar'i*). Thus, religious consciousness closely relates to business and economic orientations.

There has also been a massive spread of spiritual travel agencies that seek to meet the demands of those looking to enhance their religiosity. At the same time, however, these operations are conditioned by economic interests. Indeed, the development has overemphasized the profit orientation rather than giving attention to spirituality. As a consequence it has raised some dimensions of vagueness to religiosity: should the initiation of prayers come from one's heart or from one's lifestyle? Equating business with religious legitimacy has subtly changed some matters to become artificial aspects of religious life. It has transformed rituals to become part of a lifestyle.

Ideological Orientation

Quintan Wicktorowicz, a scholar of Salafism, classifies three categories of Salafi groups: jihadist Salafists, political Salafists and *dakwah* (proselytising) Salafists. The three can be differentiated based on their strategies. Jihadist Salafists believe in permitting violence in fulfilling religious missions. And whilst political Salafism engages the political constellation, it does not consider violence to be permissible in achieving its missions. *Dakwah* Salafists are not interested in gaining power and do not legitimize violence; they are solely interested in fulfilling religious duties.

The phenomenon of religious groups such as *dakwah* Salafists has coloured religious life in Indonesia. Compared with the other two, the *dakwah* consciousness tends to be more authentic. In general, this group does not have a political agenda. They care little about those who follow other religious ideologies, though they will tend to urge others to join their group. Accordingly, this group has moved at the ideological level, and due to their apolitical attitude the political dynamics are not particularly interesting for them.

Civilizational Orientation

A group that is categorized into this form of consciousness tends to have critical and rational thinking to distinguish between substantive and formal elements of religion. In other words, this group attempts to provide Islam in a balanced form: between systems of value and symbols. In addition, groups adopting this orientation critically reflect on the problems and backwardness of the Muslim *ummah* and seek solutions for their predicament. Examples of this orientation include calls to understand Islam's sprit for acquiring knowledge and its systems of values, as well as questions of identity.

It is fascinating that this orientation shares some common features with the political orientation mentioned earlier. This civilizational orientation views politics as essential. However, it considers politics as a medium of struggle for certain values and not merely for gaining political power. While the political orientation deals with the instrumentalization of religious symbols in order to conduct certain political agenda, the civilization orientation plays its role in the world of politics without exploiting religion. The politics of this orientation does not follow emotional concerns. According to Hajriyanto Thohari, a senior politician of the Golkar Party, it is the politics that is in line with "an ability at controlling and hiding emotion".

This kind of religious consciousness is only possible for someone who has critical consciousness about the substance, deep meaning and higher objective of religion. As a consequence, the group to have developed this consciousness is in a minority. In contrast to the first and second orientations, this orientation is likely to be left behind in terms of driving technology in campaigning for its ideas among the grass-roots masses. Considering the religious dynamics in Indonesia today, it is understandable that religious symbols will be utilised for political reasons.

Note

1. Tariq Ramadan, *Western Muslims and the Future of Islam* (Oxford: Oxford University Press, 2004).

4

Inhibited Reformist Voices: The Challenge of Developing Critical Islamic Discourse in Singapore

Azhar Ibrahim

The main goal of religious reformism is to make a religion relevant to its sociocultural context so that it may continue to provide meaning to the lives of its practitioners. Another goal is to strengthen religious presence in the civic and political lives of its members. It also implies a creative re-evaluation of past traditions, which can lead to fresh interpretations. But reform is not simply appropriating new ideas or practices. It is also about having the moral courage to exert the necessary intellectual endeavour to correct the aberrations or misleading thought and practices of the present.

The inhibited reformist voices in contemporary Malay/Muslim religious discourse in Singapore warrant special attention. While the Malay/Muslim community lives in a modern cosmopolitan city state, it would be naïve to assume their religious ideas are also marked by openness and liberality. As in many other societies, there is a challenge to nurturing a progressive and reformist religious discourse. Voices for reform are intermittent and at times timid, but at other times they are more confident and determined.

The persistency of religious traditionalism and revivalism means that there is very little space for reformist ideas to gain ground within the local community. Apart from some inherent weaknesses in reformist agendas, the moral sanctions and pressure from conservative traditionalists has meant that reformists have always been in a defensive mode. In many Muslim societies today, reformist ideas are received in a guarded way and are deemed as unnecessarily disruptive as they affect the harmonious "balance" of the people's religious lives and convictions. Indeed, openness to exogenous ideas is immediately equated to the erosion of Muslims' authenticity and identity.

In Singapore we are not faced with ultra conservatives who vehemently oppose reformists groups and deem them wayward, secular or Westernized. Opponents, however, do see reform as unnecessary or even as approaching heresy, since the religious formulations and commandments of the past are considered to be complete, final and absolutely creedal. For the modern-day religious revivalists, religious reformism is seen as a modernist project that will sap the authenticity of the religion, and it is often seen as a fatal compromise to liberal/secular (Western) ideas.

The Predominance of Religious Traditionalists

Ulamas with a traditionalistic outlook consider the zeal of reformists to be a sign of wayward human fallibility in using their rational faculty. To them, the authentic religious practices and interpretations had been formulated perfectly and comprehensively by the religious savants of the past. Hence, the parlance of or imagination for reform are not part of their discursive repertoire. Of course, the call for Islamic reform may not necessarily come from within the circle of ulamas, but indeed rather from concerned Muslims in other professions. But those without training from the religious schools are often deemed as "outsiders", as they may not have mastered Arabic or the classical *kitabs*. Hence, this group is seen as unqualified to talk about Islam. It is no surprise then that the traditionalists demand that the state (through Muis, or the Islamic Religious Council of Singapore) should seek their advice and opinions on matters that affect the interests of Muslims.

Generally, the exclusivist traditionalist groups claim to be the true custodians and interpreters of Islam. The traditionalist religious discourse is generally concerned with promoting Muslim piety, both at the individual and at the public level. Any advocacy from them for an "Islamic alternative" such as those promoted by revivalist groups is rare. The traditionalist thinking is basically of the view that religious piety can only be promoted and sustained if the environment is free from "un-Islamic" elements. Hence, morality in the public domain becomes their concern. Yet there is hardly any overt challenge from them to the status quo, which differentiates them from the politically inspired Islamists (who aspire to the restoration of sharia in Muslim society or the creation of an Islamic state).

In the main, devotional discourse is aimed at promoting correct religious observation. A common theme is a general lamentation of perceived moral degeneracy caused by an abandonment of religious teachings and neglect in providing religious education to the community, especially to the youths, who are often deemed as "deviant", "lost" and as "deserting" the religion. Thus, it is not surprising that incidents of drug addiction and alcohol consumption among Muslim youth are seen as a manifestation of religious laxity and which therefore calls for a religious solution.

Religious Reforms in History

Historically, Singapore—at the centre of the Malayo-Muslim world since the nineteenth century—was also the site where reformist Islamic ideas found their earliest inception in the region. Interestingly, before Java received a wave of reformist rejuvenation, the ground was laid in Singapore. It was through regional contacts that *Al-Imam*—alongside the Egyptian *Al-Manar*, which was also circulated here—inspired the release of other reformist publications such as *Al-Munir* in Palembang and *Azzakhirah al-Islamiyyah*, led by Ahmad Sukarti in Jakarta in 1923.

By the late nineteenth century, Singapore had become the transit centre in the region for the pilgrimage to Mecca. And as a leading centre for the publication of Islamic religious literature, it also saw the arrival of several progressive ulamas and Muslim activists of the time. One such figure was the Mecca-based Sheikh Ahmad Khatib al-

Minangkabawi, who is regarded as "the master of the first generation of the reformist ulama in Malay-Indonesia".[1] Though trained in traditional religious sciences, his activism made him promote *Al-Manar* to his followers, one of whom was Sheikh Tahir Jalaluddin. Ahmad Khatib returned to Singapore before finally settling in Sumatra. Two other figures to have been influenced by him were Syeikh Ahmad Abdullah and Sheikh Abdul Karim Amrullah. It was Ahmad Abdullah who initiated the publication of *Al-Munir* (1911–15), in Padang, Sumatra, which disseminated "jurisprudential issuance (fatwa) that spoke specifically to matters of Islamic reform in local society".[2] A famous student of Ahmad Khatib was Kyai Hj Ahmad Dahlan (1868–1923), the founder of the reformist Muhammadiyah in Indonesia.

One of the earlier expressions of Muslim reformism in the region came from the monthly journal *Al-Imam*, published in Singapore from 1906 to 1908. It was modelled after the Egyptian *Al-Manar* (1898–1937), which was the successor to *Al-Urwatu l'Wusqa*, (1882–84), the journal founded by Jamaluddin al-Afghani and Muhammad Abduh. *Al-Imam* also reached parts of Indonesia, and it later inspired the publication of *Al-Munir* in Padang, under the initiative of Haji Abdullah Ahmad, who also later set up Sekolah Diniyyah al-Islamiyyah, following Madrasah Iqbal al-Islamiyyah in Singapore. *Al-Imam* indeed became a mouthpiece for reform, although *Al-Manar* also continued its circulation in the region. The learned Islamic scholar Sheikh Muhammad Tahir was the first editor; Singapore-born Haji Abbas Taha was the second. Syed Sheikh al-Hady and Sheikh Muhammad Salim al-Kalali, an Arab-Acehnese merchant, were also actively involved with the journal.

Haji Abbas Taha published a book on education entitled *Kitab Kesempurnaan Pelajaran* (Singapore: Matbaah al-Imam, 1906). In 1911 he set up a weekly newspaper, *Neracha*, and in 1913 established a monthly journal, *Tunas Melayu*. These initiatives were very much intended to extend and popularize the ideas of *Al-Imam*, which had ceased publication in 1908. In 1936 he was made Chief Kathi in Singapore. Haji Abbas Taha, then known for his reformist stand and as a "modernist polemicist", was invited to Kelantan by the ex-mufti Haji Wan Musa to participate in a debate with the traditionalist faction on the controversy over dog saliva that had erupted in Kelantan in the mid-thirties. Abbas was accompanied by Burhanuddin b. Muhammad Noor (known also as Dr Burhanuddin al-Hilmy). Abbas in fact compiled a book entitled *Risalah*

Penting pada Mas'alah Jilatan Anjing di atas Empat-empat Madzhab about the events (Singapore: Ahmadiah Press, 1937). Whilst the controversy may seem trivial by today's standards, the context it emerged from is significant for the fact that the reformist circle was asserting their presence in a religious discourse that had traditionally been the bastion of the conservatives.

The reformist group led by Syed Sheikh al-Hady and friends in Singapore established Madrasah al-Iqbal in 1908, with an Egyptian teacher Othman Effendi Rafaat. This madrasah taught traditional religious sciences as well as arithmetic, history, geography, English, Malay and Arabic. However, as a result of local resistance, especially from among religious conservatives, the madrasah ceased to operate. The key ideas of the reformists were on the legitimacy of *ijtihad* (reasoning), championing human rationality (*akal*), and against submission to *taqlid* (absolute imitation). Some of the major reforms *Al-Imam* advocated included (a) the importance of modern education; (b) the importance of using an individual's reasoning faculty; (c) the importance of education for children, especially for girls; (d) avoiding practices contrary to religious teachings; (e) the importance of saving and frugality; (f) and good hygiene and nutrition.

Amongst Muhammadiyah (Singapore) members, the influence of local-born Ustaz Ahmad Hassan (also known as Hassan Bandung) was not uncommon, though the reforming zeal was then characterized by a more puritanical posture. A few religious scholars from the Muhammadiyah circle also demonstrated a reformist bent, such as Ustaz Yaacob Elias (*Islam dan Pedoman Hidup*, 1978). Amongst the Indian Muslim community here, reformism was initiated by Maulana Abdul Aleem Siddiqui and later by Moulavi M.H. Babu Sahid. Amongst the Malay literati, we encounter examples of reformist writings, exemplified in the fifties and sixties in the works of Ahmad Lutfi. Recent publications by two former Malay teachers and community leaders are cases in point: Suratman Markasan's *Bangsa Melayu Singapura Dalam Transformasi Budayanya* (2005) and Maarof Salleh's *Tambak Minda: Mengamat Perkembangan Islam Semasa* (2005) and *Islam, Songkok dan Bahasa* (2014).

In post-independence Singapore, in addition to the reformist ideas of Abduh being upheld among some circles, and those of Hamka, another strand of reformist idealism could be found in the writings of Syed Hussein Alatas. Alatas, who was the head of Malay Studies at the University of Singapore, was instrumental in infusing a reformist stance in the Malay community, especially among educated members. The numerous writings of Alatas in Malay are an excellent example of the dissemination of reformist ideas on Islam alongside a critical scholarship on Malay-Islamic traditions. His book *Kita Dengan Islam, Tumbuh Tidak Berbuah* (1979) is a collection of critical essays that focus on the problems of modern Muslim societies, especially in the Malay-Indonesian context. His book *Biarkan Buta* is a compilation of debates he had with the Mufti of Singapore (representing the Fatwa Council of Muis) that played out in the pages of the newspaper *Berita Harian* on the issue of organ donation. The exchange represented one of the first intellectual challenges to the religious administration, openly questioning the justification for prohibiting organ donation by the local fatwa ruling council.

Revivalists' Criticism of Reformists

In sum, the reformists could not make much headway in the community. Such a situation becomes more acute during a period of heightened religious revivalism, where Islamizing and maintaining the Islamic identity become the primary concerns. The criticisms made against the earlier reformists by the revivalist ideologues has meant there is only a very small presence of reformist discourse remaining in the public sphere. Hence, there is very little exposure to or discussions of such ideas among the people. As a pejorative label is often given to any reformist, it creates a psychological barrier for any others to be associated with them.

In the past, the term "Kaum Muda" was seen as derogatory in some circles. Today, it is the terms "Islam Liberal" and "pluralist" that connote a certain laxity in doctrinal commitment or even ritual observances in Islam. These wayward "liberals" are seen as undermining Islam, or perhaps as serving the agendas of the enemies of Islam. Those who speak of tolerance and who are mindful of the rights of religious and sexual minorities are quickly deemed as compromising the true teachings of Islam.

Generally, the traditionalist-revivalist religious discourses are often marked by a concern with issues for doctrinal creed and the dangers of deviating from it; the primacy and meanings of the Prophetic Traditions; ritualistic laws concerning prayers and warnings against those who neglect them; laws on tithes and Islamic inheritance; halal food; dressing and modesty, especially the hijab or *tudung* for women; moral decadence and social problems of Muslims; the enhancement of rituals and the importance of moral and good behaviour; the efficacy of the Sunni *mazhab* as opposed to any others schools of thought or to Shiism; the [dis]unity of the Muslim *ummah*; and the importance of *dakwah* propagation, be it to Muslims or non-Muslims. In the main, devotional discourse is aimed at promoting what the traditionalists consider to be the correct religious observations; something they consider reformists to have very little concerns with.

Moreover, the preoccupation of revivalists for cultural and political Islamization has very much departed from the reformist stance. If the early reformists called for a return to the prophetic "pristine past" whilst at the same time accommodating Western technology and scientific achievements, the revivalists called for a rejection of the West and the creation of a truly authentic Islamic identity and paradigm. Such *dakwah* fervour saw several student organizations on campuses and Malay Muslims organisations like Darul Arqam, FMSA (Fellowship of Muslim Students Association) and PERGAS (Singapore Islamic Scholars and Religious Teachers Association) become active in promoting the revivalist/Islamist ideas. In the same period, popular and devotional religious writings appeared to dominate the market in comparison to reformist liberal writings.

It seems that critical works that discuss issues such as religious reformism or civic pluralism are deemed as very much "Westernized" and/or as having doubtful Islamic integrity, or perhaps even as being outside the concern for an authentic religious life. In many cases it is easier to find works criticizing Muslim reformism and liberalism by conservative/Islamist writers than it is to find works by the reformists and liberals themselves. Reformist or modernist Indonesian writers are hardly known or well received, and the same even applies to Malaysian writers of this ilk. Yet, translations of works that are exclusivist in their orientation are readily available here. Works by revivalist figures like Maududi, Maryam Jameelah and Syed Qutb, be they English or Malay-Indonesian translated versions, can still be found on the shelves of local bookstores. Hence it is not surprising to find there is a greater receptiveness for traditionalistic and revivalist discourses and that reformist ones are kept at a distance. This can easily be illustrated by taking a sampling of published religious works, which will be found to bear a preponderance of the kinds of discourses favoured by the traditionalists-revivalists that I had listed earlier.

In recent years Muis has been active in inviting scholars of contemporary Islam to give talks to local Muslims. Speakers have included Asghar Ali Engineer, Tariq Ramadan, Abdullahi An'Naim and Chandra Muzaffar. But these talks have been delivered exclusively in English. And while they have been welcomed by English-medium audiences in Singapore, there are some circles that are not comfortable with the speakers. They see such speakers as critical of Islam and assert they are not part of the mainstream religious establishment.

Religious conservatives (both traditionalists and revivalists) have often taken it upon themselves to be watchdogs of the Islamic discourses permeating the local community. They are quick to dismiss those speakers they deem too critical, and they would pressure Muis or the government to prevent such speakers from making their deliveries, claiming such talks would undermine the local Muslim community. The 2003 criticism by PERGAS of invitations to speak made by ISEAS to Zainah Anwar of Sisters in Islam (Malaysia) and Ulil Abshar-Abdalla of Jaringan Islam Liberal (Indonesia) is a case in point. That episode demonstrates a response by a group claiming to be the custodian of religion which is not comfortable with alternative voices.

Conclusion

Today, amid heightened religious radicalism and extremism, the voices of the moderate reformists have begun to receive more attention. Indeed, there have been intermittent calls to open space for critical multi-perspectives on Islam, since "The tradition of a healthy debate within the community, as found say in places such as Indonesia and Iran, is central to the very essence and spirit of Islam."[3] At the same time, we can also observe the persistency of more exclusivist or fundamentalist/revivalist expressions of the religion, both from within and outside the community.

There is a growing realization within the Malay/Muslim community, including in the religious establishment, that we need progressive Muslim scholars with the confidence to be critical of cherished traditions, traditions sometimes afforded an almost sacred status. Good exposure to and critical appreciation of classical Islamic intellectual traditions vis-à-vis the contemporary challenges would be pertinent in infusing reformist ideas. Certainly, more needs to be done to ensure reformist ideas gain a strong foothold in the local discourse. This is not impossible. The country's past has demonstrated the background for the emergence of reformist voices, albeit not without their limitations and problems. To nurture a reformist outlook is therefore pertinent.

Ultimately, reform in religious beliefs and practices is not about abandoning religion or belittling its cumulative traditions. Instead, reform is the very effort to ensure the vitality of a religion, in order for it to remain truly human, intellectually sound, ethically conscious, and spiritual, free of religious infantilism and medievalism. Religious reforms must fundamentally posses at their core the powers of criticality and creativity. They therefore cannot be equated with academic/apologetic nomenclatures like resurgence, revivalism or revitalization, for these idioms do not capture the attributes that, as mentioned, are necessary to reform. To keep the commitment and reformist spirit alive, the stamina of reformist intellectuals must be sustained through discourses, public engagement and publications. Only with such efforts can the intellectual rigour be maintained, spurring it on to another level of engagement as society progresses.

Notes

1. Cited in Jajat Burhanuddin, "Aspiring for Islamic Reform: Southeast Asian Request for Fatwas in al-Manar", *Islamic Law & Society* 12, no. 1 (Feb 2005): 13.
2. Howard M Feederspeil, "Modernist Islam in Southeast Asia: A new Examination", *The Muslim World* 92 (1992): 376.
3. Speech by Yaacob Ibrahim, "Doctrinal and Strategic Implications of Global Islam", delivered on 4 September 2002, Singapore.

Progressive Islam as Alternative Voices

5

Religious Resurgence amongst the Malays and Its Impact: The Case of Singapore

Noor Aisha Abdul Rahman

Since the 9/11 attacks there has been a proliferation of strategic studies and publications on terrorism and radicalism in the region, given their potent social, economic and political ramifications. However, critical studies on the phenomenon of the non-violent resurgence of Islam among the Malays remains wanting, despite its dominance and impact. Those studies that do exist tend to disproportionately focus on its emergence and manifestations within a generally positive evaluative perspective. This chapter focuses critically on the major fixations and agenda promoted and embedded in resurgence discourse, and analyses how they are sustained and reinforced. It argues that the phenomenon has become so dominant that it negates, marginalizes and silences competing Malay thought and perspectives that are vital to the development and well-being of the community and the larger society. Instead of identifying relevant problems and providing much-needed solutions grounded in an enlightened concept of religion and other philosophies that could facilitate Malays' adaptation to change, resurgence discourse impedes this process and exacerbates the challenges. While special attention is given to the case of Singapore, the issues and problems discussed here are no less relevant to but intertwined with the country's predominantly Malay/Muslim neighbours.

Religious resurgence has become so prevalent today that there has been a strong tendency amongst both Muslims and non-Muslims to misleadingly conflate manifestations of the phenomenon with the teachings and values of Islam itself. So influential has the phenomenon been that it has profusely penetrated not only religious thought and practice at the individual or community level but has also expanded to the public sphere, where proponents articulate their views and demands on a thousand points, leaving hardly any domain untouched. Its overwhelming imprints are evident in the innumerable and diverse issues that encompass identity issues; the sense of morality; perceptions of customs, traditions and social norms; the expanding range of dietary taboos and restrictions; gender relations; and intra-community issues, issues relating to relations with non-Muslims. Perceptions and discourse on popular culture involving music, dress, lifestyles, dance, film, literary forms and expressions also bear its unmistakable imprints. At the institutional level, attitudes towards modern education, the revival of madrasah education, the call for Islamizing knowledge, the expansion of sharia law beyond the established constitutional limits, the insistence on *hudud* as mandatory, pressure for radical changes to conventional finance and banking systems, and development policies that have led to a vast expansion of halal and religious businesses, all bear their salient traits. Not only have traditional religious institutions like mosques, religious schools and religious organizations imbibed resurgence slogans and rhetoric, even those academic institutions, social movements and NGOs that call themselves Islamic manifest the phenomenon's outlook. While traditional media such as newspaper columns, television and radio programmes have proliferated with its views through *ceramahs*, dramas, advertisements, entertainment programmes and others, new media have also become another major attractive platform that promotes and disseminates its fixations. In the domain of politics, it permeates not only the political agenda of opposition parties calling themselves Islamic but also the very ideology, policies, fatwa (Islamic legal opinions), laws and regulations of the state, which has either unwillingly relented to these demands or has endorsed them. Contesting interpretations on the status of Islam in state constitutions also reveal its imprints. It is for instance at the heart of the re-emergence of the political battle for the reinstatement of the original version of the Jakarta Charter, which would see the sharia as basis of the Indonesian state. Prevailing contestations over the meaning of the status of Islam in article 3 of the Malaysian Federal constitution also manifest its influence. In Singapore, where politics and religion do not mix, resurgence discourse is by no means muted, but is evident in the agendas of proponents aiming to out-Islamize competing groups and position themselves as the guardians and interpreters of Islam in the eyes of the community and of the government. Differences in strategies in achieving their puritan vision of Islam are not tantamount to differences in the basic outlook or perspectives among them. On the contrary, an interplay and interaction of views between resurgent groups within and beyond the region are evident.

Salient Traits

Scholars attempting to understand this phenomenon have referred to it by various terms such as *dakwah*, Islamic revivalism, resurgence, reflowering of Islam and, more recently, religious extremism, Salafism and Wahhabism. Our concern here is not with the terminologies employed in describing the phenomenon but in examining its central fixations and ramifications for Muslims and the larger society. While non-violent, the resurgence is characterized by ambivalence, dislike, opposition to or disapproval of the existing social order, which proponents consider to be inconsistent with the teachings of Islam—or, in short, "un-Islamic"—and they have a radical single-minded agenda to replace it with something they deem authentically Islamic. But, as Maaruf in his perceptive study of the style of thought of resurgence groups has asserted, "more often than not, they are not clear as to what they are objecting to or disapprove of".[1] Central to their discourse is the dogma of their version of *ad-din*, the complete religion. While Muslims have long understood Islam's comprehensiveness in terms of the universal values it provides for man and society—which must inevitably be experienced contemporaneously within specific social and historical conditions—*ad-din* in resurgence discourse essentializes and reduces the religion to fixed social, political, legal and economic systems, quite at odds from how the religion had actually evolved within distinct civilizations and institutions. This dogma underlies the discourse and activism for the establishment of an Islamic state, society or order, as the teachings of Islam, in the view of the proponents of this, "cannot be implemented in perfection without political power to implement its criminal laws and justice."[2] It also entails accepting the *syurah* and *hudud* (Islamic law on punishment) instead of parliamentary sovereignty as national law, since in their view the *syurah* derives its power and legitimacy from the sovereignty of the Qur'an and the Sunnah.[3] They employ the justification of *rukhsah* (exemption) to suspend their belief for *syurah* when they are unable to realize their utopian plan. Indeed, *ad-din* in their thinking clearly reveals a more "conscious political formulation",[4] one that is incongruent with the entire social order and the institutions that have developed to cohere it. They label these as "secular", which in resurgence discourse is essentialized to mean all that is not "Islamic". This recurrent motif in their discourse has spewed an endless stream of terminologies such as "secular knowledge", "secular education", "secular economic system", secular political system", "secular law", "secular state", and which they dichotomize from what they deem "Islamic".

With the attitude of self-sufficiency and intellectual "hermitism" reminiscent of the mass man syndrome which Ortega so well explicates,[5] proponents resort to totalistic claims completely indifferent to intellectual debates on these very issues. While Muslim scholars have long utilized complex social science theories and concepts that expound and provide insights into meanings of secularism and its compatibility with Islam, for instance, resurgents are oblivious to these and are content with their indifference.[6] In their discourse, secularism is simply symbolized by the West, which they attack and vilify as synonymous with atheism, nihilism, relativism, hedonism, materialism, promiscuity and other beliefs and values destructive to society. They dissociate themselves from this caricature or myth that they have constructed, and they attack it as undermining and conflicting with the ethics and world view of Islam and as threatening the very integrity of the religion itself. Their indifference to engaging with competing views and of having their own views subjected to intellectual scrutiny reflects the basic limitation of their mode of thought. Instead, self-proclaimed assertions of a conflict between Islam and secularism litter their discourse, as instanced in the following:

> Secularism segregates the role of religion from matters of society and state, limiting it only to individuals and places of worship. In contrast, Islam has guidelines for all aspects of life and demands its believers' commitment to all its teachings. Therefore, whatever the form of secularism, whether it be one which totally rejects religion or limits it to just moral aspects of society with the purpose of eliminating religion from society or which accepts religion to secure harmonious living, it is in principle conflicting with religion.[7]

While they deem themselves as ulama, their writings do not reveal any attempts to partake in debates or engage with opposing ideas advanced by prominent scholars. For instance, while they attack humanism, modernism and relativism as un-Islamic, they do not strive to understand these philosophies through scholarship, but instead resort to definitions drawn from dictionaries or encyclopedia entries.[8] Their writings, views, judgements, opinions and publications are generally not known outside their limited circle, and definitely not in the region or the larger Muslim world that would serve to signify the strength of their scholarship. In the absence of intellectual benchmarks, proponents resort to vilifying opponents through derogatory labelling and caricatures. With a stroke of the pen they condemn "abangan" Muslims as "minimalist", Kamalism of Turkey as secular, and imply that the entirety of the Malays in the 1950s were not following the teachings of Islam.[9] They caricature those who attempt to reinterpret Islamic traditions to make them relevant to the modern world as "liberal or modernist Muslims", and claim that they reject, destroy and marginalize Islamic tradition and scholarship.[10] Their emotive rhetoric functions to cast doubt on the religiosity of others, which they deem to threaten or undermine their own "authority", thereby impeding constructive analysis of ideas and their relevance. As Maaruf, who delineates resurgence thought as utopian in the "Mannheiman" sense, succinctly submitted, "In claiming predictability and comprehensiveness for its own theoretical and intellectual position, utopians are in a position to exclude all potential ideas which are not compatible with its own ideas and interests. When a system is perceived to be all-inclusive and all-embracing, there could be no room for anything else."[11]

Context of the Emergence

The beginnings of this phenomenon in the region can be traced to the period shortly after Independence in the mid-1970s, when the Malays, saddled with the baggage of their colonial past, were grappling with immense challenges of political-economic experimentation and extensive change, compounded in some cases by corrupt and authoritarian rule that ruthlessly clamped down on critics in the name of development.[12] Some of these fertile conditions for its emergence were also relevant to Singapore, where amid rapid and unprecedented social, political and economic development, the Malays continued to lag behind non-Malays. Structural displacement and maladaptation to change exacerbated a host of problems in which they were relatively over-represented, including educational under-attainment, unemployment, drug abuse, early marriage and divorce, especially among those on the lower rungs of the socio-economic ladder. These indicators began to raise concerns among community leaders that the community had been reduced to a weak minority within a predominantly Malay/Muslim region, and that more should be done to alleviate these problems, which did not bode well for the nation as a whole.[13] The fact that such efforts initially fell squarely on Malay self-help community bodies, given the government's firmness in upholding meritocracy and multiculturalism, meant that progress was slow. The challenge was compounded by the lack of an objective analysis of these problems. Dominant narratives problematized the community as lacking the value orientation required for the changing socio-economic conditions of Singapore. Malays were repeatedly urged to delay immediate gratification and to change leisurely lifestyles in order to catch up with the rest of the society. Calls for "mindset" and attitudinal changes in tandem with Singapore's development as a premier manufacturing, industrialized hub and financial centre, were not uncommon.[14]

Signs of insecurity became evident as the community's religious and cultural leaders began articulating concerns that Malay cultural and religious values and identity were being threatened and undermined by the growing influence of Westernization. The apparent corrupting impact on Malay youths in particular were frequently highlighted in the Malay press. Youths were deemed vulnerable targets of undesirable Western influences essentialized by the "hippie" culture of drug abuse, loose gender interaction, cohabitation, males keeping long hair, smoking and consuming alcohol. Fear of what was seen as the rise of "yellow culture" resulting in atheism and inter-religious marriage mirrored as much as exacerbated moral panic.[15] Religious elites began to urge parents to instil faith in their young, build trust and confidence in Islam, and cultivate moral values in their children to help insulate them against such threats to their identity as Malay/Muslims. Discomfort and dissatisfaction among some about the need to adapt religious life and practices to the demands of urbanization and change aggravated the problem.[16] This prompted Muslim scholars and leaders to emphasize the imperative for the development of morally upright leaders capable of identifying genuine problems confronting the community and to plan systematically for their amelioration.[17]

While religion had all the while served as impetus that facilitated adaptation to change, the period witnessed the rise of a new religious outlook promoted by upwardly mobile, largely English-educated social groups who were themselves the product of the changing social structure within the community. Their discourse on the problems of their community using religion revealed a radical shift from the perspective of the Malay intelligentsia concerned with the causes of the community's socio-economic lag and systematic attempts at improvement. It also differed from the concerns of the traditionalist religious elite, trained in theology and religious knowledge, who had had all the while a monopoly over religion. Conditioned by insecurity in the wake of change reinforced by the baggage of a "backward" minority, proponents revealed a puritan and authoritarian religious outlook on Islam and Malay identity that radically differed from that of the past. While the teachings of the traditionalist religious elite centred on personal salvation and individual piety, religious devotion, rituals and matters of life after death, the resurgents paddled the rhetoric of returning to the Qur'an and the Sunnah as the panacea for the problems of the modern world. While traditionalist religious leaders, organically intertwined as they were with the community, promoted the teachings and values of Islam in Malay based on texts transmitted from classical scholars and savants of the past, they latched on to translated and English ideological religious writings of "global" spiritual personalities and ideologues from South Asia, Egypt and Africa contained in handbooks and manuals. Amongst these authors were Hassan al-banna, Syed Qutb, Abul ala Maududi,

Kurshid Ahmad, Ismail Faruqi, Abdul Hassan ali Nadwi, Maryam Jamilah, Yusof Qaradhawi and Rashid Ghannouchi. Leaders of social movements such as ABIM, including Anwar Ibrahim, Siddiq Fadil and those from Himpunan Mahasiswa Indonesia (HMI), were also turned to for guidance. The rise of global Islamist networks and organizations such as the International Federation of Students Organisations (IFSO) and the World Assembly of Muslim Youth (WAMY) provided new transnational platforms for funding and organizational backing for the promotion of this new religious activism and ideology.

The outbreak of the Iranian revolution in 1979 provided a further emotional catalyst for resurgents to imagine the possibility of Islam as the basis for the establishment of an alternative state and society, though in this aspect, too, they were a long way from fully understanding the complexities of Iranian history, religion and politics. Over the decades the resurgence has intensified, with new and more complex configurations of political and social factors. Technological advancement and the rise of new media further facilitated the spread of resurgence discourse in cyberspace. A number of other factors have served to exacerbate the situation, including the impact of returning Islamic studies graduates from the region and beyond imbued with modern knowledge from "Islamic perspectives", the geopolitics of the region and of the Middle East, the persistent socio-economic problems of the community over the decades, and the community's dissatisfaction with the establishment elite for their perceived dismal record in addressing the socio-economic plight of the Malays.

While some of the old ideologues continue to be upheld, new spiritual mentors have also come on board. Mufti Menk, Zakir Naik, ibn Taymiyah, Yusof Qaradhawi, and Malaysians Mohamed Nur Manuty and Muhammad Kamal Hassan are among them. Whilst in the beginning resurgents were generally the product of modern education, over time the phenomenon has even penetrated traditionalist religious circles, who have now assimilated these idioms and rhetoric. The interaction between such groups and across boundaries has also expanded the discourses and their influence.

Given the conditions for its emergence, it is not unexpected that the phenomenon was strongly characterized by defensiveness and conservatism in the sociocultural and religious outlook that began to intensify over the decades. Discussions on marriage laws in the late

1970s in the Malay daily for instance began to reveal signs of restrictive views, though relevant provisions in the Administration of Muslim Law Act (AMLA) at that point had not been amended accordingly. A consistent rise in the number of attacks against *ajaran sesat* (deviant teachings) as undermining faith, as well as against the Ahmadis within the region, also became evident during this period. One also cannot help noticing the decline of a pluralistic outlook and interest in the thought and contributions of thinkers from beyond the Malay Muslim world, which prior to the late 1980s were featured in the columns of the Malay daily to inspire the community to progress.[18]

Despite the decades since its emergence, resurgence discourse and activism centred on the dogma of *ad-din* continue to reveal strong signs of insecurity, compounded in Singapore by the syndrome of minority complex stemming from their self-perception of a community without strong socio-economic or political power. Such signs underline the fixation with preserving an "authentic" Islamic identity, one that seeks to embrace modernity as the pathway to socio-economic progress for the community while remaining firmly rooted in Islam. The attitude towards *hijrah* articulated by PERGAS (Singapore Islamic Scholars and Religious Teachers Association) is but one of numerous examples that illustrate the point:

> Muslims in Singapore are backward compared to other communities in Singapore. This is unlike some minority communities in other places who are better off than the majority, like the Indian minority in Fiji and the Chinese minority in Malaysia. To change this situation, the Muslims need to reach out and draw on as many people from their community, especially from among the educated and experts in their fields, in its efforts to uplift the community, to strengthen its commitment to religion and to safeguard its interests. The flow of Muslims migrating out of this country will decrease the total number of Muslims here. This will certainly have a negative socio-political effect on the Muslim community. Such a move will also mean that one surrenders his right as the indigenous people of the country.[19]

In their bid to create an identity based on their selective version of *ad-din*, they however remain preoccupied with outward forms and symbols. This mental outlook thwarts their ability or willingness to raise and deal with concrete problems facing the community, problems that demand a good understanding of the realities and of the ideals and actual principles embodied in Islam and other progressive thought. While numerous examples of such problems abound in their discourse, just a few are highlighted here to illustrate the point.

Fixation and Impact

The superficial fixation with form of the resurgents is evident in their notion of a comprehensive Islamic education that they deem a crucial foundation for the creation of a pristine Muslim identity. Using the trump card of *ad-din*, they reject or reveal ambivalence towards modern education, which the Malays have clearly embraced as a social enabler and as a major means of alleviating their socio-economic problems since Independence. Instead, they call for the Islamization or integration of knowledge that they deem vital in creating an identity socialized with "Islamic perspectives". Such rhetoric is part of a wider ideological movement against Westernization, secularism and science in the name of religion.[20] It is alienated from contemporary scholarship and discourses on the changing aims of modern education under the impact of social change that lend themselves to a re-evaluation of traditional pedagogy and approaches to teaching and learning in specific contexts. It is also divorced from educational reforms centred on developing critical literacy amidst the complexity of a changing society and technological advancement. Concerns with the "banking" concept of education amid the proliferation of information today is also absent in their discourse.[21] Instead, proponents are preoccupied with their own rhetorical caricature of modern education as secular and a potent threat to Islamic identity. The constant dichotomy has generated ambivalence in the minds of Muslims towards mainstream education, seeing it as inconsistent with Islamic values. While some attempt to revamp modern education deemed secular/atheistic to one centred on the belief in God, others seek to "integrate" both secular and Islamic knowledge, though what this entails remains fuzzy. In Singapore, proponents promote madrasah education as an institution able to guarantee an Islamic milieu and a curriculum that will socialize students into becoming Muslims with a "tauhidic (monotheistic) worldview" that will safeguard and insulate them against the threat of secularism and adverse influences from the West. Such rhetoric appeals to many resigned to the fact that Islamization cannot be achieved by political means or who are wary of the uncertainty of change to their identity.

However, underlying the discourse is the fixation on forms at the expense of a philosophy of progressive education and the consequent impact this has on concrete pedagogical frameworks. While the latter is negated or absent in resurgence discourse, overriding emphasis is given to the madrasah's "Islamic" milieu in the creation of Islamic scholars and professionals, where female students don headscarves, rituals can be performed congregationally, and a curriculum that integrates both types of knowledge is offered. Despite the extremely high attrition rate at the national examinations (prior to government intervention in 1999), enrolment applications to the schools far exceed the number of places available. Furthermore, though the fee structure is much higher relative to that for the national schools, and despite the infrastructural, resource and pedagogic limitations in these schools, parents have not been deterred from enrolling their children in the madrasahs. When madrasahs came under the spotlight in the context of the debate on compulsory education in the late 1990s, stakeholders mobilized hundreds of people in a bid to win support to protect the madrasahs against what was deemed a "sinister motive" on the part of the government to close them down. Though the episode reached a conciliatory closure, with the government allowing madrasahs to be part of compulsory education on the condition they would prepare students to sit for the Primary School Leaving Examinations (PSLE) and that they met the minimum passing standard set, this incurred unwarranted consequences for the community. Various measures were implemented with the support of the Religious Council of Singapore (Muis) to ensure the madrasahs could meet the benchmarks. For instance, Muis collaborated with Mendaki to help all six full-time madrasahs prepare their pupils for the state examinations in English, mathematics and science. It provided resources to develop the capacity of madrasah teachers to teach non-religious subjects and support for remedial programmes.

Clearly, the fixation on forms has borne serious ramifications for the community. It has witnessed growing demand among Malay middle-class parents to enrol their children into the madrasahs instead of mainstream national schools, which has resulted in the community having to bear the cost of heavily subsidizing the education of madrasah students.

The fact that a substantial number of these students did not intend to become religious functionaries or scholars but merely preferred to study in an "Islamic" environment was not even considered a relevant issue in funding the madrasah. Much of the community's resources have been utilized to develop the capacity of teachers to teach non-religious subjects, when clearly this could have been obtained at no cost to the community through mainstream education. About $700,000 of community funds obtained through zakat collections were utilized for this purpose in 2008.[22] It has since become clear however that despite the significant funding support and assistance, the dual objectives of the madrasahs could not be met. Today, three of the six madrasahs have been unable to meet the minimum benchmark and have ceased offering the PSLE.

While Muis has acknowledged that the additional costs of education assigned to the madrasahs will only increase the challenge to the community to fund them, neither the council nor the madrasahs have revaluated the practicality of the dual aim of creating not only theologians and Islamic scholars but also Muslim professionals. There has only been a reaffirmation of the madrasahs' dual purpose, albeit "with different levels of emphasis between the two". Muis continues to assert that it will provide a "holistic and realistic educational experience" that will "allow students to navigate the mainstream educational and professional markets and also support the Islamic studies curriculum".[23] The problem is exacerbated by the fact that the madrasahs' standards of teaching for the national curriculum compare poorly to those provided by the mainstream schools, given their infrastructural and resource limitations. Furthermore, a critical appraisal of religious education and pedagogy remains wanting, even as madrasahs are lauded for their success in integrating "secular" and religious knowledge for the development of progressive Muslims. There has hardly been a serious re-evaluation of the content and pedagogy of the religious component of the madrasah education to ensure it is compatible with the demands of Singapore society and the modern world. Students remain unaware of the contributions of prominent Muslim thinkers from the Malay world and beyond, despite the relevance and contributions they have made to the progress of the community. The position adopted by Muis and the support it has given to the madrasahs reflect as much as it reinforced the demands of the resurgence.

Demand for madrasah education shored up by the resurgence has also given rise to stiff competition for admission into elementary madrasahs, which the government has capped at four hundred places as part of its compulsory education policy. To meet the growing demand, aptitude entrance tests have been institutionalized to ensure the best students are admitted to the madrasahs. Students unable to cope with the workload and pace of learning after enrolment are channelled into the national schools. Madrasah stakeholders endorse the rigorous enrolment scheme so as to ensure success in the PSLE and the survival of the madrasah. The scheme is also justified as offering an attractive pathway for higher achievers who would excel in both religious and "secular" knowledge.[24] However, there remains a dearth of critical attention on the consequences of the programme for the education of future religious leaders. And the strong tendency for the system to favour the more privileged in the community whose children can satisfy the stringent enrolment criteria is hardly problematized. Despite critical national debates on social inequality and its impact on access to education, madrasahs, considered the bedrock for religious socialization, are ironically isolated from this discourse.

The preoccupation by resurgents with forms at the expense of values is also manifest in their discourse on Islamic and civil law. In Singapore, proponents refrain from advocating for the implementation or expansion of sharia beyond its application in the areas of marriage, divorce and inheritance, unlike the situation in neighbouring countries. They also do not engage in discussion of basic problems in the administration of the Muslim law in operation. However, fanciful projections for sharia, incongruent with the operative Muslim law and how it has evolved in Singapore, litter their discourse. Basically, sharia is essentialized as a fixed system of rules legislated by God, separated from history and society and fundamentally distinct from civil laws, which they regard as "secular". Any commonalities in terms of values and aims between Muslim and civil laws within the Singapore legal system tend to be downplayed, negated or overlooked.

The manifestations of this binary mode of thought are far too many for us to discuss. One to have generated a great deal of controversy is the fatwa enunciated by the Legal Committee of Muis in 1998 against the common law instrument of joint tenancy as being inconsistent with the Islamic law of inheritance (*faraid*). Joint tenancy presumes the right of survivorship of the remaining tenant when the other passes on. This presumption commonly occurs with matrimonial property, as such properties are usually jointly purchased by both spouses. The closeness of the relationship raises the presumption that the property was purchased with the understanding that should one of them die the other would have full ownership. Most such properties involve subsidized public housing, which are subject to various restrictions for second-time buyers. When the fatwa posed challenges to some survivors of joint tenancy agreements who were pressured by *faraid* beneficiaries such as children and relatives to sell the property, Muis passed another fatwa in 2008 that attempted to harmonize the joint tenancy agreement with the *faraid*. While still not recognizing the compatibility of the law with Islam, it introduced two instruments—*hibah ruqbah* (rukbah-gift) and *nuzriah* (vow made to give one's wealth, in full or part, to another party before death)—as expressions of religious intent by the joint tenant to vest the estate to the surviving tenant. These instruments reinforce the dichotomy between civil and Islamic law, though it is unclear why joint tenancy is considered incompatible with Islam.[25] The problem is compounded by the fact that these instruments have been legally contentious. It has been appraised negatively in the judgement of a High Court case as unknown in the region, and in addition it has other serious problems in its formulation.[26] And whilst confusion over the legality of joint tenancy for Muslims was finally put to rest with a Court of Appeal judgement that ruled that *faraid* did not apply to joint tenancy agreements as it is concerned with the distribution of the estate of a Muslim and not with determining the assets that constitute the estate,[27] Muis continued to promote the *nuzriah* and Muslims continued to create it against potential pressure from *faraid* beneficiaries claiming an interest in the estate. This standpoint clearly reveals the binary Muis constructs between civil and Islamic law. Rather than embrace joint tenancy agreement on the ground of commonality of values, Muis exhibited ambivalence towards it. Its preference for an alternative instrument, no matter how remote from the historical and religious traditions of the Malays, also reinforced exclusivism from national laws. It was only in May 2019 that Muis reversed its position and enunciated in its revised fatwa that, hence, *nuzriah* and *hibah ruqbah* are no longer required to validate joint tenancy.[28]

Another example of a binary approach and a fixation with form at the expense of values is evident in the discourse by the resurgents on *syurah* verses parliamentary sovereignty. Resurgence rhetoric mandates belief in *syurah* as obligatory and sees it as a fundamental aspect of faith equivalent to prayers and charity, two of the foremost pillars of Islam. While they proclaim that the *syurah* has the power only to make laws not predetermined by the Qur'an and the Sunnah, they refrain from explicating who it is accountable to and which version of these laws from the vast and complex legal history of Muslim civilizations are divinely ordained and immutable. They also simplistically and misleadingly essentialize Parliament as having the power to pass any law on the basis of a majority vote system, and they express resignation at accepting this, given their political emasculation and acknowledgement that generally laws enacted by Parliament do not oppress them or violate their religious beliefs.[29] Their assertions reflect an arbitrary and misleading understanding of both parliamentary democracy and of the beliefs of Muslims. Their view that only Muslims can be appointed to the *syurah* is also revealing of their alienation to the pluralistic society in which they live. Resurgents are also fixated with what they maintain as the comprehensiveness of the Medina Charter, while at the same time ignoring or not wishing to understand the Singapore Constitution itself and the liberties it guarantees for all citizens.[30]

The preoccupation by resurgents with form at the expense of basic values also pervades their discourse on *hudud*, which they proclaim is mandatory in Islam. As PERGAS asserts: "hudud is part of our religion and one needs to understand it as best [as] possible before we talk of its implementation or criticize it. As hudud is enshrined in the Holy Quran and as Sunnah, it is compulsory for Muslims wherever we are to believe in the sanctity of hudud". Questioning *hudud* is synonymous with "doubting and disputing it", which may lead to apostasy. The Qur'anic verse urging Muslims to judge on the basis of what Allah has revealed is taken to mean that God has determined definite and fixed forms of punishment that cannot be compromised if conditions are met for its execution.[31] Despite their acknowledgement of the need to understand *hudud*, little can be gained in terms of that effort in their writings. Critical debates on their very understanding of *hudud* based on Muslim legal history and tradition are completely absent from their rhetoric.[32] Their recent statements on *hudud* for apostasy serve to illustrate this. While they do not support the death sentence for apostasy, they assert without substantiation that it represents the "dominant" view in Islam. They also acknowledge what they call a "minority view" on the issue in which a discretionary form of punishment determined by "an Islamic authority" is prescribed. Though both views regard apostasy as a punishable offence, resurgents remain silent on them. Their support for Qaradhawi—who while proclaiming that there is no compulsion to accept Islam nevertheless subscribes to the view that whosoever embraces the religion of his own free will is not permitted to abandon it—is also revealing of their fixation with form.[33] This is further evidenced by their complete disregard for competing standpoints amongst Muslim scholars who reject punishment for apostasy as offensive to Islam's emphasis on freedom of conscience and individual accountability, mercy, compassion and justice. Like the case of the *syurah,* resurgents simply exempt themselves from *hudud* only because they maintain that they are politically emasculated as a minority.

The resurgents' discourse relating to the rights to custody of children from parents who abjure Islam also clearly reveals their partiality, which again may be conditioned by their fixation on forms at the expense of values. For instance, they maintain that one who commits apostasy automatically loses her/his right of guardianship/custody over the children in divorce. This position is in conflict with the basic principle in Muslim legal tradition that puts the welfare of the child as the overriding consideration in the determination of custody disputes. It is also at odds with the principle adopted by the Singapore Shariah Board of Appeal in determining custody disputes in the face of allegations that the parent who converted to Islam had or would revert after the divorce (Zakaria bin Abu Kassim v. Natasha Chooi Abdullah [alias Chooi Lye Chan] [No 21 of 1998]; Heng Hock Lim, Lena alias Lena bte Abdullah v. Mohd Zaini bin Salleh [1999] 3 SSAR 98–103). Resurgents also assert that it is obligatory for such cases to be tried in the Shariah Court, though this claim has no legal basis in AMLA.

In the realm of politics, the fixation of resurgents on forms at the expense of fundamental values is no less evident. This is manifest in their idea that government and administration must be held solely in the hands of Muslims. As with PAS (Islamic Party of Malaysia), which espouses the concept of an exclusive Islamic leadership as one of the defining features of its Islamic state, resurgents in Singapore also succumb to similar rhetoric, though they are not involved in direct political action. They assert that politics is integral to Islam and that believing in the Islamic state is imperative to faith, though they concede that in practice the Islamic state differs little from the modern state. According to them, Islam does not permit Muslims to appoint non-Muslims as their leaders, a conclusion they arrived at based on their interpretation of chapter 3, verse 28 of the Qur'an. They read the verse to mean that Islamic law is integral to an Islamic state and that since only pious Muslims can implement Islamic laws to regulate the affairs of the state and politics, non-Muslims cannot be expected to fulfil this role. Given their political reality as a minority, however, they concede they are exempt from the binding effect of this religious mandate. They also concede that in Singapore, freedom of religion is guaranteed and secularism takes the form of a neutral government that does not take the side of any religion. For that reason, and by default, they acknowledge that the Muslim community should always respect the legitimate authority appointed via the democratic process. They further maintain that although the government does not establish Islamic law, it is nevertheless clean and fair and should not therefore be placed in the same category as those that are oppressive and hostile to Islam. In the event of a clash between the government and the community on matters of Islam, they urge the community not to remain quiet but to present disagreements through the appropriate channels and without resorting to force. Engaging in *dakwah* with the government is deemed necessary if the benefit to be derived from it would be greater than any harm inflicted.[34]

Resurgents' preoccupation with an Islamic state and concessions for accepting the secular state blinds them from problems of common concern of the government and of their relevance to all, irrespective of faith. While issues such as the morality and accountability of the leadership, transparency and the capacity for resolving socio-economic disparity, inequality, the minimum wage, poverty, retrenchment, unemployment, rising prices of goods and services, technological displacement, vulnerable families, youths at risk, aging and others have taken centre stage in the public sphere and demand critical attention and reform in the interest of social justice for all, they do not feature in resurgence discourse. Furthermore, while respect for democracy calls for all citizens irrespective of creed, gender, ethnicity and class to be ensured of effective safeguards against authoritarianism, corruption, nepotism, and arbitrary rule that denies the rule of law, they are instead preoccupied with essentialist and binary categories of Muslims and others, at odds with reality and the actual challenges confronting all citizens. Their discourse fails to distinguish forms from principles, polarizes society on the basis of creed, and fanatically deems that on the basis of Islamic teachings, Muslims must only be led by Muslims unless they have no other choice. That such leadership is deemed integral to Islam's teachings because only a Muslim leader can implement Muslim law (even though they concede that the government is nevertheless fair and hence should be obeyed) provides further evidence of their exclusive and puritan mode of thought.

Such rhetoric also breeds scepticism and ambivalence towards national institutions. It parochializes the community and prevents it from developing a positive attitude towards or constructive involvement in the advancement of common institutions beneficial to all. It constrains and severely limits the development of Muslims and fosters an apologetic, defensive attitude that leads to conflict and impedes their progress. Trapped within their theological cocoon, they spin irrelevant debates on the permissibility of Muslims residing in a non-Muslim country or of holding positions in a non-Islamic government, though at the end of the day they proclaim they have no objections against these. Ignoring completely the reality of their status as citizens of a pluralistic nation state, one providing equal rights for all based on common citizenship and constitutional democracy, they dabble at length in legal debates of the tenth century on the status and relations of Muslims with non-Muslims, employing anachronistic terms like *darul Islam*, *darul harb* and *darul amman*, as if these are relevant to Muslims in Singapore.[35] It may be argued that at the end of the day their discourses are not dangerous, as they do not reject the basic institutions of the state; however, it cannot be denied that this creates an unwarranted dilemma for Muslims and results in a preoccupation with issues irrelevant to the context of Singapore and the community's historical experience. It also impedes Muslims from developing a social consciousness on issues that matter and from transforming them in accordance with the ideals and values of progressive religious philosophies.

The exclusive tendencies of the resurgents—which exacerbate divisiveness, doubt, scepticism and ill will towards others—is also manifest in their support for preachers whose teachings have been deemed by the authorities to be insensitive to other faiths and beliefs. Among them are evangelical preachers including Zakir Naik and Mufti Menk. When these preachers were prohibited from preaching here, proponents protested and voiced their dissatisfaction over social media. In response to fatwas issued by neighbouring muftis banning congratulatory messages to non-Muslims in conjunction with their religious festivals and participation in their religious events, they provide carefully crafted apologetic standpoints, underlined no less by exclusivism. For instance, they assert that it is permissible to express greetings to non-Muslims on these occasions, given our pluralistic society. Yet they conceded to and did not reject alternative views that maintained that to do so would undermine one's belief. They merely expressed preference for the former, given the context of Singapore society, irrespective of the fact that Islam had from its inception been addressed to pluralistic societies.[36]

Group Preservation

Despite its adverse impact on the well-being and development of the community, the resurgence continues to gain credibility and to expand and sustain its influence. Embedded in the resurgents' discourse are their consistent efforts to position themselves in the eyes of the community and the government as guardians of authentic Islam with the legitimacy of articulating the religious thought, demands and aspirations of the community. In response to the call by the government for moderates to speak up to counter violence and terrorism post 9/11, they strategically positioned themselves as champions of moderate Islam who reject extremist religious ideas. Their firm stand against radicalism has given them greater credibility in denouncing the threats of al-Qaeda and ISIS (Islamic State in Iraq and Syria). They also take the lead in public forums combatting extremism using religion. Their profile has been further boosted in recent years as they are also consulted by the private sector and the government on matters relating to Islamic banking and finance.

Resurgents also consciously preserve their influence as guardians of Islam in the eyes of the community by profiling themselves as embracing modernity while being rooted in an Islamic identity. They cloak their exclusive views by riding on and appropriating modern idioms and terminologies such as human rights, gender empowerment and multiculturalism, through which they weave their fundamentalist thought. Unlike religious traditionalist discourse, which remains largely centred on devotional matters and rituals, theirs is littered with pronouncements on contemporary issues such as environmental degradation and LGBT (lesbian, gay, bisexual and transgender) issues from "Islamic perspectives". These appeal to youths and others searching for an Islamic panacea to contemporary phenomenon.[37] Proponents undermine traditionalist *ulama* as incapable of addressing the aspirations and needs of youths. The lack of English proficiency by the traditionalist *ulama* is at times also cited as a limitation that hinders them from being in touch with contemporary issues affecting Muslims. Even the *maulid*, *zikir* and other religious rituals and devotions that religious traditionalists celebrate as part of the sanctity of Islamic traditions are condemned in resurgence discourse as petty indulgences that are alienated from the real problems of the day. Instead of demanding good scholarship from an *ulama*, they give overriding attention to the latter's *ceramah* translations into many languages and their ability to attract large crowds. Yet, resurgence writings by no means mirror a depth of understanding of problems and solutions.[38] Several of their spiritual mentors have even been castigated for promoting negative views that impair the well-being of Singapore's pluralistic society. Mufti Menk for instance has been banned from preaching in Singapore for provoking enmity against non-Muslims. Qaradhawi's minority fiqh that they revere is underlined by negative sentiments and suspicions against non-Muslims. His endorsement of suicide bombings in Israel targeting civilians, which he justified as "martyrdom operations", has also been strongly criticized by many prominent Muslim scholars.[39]

Far from an objective and critical appraisal of their opponents' views, proponents resort to authoritarian means to wield influence. This is done in several ways. First they appropriate traditions ascribed to the Prophet Muhammad to the effect that the ulama are the successors of the prophet (*ulama pewaris nabi*), implying thereby that others should defer to them as guardians and interpreters of Islam. In the bid for guardianship of Islam, they vilify others who differ from the views they proclaim, irrespective of competing views amongst Muslim scholars. Their standpoint on the *tudung* (headscarves) captures the problem. Contrary to historical experience and the diversity of theological rulings on this issue, they simply assert that not putting on the headscarf signifies Malays' ignorance of Islam. In their words: "Even though 50 years ago Muslims did not practice certain religious obligations because of ignorance, that is no excuse to continue neglecting them today. The practice of religious obligations which were once neglected should not invite suspicions if they are established in Islam, this is part of the process of change. If we can accept the importance of changing the economic mindset due to changes in the environment we should be able to accept the changing social mindset due to socio-religious changes in society."[40]

While no one can deny that adaptation to change is indeed imperative, the issue at stake is their unquestioned presumption against all others (including traditional custodians of religion), whom they imply are ignorant. Though they do concede behind closed doors to differences of views among scholars on the *tudung*, they nevertheless patronizingly maintain that allowing for plurality of views on this issue would only confuse the community. The statement by PERGAS against the directive of Muis on the *tudung* in schools after four girls were suspended for defying the rules by insisting on donning the hijab to school, illustrates their bid to out-Islamize official religious authority. While Muis declared that when a choice has to be made education is more important than the headscarf, PERGAS proclaimed that the *tudung* is *wajib* (mandatory) for Muslims who have reached the age of puberty and that their ruling, which "cannot be refuted", "is based on the teachings from the Quran and the Sunnah" and affirmed through the consensus of Islamic scholars. They further asserted that "No Muslim is allowed to remain complacent and feel satisfied with such hindrance towards the religious obligation for the modest covering of aura", and that "it is the responsibility of every individual Muslim to strive as best as he/she can to remove whatever causes which obstruct the fulfilment of our religious duties ... through proper planning and approaches".[41]

The exclusive and dogmatic standpoint of resurgents on this issue bear serious adverse consequences for Muslims. It reflects an authoritarian and essentialist orientation—one that attempts to speak in the name of God for all. Its fixation on forms rather than the value of modesty creates unwarranted adversity for those who—as a matter of belief, preference, policy, circumstances or other reasons best known to themselves—do not don the headscarf. It also raises an unwarranted dilemma for girls who may wish to partake in and contribute to professions that require uniforms without a headscarf. The fact that for years Malay/Muslim women have been contributing to the health sector without being made to feel that their faith is compromised is simply overlooked or self-righteously presumed to be due to their ignorance of the dictates of their faith. Similarly, pressures imposed on girls to enrol into a polytechnic, where they may wear a *tudung*, instead of a junior college, which prohibits it, reveals another unwarranted dilemma posed to Muslims as a result of the fixation on forms. The standpoint of PERGAS also induces contestations against the authority of Muis, implying that it lacks the courage to speak truth to power. Such views also perpetuate the notion that Malays are marginalized and fuel critiques against multiculturalism in Singapore, which is then said to ignore the rights of the minority. These critiques tend to homogenize the community and to overlook the plurality of intra-community religious views and thought on the issue.

Resurgence discourse also utilizes moral panic, which functions to guard their turf against competitors. This is evident in their constant call for unity within the community and using the fear of disunity as a major threat confronting it. Yet, while they clamour for unity, they neglect to explicate its very purpose. In the name of unity, resurgence proponents have been at the forefront in rigorously urging the authorities and religious institutions for stronger efforts to execute *dakwah* and strengthen religious education to eradicate competing religious voices that they deem erroneous. Religious traditions are selectively construed to convey the importance of their role as bearers and keepers of unity of the community, at the expense of other equally pertinent values cherished in Islam, including the importance of individual judgment and accountability, tolerance for a diversity of views, rationality, fairness, and basic rights. This is clearly manifested in the protests they publicly register when activists and scholars from the region have been invited to speak on Islam, and by their insistence that they should be consulted on matters to do with Islam. They latch on to justifications by like-minded religious authorities in the region to disqualify these personalities as deviants, rather than evaluate their opponents' views independently.[42]

In recent years even the Shia have been targeted and denounced by proponents as falling outside the fold of Islam and as threatening the unity of Muslims. Such views mirror fatwa in neighbouring countries that declare Shia deviant irrespective of stern critiques by prominent Muslim scholars. Even in Singapore, where antagonism against Shia is not externalized, given the strict laws against any promotion of religious hatred, there remains evidence of voices demonizing the sect and of attacking it as heresy. Those in power have refrained from dealing with critics who maintain that Shia are heretics or from making clear their standpoint, even when urged by members of the public to do so. Such destructive thought has penetrated the religious perspectives of the very people who control and manage public institutions, thereby reinforcing the resurgence influence. The fact that there have been instances of kadi refusing to solemnize marriages to Shia is revealing of the prevalence of the exclusive traits of the phenomenon.[43]

The same attempt to trump competing thought using moral panic was evident when proponents of resurgence publicly invoked God's wrath to justify their discontent over the appointment of a Muslim civil law practitioner as president of the Syariah Court in 1990. Utilising the Malay media and the pulpit to express their unreserved attack, they argued vehemently that the Syariah Court as a religious institution administering God's law should not be headed by one without expertise in sharia. Fearmongering was clearly invoked as proponents warned that misfortune and sin would befall the community, whom they claimed had deviated from God's law by unjustly appointing one without knowledge of sharia to the "religious" court. Such attacks were made irrespective of the judge's professional credentials, legal experience and contributions towards reforming the administration of the court, as well as the considerable degree of interaction between the Syariah Court and the civil court. The attack was also inconsistent in so far as it refrained from examining the composition of the Board of Appeal, the higher tribunal that reviews Syariah Court judgements, which had for some time been presided by civil-trained judges and lay persons.

A similar attempt to trump competitors with moral panic was also reflected in their emotive response to the 1999 amendments to the

AMLA, which provided for concurrent jurisdiction between the Syariah Court and the civil court on issues relating to the custody of children and the division of matrimonial property under Muslim divorce. The proposed amendment would effectively allow parties their choice of legal forum to hear such disputes if both agreed or with the consent of the Syariah Court if one objects. Here again, PERGAS was one of the major organizations that vehemently registered its objections. Its major contention was that giving Muslims the choice to resolve such issues in the High Court would result in weakening the power of the Syariah Court. PERGAS also alluded to the presumption that the High Court would award custody to parties who have renounced Islam in disputes.[44] Such concerns were not confined to PERGAS. A study has revealed that "even the ulama in Muis opposed the amendments but chose to assist their colleagues in PERGAS from behind the scenes due to constraints placed on them as civil servants".[45] This is despite the fact that the overriding principle governing the Muslim law on custody, like the civil law, is the paramount welfare of the child. In fact, prior to the amendment the Syariah Court and Board of Appeal had, based on this overriding principle, awarded custody orders to mothers despite the fact that they had renounced Islam.[46] The vehement attack by PERGAS against those who attempted to give Muslims a choice in matters which the religious law has adequately and exclusively provided for as tantamount to a "display of intolerance for the religion itself" provides yet another example of its ideological streak.[47] Its objections cannot be isolated from its concern that the proposed amendment would limit the extent of the influence of theologians in a domain that had been their purview all the while. The fact of the proposed concurrent jurisdiction being seen largely as "surrendering" the power of the Syariah Court to the High Court was no less telling of their insecurity. In response to the question posed by a member of the Select Committee as to whether it would be fair for a secular government to allow Muslims to avail themselves of the civil court to resolve these issues, PERGAS even retorted that "The purpose of AMLA was for Muslims and those who were married under the Muslim law. If we allow matters relating to Muslims to be considered in another court, we are allowing them to do something which is against the religious law...". When informed that Muslims have been resolving specific matrimonial issues in the civil court such as maintenance disputes,

PERGAS asserted that "[t]hey went there because they were ignorant that these are laws contrary to Islamic law."[48]

Such a perception failed to give adequate consideration to commonalities of principles between Islamic and civil law as well as the rights and well-being of the parties and their children. In fact, prior to the proposed amendments, issues of custody and matrimonial property have all the while been heard and determined in the High Court while divorce proceedings were pending in the Syariah Court, without objections from Syariah Court judges themselves and irrespective of the fact the Syariah Court had exclusive jurisdiction on these matters. In this sense, the proposed amendments would merely institutionalize what had been going on empirically. Moreover, such cases have not been met with objections by litigants or the general Muslim public, which implies that their overriding interest is to have their cases resolved fairly and expediently.

Resurgence influence is also reinforced and mirrored by the writings of some prominent academics who are themselves guilty of coming under its powerful grip. They mirror as well as exacerbate its predominance through their non-critical publications on the phenomenon in which they conflate its imprints with Muslims being stricter in their observation of Islam. Their mode of thinking equates the selective puritan rhetoric of the resurgents on various issues as representing the teachings of Islam itself. For instance, a prominent local academic attempting to explain the fixation with halal requirements misleadingly asserted that "What was to surprise the Singapore government was the revelation that since the 1980s, Singapore Malays, including its educated professionals, have become more religious."[49] Such statements clearly imply that Muslims who were not prone to such fixations were not as religious. The heightening of the resurgence since the 80s is also commonly viewed non-critically and positively as synonymous with Muslims becoming *more fervent* about their ethno-religious identity amid the "materialistic and capitalistic foundations of the Singapore state and the general modernisation of Singapore society as a whole".[50] The government's wariness over this type of religiosity as impeding social integration was viewed as attempts to stem greater Islamic assertiveness. Demands by specific groups that girls be allowed to don long sleeves and scarves at customs points have been confusingly equated with the "rising tide of Islam amongst Malays in Singapore".[51] Such tendencies to equate the resurgence orientation with Islam reinforces the appeal of the resurgence. The fact that the few critics who engage with such discourse are often demonized and derogatorily labelled as "liberal", "secular", "anti-Islam", "destroyers of faith" (*perosak agama*) and those who "confuse or disunite Muslims" or are "deviants", exacerbate the problem. Though in Singapore critics have not suffered grievously through medieval modes of punishment at the hands of proponents—including having had their books banned or burned, as has been the case in neighbouring countries—such labelling is nevertheless destructive and intended to mar an individual's reputation as a good Muslim.

It is clear that resurgents have turned *ad-din* into an ugly dogma that has not contributed to reform the community nor constructively facilitated its adaptation to the demands of the pluralistic society and the modern world. On the contrary, it has given rise to fierce obsession with forms and symbols, emotive and exclusive rhetoric devoid of social reconstruction and institution building based on democratic values. It has also retarded intellectual development and social consciousness and created false consciousness amongst the Malays. While the contemporary Malay world has given rise to numerous intellectuals with powerful reform ideas crucial to developing a rational, progressive and dynamic society, the resurgence threatens or marginalizes their significance.

Conclusion

There is no doubt that such an exclusive and authoritarian orientation must be curbed if not eliminated in order to improve the well-being of Muslims and the larger society. Given the dominance and danger it poses to our social fabric, the challenge to eliminate it cannot be left solely to the community. However, attempts to tackle the problem have to some extent been marred by overgeneralizations and misunderstanding, which can aggravate the phenomenon and reinforce empathy for it. The strong tendency to presume that the more religious one is in terms of observation of religious teachings/rituals, the greater the tendency to be more fanatical and exclusive, is a case in point. Adhering strictly to prayers, not consuming alcohol, and observing dietary taboos (halal) at public events have been highlighted in national discourses as signs of Muslims becoming fanatical and as impeding social interaction, engagement and cohesion. The opposite practices amongst them on the other hand tend to be positively sanctioned. These have to some extent aggravated dissatisfaction and defensiveness amongst religious Muslims who are not part of the resurgence tide. While they conform to these basic religious teachings, they do not harbour the exclusive traits of resurgents that undermine social integration. Dissatisfaction with such attacks against the precepts of their religion have to some extent shored empathy for resurgents, who have used such discourse to reinforce insecurity that the religion has once again been threatened by secularists who are undermining and attacking their faith and identity as Muslims. This clearly does not bode well for society and should be avoided.

Efforts at countering the phenomenon should also not mirror the very limitations and pitfalls of essentialism, as this may further push Muslims into the grip of the resurgence. The recent discourse against Arabism in Singapore to counter religious extremism, which mirrors common sentiments of some Muslims in the region, serves to illustrate the point. Such a sentiment has been conditioned by what is perceived as the impact of Wahhabism or Salafism from Arabia and the Middle East into the region with globalization and new media. Critiques maintain that this has resulted in the phenomenon of cultural encroachment that undermines and supplants Malay identity and how Islam has been experienced locally. Everyday life examples such as the use of the *tudung* and Arabic garb, the creeping of Arabic terminologies into the Malay language are invoked as manifestations of such encroachments on Malay culture and identity.[52] Yet the crux of the issue is not in the imitation, borrowing or assimilation of these symbols and forms, unless they are accompanied by puritan and authoritarian streaks that mandate them as non-negotiable Islamic rulings superior to the culture and practices of the Malays. The danger lies in such fanaticism that ascribes exclusivity to such forms and thought. It must be noted that such exclusive influences are not merely confined to the Arab world. Indeed, cultural, economic and religious exchanges and assimilation between the Malays and the Arab world have been in progress for centuries, even before the coming of Islam. Reform ideas from the latter have also influenced religious, political, legal and cultural life of the community. Ideas on religion, history, women, law, governance and many others have contributed to the development of local communities in the past. The challenge today is not for the Malays to shun the Arab world and its influences, but to enhance exposure to progressive discourses on diverse areas relevant to the Malay world. Progressive voices in the Arab world are themselves confronted by serious challenges posed by fundamentalism in their own societies, much as is the case for the Malays in Singapore and the region. Their contributions should be understood and developed as an antidote to the dangers of parochialism and radical religious ideologies in our midst. Instead of curbing the flow of students studying religion in the Middle East, they should be strongly encouraged to develop greater awareness of the variety of intellectual currents there and to develop critical perspectives through interactions with varying streams of Islam, traditions and ideas that are useful to the community and a bane to religious fundamentalism in the region.

The response of certain groups within the community to promote Nusantara Islam as a response to religious radicalism must also not be tainted by similar limitations, which could dampen its potential to counter the ill-effects of the resurgence. Within Nusantara there exist a variety of religious orientations, not all of which can be said to be progressive and worthy of emulation. For instance, Islam has been woven into a feudal and authoritarian political culture that has impeded its potential as a basis for facilitating a progressive society within the region. The type of Islam that has been conditioned by the dominant authoritarian political culture has inhibited and denied the development of a strong consciousness of positive individualism, rationality, equality, respect for the rights and dignity of the individual, loyalty based on humanitarian principles of leaders, and many other positive traits. This type of religious orientation is surely not conducive to the well-being of the community.

One should also be mindful of promoting syncretism as part of local Islam that overemphasizes non-rational, magical and mythical world views that impede adaptation in the value sphere conducive to values of modernization. The syncretism of local culture with Islam must continue to evolve dynamically with the changing conditions of society and not remain trapped in a static world view of the past. Critiques on Nusantara Islam in Indonesia have also pointed out that the project may well degenerate into exclusivism and labelling if essentialism in understanding local Islam and Islam from the Arab world goes unchecked. The effort to contextualize Islam must, they argue, be a constructive and insightful one that awakens a strong understanding of the dynamism of the religion and cultural tradition. In this respect, the reform efforts at indigenizing Islam (*pribumisassi Islam*) that had been spearheaded by Indonesian intellectuals such as Nurcholis Madjid and Abdurrahman Wahid are useful sources that can pave the way for development. Their contributions provided a strong critique against the dominant views that tended to see the Indonesian experience of Islam as a kind of abnormal, superficial outlier that did not bear a strong influence on society. It reawakened cultural awareness of Indonesian Islam among Indonesians as a distinctive and unique kind of Islam that is culturally embedded in the conditions of society and geography and which emphasizes tolerance, respect for relevant cultural traditions, religious diversity, pluralism, peace and other values conducive to society's well-being. Such efforts to revaluate and to selectively and creatively synthesize Islamic teachings and values with relevant cultural traditions have boosted efforts at institutional reform, and they should be developed as an antidote to exclusivism.[53]

It is also highly pertinent that governments should understand that perceptions of Islam in all its dimensions are by no means monolithically understood by Muslims. Competing views and sources of authority have existed all the while, more so with the increasing complexity of society today. This means simply that governments should not rely on a single group on matters to do with Muslims simply for pragmatic reasons or even based on the presumption that to do so is in the interest of and respectful to the minority community. It is not unreasonable to conclude that it is often the dominant groups who are deemed the sole and rightful authorities on Islam, and who are thus consulted on matters to do with the religion on behalf of all. This approach may only enhance the role and influence of the resurgents. Given their dominant influence and mode of thinking, it is not unexpected that such groups would assert a monopoly of authority over Muslims in the name of religion. The persistence of such an arrangement may lead to unwarranted repercussions, not just on the well-being of the community but also on that of the larger society. While the adverse ramifications of such collaboration is more evident in the experience of neighbouring countries, where religion and politics have become conflated, Singaporean Muslims are not altogether isolated from a similar harmful trend.

It is important as a matter of principle to acknowledge that the government is the ultimate custodian of the well-being of Muslims. This is especially pertinent as diversity of religious views and experiences within the community exist. Wherever possible, therefore, Muslims should be subjected to the same policies and laws as non-Muslim citizens. This will go a long way to check and curb the expansion and influence of resurgence and to eliminate risks of Muslims being subjected to the demands of the resurgents. As an extension of this principle, the government should seriously consider giving Muslims the right of choice in being bound to a common system of laws. Those who wish otherwise should be allowed to do so. Such a policy will also contribute to curb the influence of resurgents in determining matters of Muslim law and alleviate fetters on the rights of Muslims who wish to opt out without having to abjure Islam.

Last but not least, consistent efforts must be made at developing and propagating the rational, progressive and humanistic tradition of Islam vital for the well-being and emancipation of the community. Without such efforts, humanity and universalism will be undermined, while dogmatism, parochialism, distrust, fanaticism, bigotry and prejudice so dangerous to the well-being of pluralistic society will thrive.

Notes

1. Shaharuddin Maaruf, "Religion and Utopian Thinking among the Muslims of Southeast Asia" (Singapore: Department of Malay Studies, 2001), p. 2.
2. PERGAS, *Moderation in Islam: In the Context of Muslim Community in Singapore* (Singapore: PERGAS, 2004), pp. 116–18.
3. Ibid., p. 120.
4. Maaruf, "Religion and Utopian Thinking", p. 4.
5. Jose Ortega Gasset, *The Origin of Philosophy* (New York: Norton, 1967), pp. 54–60.
6. Refer, for instance, to explications on secularism by Maaruf, "Religion and Utopian Thinking", pp. 9–19. See also Azzam Tamimi, "The Origins of Arab Secularism", in *Islam and Secularism in the Middle East*, edited by Azzam Tamimi and John L. Esposito (London: Hurst, 2000).
7. See PERGAS, *Moderation in Islam*.

8. Ibid., pp. 170–82
9. Ibid., pp. 158–59.
10. PERGAS, *Wasat Online*, no. 21 (2018), https://wasatonline.wordpress.com/2018/06/01/dari-meja-penyunting-wasat-edisi-no-21-jun-2018/.
11. Maaruf, "Religion and Utopian Thinking", p. 5.
12. Chandra Muzaffar, *Islamic Resurgence in Malaysia* (Petaling Jaya: Fajar Bakti, 1987).
13. Ismail Kassim, *Problems of Elite Cohesion: Perspective from a Minority Community* (Singapore: Singapore University Press, 1974).
14. These problems were discussed by Standley Sanders Bedlington, *The Singapore Malay Community: The Politics of State Integration* (Ithaca: Cornell University, 1974), p. 331. See also Lily Zubaidah Rahim, *The Singapore Dilemma: The Political and Educational Marginality of the Malay Community* (Kuala Lumpur: Oxford University Press, 1998); Noor Aisha Abdul Rahman and Azhar Ibrahim, *Malays* (Singapore: IPS and Straits Times Press, 2017), pp. 35–37.
15. "Tak boleh khawin dgn bukan islam: jamiyah", *Berita Harian*, 9 September 1970; "Bendong belia2 liar", *Berita Harian*, 7 September 1970; "Kemerosotan akhlak: Semua pehak mesti berusaha –Jamiyah", *Berita Minggu*, 3 February 1971; "Chara2 untok atasi soal kemerosotan moral di-fikir", *Berita Harian*, 21 January 1971; "Ajarlah anak2 cara hidrup yg sihat: 'Jangan puja kebudayaan dari barat'", *Berita Harian*, 18 December 1972; "Cara cegah ajaran sesat", *Berita Minggu*, 4 January 1976; "Hak kebebasan wanita: Tuntutan perlu sesuai dengan keadaan setempat", *Berita Harian*, 29 November 1973; "Badan2 Islam diseur atasi masalah belia rosak", *Berita Harian*, 1 October 1977.
16. "Ribut awal Shawal: usul kpd MUI", *Berita Harian*, 3 December 1970.
17. "Masyarakat Islam diseru hapuskan kebiasaan yg tak ada kaitan dgn ajaran ugama sebenar", *Berita Harian*, 11 February 1974.
18. See, for instance, publications on philosophical thought and contributions from both Muslim and non-Muslim intellectual traditions in the weekly column "Pemikir Agung" in *Berita Harian* in the 1980s.
19. PERGAS, *Moderation in Islam*, p. 234.
20. Refer, for instance, to Ismail Faruki's work on Islamizing the social sciences in *Islam and Sociological Perspectives*, edited by Abubaker A. Bagader (Kuala Lumpur: Muslim Youth Movement of Malaysia, 1983). For a good critique, see Shaharuddin Maaruf, "The Social Sciences in Southeast Asia: Sociology of Anti-sociology and Alienated Sciences", in *Reflections on Alternative Discourses from SEA: Proceedings of the ISA Regional Conference for Southeast Asia*, Singapore, 30 May – 1 June 1998.

21. Noor Aisha Abdul Rahman, "Challenges to Madrasah Education in Contemporary Muslim Societies", in *Rethinking Madrasah Education in a Globalised World*, edited by Mukhlis Abu Bakar (Abingdon, UK: Routledge, 2018).
22. Farah Mahamood Aljunied and Zalman Putra Ahmad Ali, "Madrasah Education: A Journey towards Excellence", in *Fulfilling the Trust: 50 Years of Shaping Religious Life in Singapore*, edited by Norshahril Saat (Singapore: World Scientific, 2018), p. 99.
23. Ibid., pp. 100–101.
24. Ibid., p. 102.
25. Nazirudin Nasir, "Contextualisation and Modernisation: Islamic Thought through Fatwas in Singapore", in *Fulfilling the Trust: 50 Years of Shaping Religious Life in Singapore*, edited by Norshahril Saat (Singapore: World Scientific, 2018), p. 70.
26. Mohamed Ismail bin Ibrahim v. Mohd Taha bin Ibrahim Mohamed (2004) 4 SLR 756.
27. Shafeeq Salim & Anor v. Fatimah bte Abd Talib (2010) SGCA 11.
28. https://www.muis.gov.sg/officeofthemufti/Fatwa/English-Joint-Tenancy.
29. Muhammad Haniff Hassan, *Contextualizing Political Islam for Minority Muslims*, Working Paper no. 138 (Singapore: RSIS, NTU, 2007), p. 17; See also PERGAS, *Moderation in Islam*, p. 120.
30. Refer, for instance, to the findings in the study by Mohamed Alami Musa, *Islam and Secularism in Singapore: Between Embracement and Belief*, Occasional Papers of Studies in Inter-Religious Relations in Plural Societies Programme, RSIS, NTU, 3 April 2019.
31. PERGAS, *Moderation in Islam*, p. 129.
32. Refer, for instance, to the work of Muhammad Said Al-Ashmawy, *Islam and the Political Order* (Washington, DC: Research Council for Values and Philosophy, 1994). See also Rose Ismail, *Hudud in Malaysia: The Issues at Stake* (Kuala Lumpur: SIS Forum, 1995).
33. Sheikh Yusof al-Qaradawi, *Fiqh of Muslim Minorities: Contentious Issues & Recommended Solutions* (Cairo: Al-Falah Foundation, 2003), p. 62.
34. PERGAS, *Moderation in Islam*, pp. 286–91.
35. Ibid., pp. 211–36.
36. PERGAS, "Religious Guidance in Sending Greetings to Non-Muslims on Their Festivals and Celebrations", 5 February 2016, http://www.pergas.org.sg/media/MediaStatement/IslamicGuidanceFestival.pdf (accessed 23 April 2019).
37. Azhar Ibrahim, *Contemporary Islamic Discourse in the Malay-Indonesian World: Critical Perspective* (Kuala Lumpur: SIRD, 2014), pp. 35–90.

38. See, for example, Khairudin Aljunied, *The Ulama in Singapore and Their Contemporary Challenges*, PERGAS Working Paper no. 1/2015, http://www.pergas.org.sg/media/Comment-Working/The-Ulama-in-Singapore-and-their-Contemporary-Challenges.pdf (accessed 25 April 2019).
39. Refer to Muhammad Munir, "Suicide Attacks and Islamic law", *International Review of the Red Cross* 90, no. 869 (March 2008).
40. PERGAS, *Moderation in Islam*, p. 158.
41. Ibid., pp. 344–455.
42. See for instance the protest by PERGAS against ISEAS for inviting Zainah Anwar, former president of Sisters in Islam, and Ulil Abshah, founder of Jaringan Islam Liberal (JIL), to speak at its Regional Outlook Forum in 2003. Their standpoint on gender equality and hudud amongst other issues had incensed religious conservatives in their own countries. *Straits Times*, 25 January 2003, p. 30.
43. See, for instance, the case of Izza Amalina bte Ibrahim v. Ahmad Murthdha bin Mohd Rosli (appeal no. 25/2016). In this case the kadi declined to solemnize and register the marriage of a daughter to her choice of spouse, an adherent of Shiism, after her father had refused his consent simply because the prospective groom was a Shia. Although Shias are clearly within the fold of Islam, they have as a whole been castigated, attacked, labelled and demonized by some fundamentalist segments of the community in recent times. The kadi's dismissal of the marriage bears serious implications on the wishes and rights of the daughter to choose her spouse. In his judgement, the kadi had alleged that under the Shafie school of law, the father as *wali* has absolute power over the marriage of his ward. This view deviates starkly from judgements of the Registrar as well as the BOA since the 1980s. In reversing the kadi's judgement, the BOA reasoned that it is commendable for the *wali* not to abuse his power where his daughter seeks to marry under no compulsion. It also found no evidence of any potential for family disharmony to arise.
44. *Report of the Select Committee on the Administration of Muslim Law (Amendment) Bill*, bill no. 18/98, 181 (1999).
45. Mohamed Nawab Mohamed Osman, "The Religio-Political Activism of Ulama in Singapore", *Indonesia and the Malay World* (Feb 2012): 7.
46. See, for instance, the case of Heng Hock Kim, Lena (alias Lena bte Abdullah) v. Mohd Zaini bin Salleh (appeal no. 21/1998), in which the BOA submitted: "we appreciate the concern of the husband, it is in the interest of the children and in the interest of the ummah that they should be brought up as Muslims. However, we do not think that evidence points towards the children being brought up as non-Muslims ... by the wife.

We note the affidavit of the wife ... which should dispel the husband's fear that the wife would turn the children away from Islam." The Board also highlighted that: "It is apparent, however that all rules of Muslim law relating to guardianship and custody of the minor children are merely the application of the principle of benefit of the minor to diverse circumstances. The welfare of the minor children remains the dominant consideration." See also the case of Zakaria bin Abu Kassim v. Natasha Chooi Abdullah@ Chooi Lye Chan (no. 6 of 1993).

47. *Report of the Select Committee on the Administration of Muslim Law (Amendment) Bill* [bill no. 18/98], pp. 153–65.
48. *Singapore Parliamentary Debates*, 70, *Official Reporter* at cols. 1249–50 (15 April 1999).
49. Hussin Mutalib, *Singapore Malays: Being Ethnic Minority and Muslim in a Global City-State* (London: Routledge, 2012), pp. 66.
50. Ibid., p. 66.
51. Ibid., p. 64.
52. See, for instance, "Arabisation of Islam in S-E Asia a Danger", *Straits Times*, 30 October 2004, p. 22; "Mahathir's Daughter Speaks Out against Arab Colonialism", *Sunday Times*, 24 May 2015, p. 24; "Keeping Singapore Safe and Inclusive", *Straits Times*, 30 June 2017; "Anchoring Malay Culture in Singapore, *Straits Times*, 7 August 2017; "Arabisation of Islam in Asia: A Clash within Civilisation", *Straits Times*, 19 July 2016; "Indonesian Islam: What Went Right", *Straits Times*, 30 December 2010.
53. Ahmad Najib Burhani, *Islam Nusantara as a Promising Response to Religious Intolerance and Radicalism*, Trends in Southeast Asia, no. 21/2018 (Singapore: ISEAS – Yusof Ishak Institute), pp. 6–9.

6

The Trials of the Progressive: Malay Literary and Cultural Expressions in Singapore

Azhar Ibrahim

> *The creative thought is always a critical thought because it does away with certain illusion and gets closer to the awareness of reality. It enlarges the realm of man's awareness and strengthens the power of his reason. The critical and hence creative thought always has a liberating function by its negation of illusory thought.*
>
> —Erich Fromm

The emergence of modern Malay literature at the turn of the twentieth century came alongside the growing nationalistic and reformist consciousness clamouring for the Malays to address and confront the challenges of development. These challenges included the economy, education, culture, and religious and intellectual thought. Generally, progressive religious and cultural ideas in Malay society are largely expressed via the literary medium, which is more pronounced than mainstream religious discourse. Reformist ideas of the time were articulated and debated through novels, short stories and essays. The role and contribution of literature in Malay society cannot be underestimated.

Thus, any study on Malay society that ignores the literary tradition will miss one of the important cultural and intellectual expressions of the Malays, be it in the past or the present.

This chapter does not seek to chart the development of Malay literature.[1] The aim is to highlight that the literary realm is a creative and critical site where progressive ideas are articulated. Therefore, an appreciation of the historical and sociological dynamics, beyond dissecting texts, an approach that is often taken up in mainstream formalistic literary studies, is necessary. The literary realm can be viewed as contending sites where progressive writers apply the literary medium to annunciate and denunciate ideas in society, inasmuch as regressive and problematic ideas have found their way into literary works too.

By progressive writers, we mean those who have articulated and advocated reformist ideas against religious traditionalism and obscurantism, while recognizing the primacy of human reason, human dignity and rights, political and social freedom, economic and social justice, intellectual and cultural creativity and the overall sense of humanity and rootedness in history and society. Not all of these attributes can be found in any single writer among those whom we classify as "progressive". In reality these ideas had been articulated by a number of writers, with some articulating them more consistently and persistently than others. In some cases reformist writers also express conservative ideas, reflecting competing streams of ideas in society. Most importantly, their articulations of certain ideas have been the common markers to achieve significant presence in the cultural and literary imagination of the larger society, or at least amongst literary circles.

Progressive ideas are articulated in various forms and sites. Literature is one of them, although this is not to say all literary expressions are progressive in nature. In fact, for progressive ideas to be projected in literature, there is a need first for writers to be exposed to critical perspectives and reformist cultural and religious ideas floated in society. As sociological literary theory would argue, the emergence of a talented and progressive writer is not so much due to his artistic talents but to the kinds of ideas that permeate society or the social circles he is associated with. Most importantly, the role of the literati has been recognized as the agents or carriers of change and emancipation. As eloquently put forth by Georg Lukacs:

> Literature has a great part to play in solving the new tasks imposed by the new life in every country. If literature is really to fulfil this role, a role dictated by history, there must be as a natural prerequisite, a philosophical and political rebirth of the writers who produce it.... It is not only the opinions that must change, but the whole emotional world of men; and the most effective propagandist of the new, liberating, democratic feeling are the men of letters.[2]

When progressive ideas are constantly pronounced and circulated, they invariably influence the literary and artistic realms, whether this includes writers and critics or even publishers. Concomitantly, progressive writers can play the role of the beacon of enlightenment for critical thoughts aimed at improving the conditions of society. Nevertheless, it would be naïve to assume that the posture of progressiveness is constant for a particular writer throughout his or her literary career. A closer study of the works of some writers suggests varying postures and responses. This in turn warrants our critical analysis of ideas permeating society, especially amongst the literary and cultural circles; to ask why a progressive outlook can become a recurrent theme in one period while in another it becomes dormant and relegated.

Within the literary fraternity there are conservatives who are parochial in their outlook as well as those who remain apolitical and ahistorical in their thinking. Such limited and myopic exposure is often translated into their literary productions. In the absence of substantive literary criticism, many of these ideas remain unchecked and are not subjected to scrutiny or evaluation. This is further accentuated when the aesthetical finesse or literariness becomes celebrated as a mark of literary accomplishment, rather than any substantive ideas encapsulated in the works. It is within this context that it has become imperative for us to identify and evaluate some of the progressive articulations alongside the regressive ones. This phenomenon can be referred to as the "trials of progressive ideas".

Evaluating the Progressive Postures

In the literary realm, we can denote progressive voices through two main articulations; namely, the annunciation and denunciation of matters pertaining to the interests and concerns of the community and the larger nation. The thrust of critical consciousness is the common thread that may be detected in all progressive pronouncements. Progressive literature and culture constitute several ingredients; among others, a sense of historical consciousness and pride; affirmation of dignity of life for individuals and the community; the ethical commitment to social justice against any form of dehumanizing practice; and the need to embrace modernity, without succumbing to Westernization. The trials of these progressive writers come into full play when we understand that they were, and are, not only struggling in a context of prevailing cultural and religious conservatism, but they were also subject to the conditions in society whereby non-provocative, apolitical and highly aesthetical expressions are much celebrated and tolerated, as opposed to articulations of critical thought that is often deemed too "liberal", "socialistic", or simply "subversive" and "not sufficiently literary".

Progressive writers, like any other critical intellectuals, are invariably a minority in Singapore. Yet, their contributions cannot be underestimated. The emergence of some prominent writers obviously has an impact on the literary scene: they inspire younger writers, and are generally respected by the community for their moral voice, rootedness and intellectual courage. In the Malay literary scene in Singapore, prominent figures like Harun Aminurashid, Mahmud Ahmad, Ahmad Lutfi, Muhammad Ariff Ahmad, Masuri S.N., Suratman Markasan, Mohamed Latiff Mohamed, Rasiah Halil, Hamed Ismail and Isa Kamari are some of the creative writers who have adopted themes in their work discussing the predicaments of society. This list is not exhaustive, but the names mentioned are the leading writers in Singapore Malay literature, and their works are part of the nation's literary canon.

Historically, the Malay literary scene in Singapore was part of the larger cultural orbit of Peninsular Malaysia. To some extent this continues today, although the evolution of Singapore Malay literature has experienced its own trajectory since Separation in 1965.[3] The turn of the twentieth century saw the emergence of Muslim reformist ideas in this part of the world. Singapore was one of the centres for reformist ideas in the region, where prominent figures like Syed Sheikh al-Hadi, Sheikh Tahir Jalaluddin and Haji Abbas Taha flourished. The publication of *Al-Imam*, modelled after the famous Egyptian journal *Al-Manar*, in 1906, testified to the brewing consciousness then. The establishment of Madrasah Al-Iqbal in 1908 in Singapore, although short-lived, was another important landmark in the circulation of progressive religious thought, which generally called for embracing a rational outlook on life, with openness to modern knowledge and participation in the modern economy, the importance of education for girls, and the need to change the curriculum for religious education.

Essentially, the reformists were confronting religious traditionalists who objected to the reform agenda. Reformists like Al-Hadi and Sheikh Tahir Jalaluddin were instrumental in bringing progressive thought into the public sphere. Their ventures into publication and the literary medium, as demonstrated by Al-Hadi's novels, were the means by which reformist ideas could be disseminated to the community.[4] The call for the application of human reasoning, including embracing modern education for both boys and girls, was part of the reformist agenda that gradually gained acceptance. The socialization of such ideas took some time, but the growing challenges of the day inevitably led the community to recognize the importance of adopting the ideas the reformists were pushing.

In the following decades, especially after the Second World War, a reformist-minded writer and publisher Ahmad Lutfi rose to prominence. Works during this period were characterized generally by exhortative tones. The call for modernity was made alongside the need to practise religion in an enlightened way, departing from *taqlid* (blind imitation) and an unnecessary fear of *akal* (human reasoning).[5] But it was also not uncommon for such reformist calls to be interspersed with moralism or moral panic, in which monocausal views were often expressed to explain certain instances of social breakdown or disruption. Lutfi, through his publishing house Qalam Press, wrote a number of novels covering provocative themes that his opponents considered to be immoral, if not pornographic. The themes he covered also pertained to the plight of women, particularly under poverty, the hypocrisy of the religious elites and the moral breakdown and pervasiveness of ignorance due to a lack of education or religious upbringing. Lutfi's vocal criticism, which invariably made some groups uneasy, was nevertheless characterized by a puritanical stance, especially in regard to women in public places.[6]

As Singapore was a transit centre between the region and the outside world, several prominent figures made their presence felt among the locals. Muslim reformists like Syeikh Tahir Jalaluddin and Syed Sheikh al-Hadi were active in promoting Islamic reformist ideas, which saw the establishment of the journal *Al-Imam* and Madrasah Al-Iqbal. At the same time, the regular presence of Hamka in Malaya and Singapore, a leading proponent of reforms from Indonesia, was a major boost to the proliferation of progressive ideas, especially in the areas of education and social and cultural thought. Hamka was not only a respected religious figure but he was also a writer to have penned a number of novels, short stories and essays.[7]

The fact that the post-war Malay movie industry was also centred in Singapore brought writers, performance artists and musicians to make the island their home base. At that time there were already Malay journals and magazines and a Malay newspaper circulating on the island. *Utusan Melayu* had prominent journalists and writers within its ranks. Among them were A. Samad Ismail, Keris Mas, Usman Awang, and a few others. The formation in 1950 of a literary association of writers, ASAS '50, became the hallmark of a literary ethos that affirmed "literature for society". The polemics on "Art for Society" versus "Art for Art's sake" between Asraf and Hamzah Hussein,[8] although short lived, signalled the importance of linking literature to social and cultural development.

Apart from the religious reformist spirit pulsating within the local community during this period, the consciousness of Malay nationalism was also more apparent and gaining momentum. Amongst the intelligentsia, the idea of social justice, equality, democracy and economic development gained increasing prominence. Small pockets amongst them were also attracted to socialist ideas and were critical of capitalism and colonialism. In the mix were also ethno-chauvinists who invariably linked the plight of the Malays in Malaya to economic strangulation by non-Malays.

A sociocultural and political ambience had developed that was open to new ideas for the construction of Malay/Malayan society. These robust expressions of nationalistic and reformist sentiments took place during the period that Malaya/Singapore was agitating for self-governance and which led to eventual independence. The formation of the Malay Studies programme in 1955 at the University of Malaya's Bukit Timah campus provided another setting where an interest in Malay intellectual, literary and cultural discourse was being enhanced. Led by Za'ba (Zainal Abidin Bin Ahmad)—an expert in Malay language, literary and cultural studies—the Malay intellectual discourse in the academic setting was laid out. It would later have a considerable impact on Malay intellectual life in Singapore and Peninsular Malaya. Za'ba was a respected cultural figure who was a vocal advocate for Malay progress and who was critical of the conservative religious elite.[9]

Amongst the Malay teaching fraternities, which made up the bulk of the Malay intelligentsia, the interest in Malay language and education also spurred an interest in Malay literature, including the literature of Indonesia. It was not uncommon in Singapore at that time for Indonesian works to be read and for them to be easily available. The development of the Indonesian literary scene was much followed, and prominent Indonesian writers became literary icons for local writers. Celebrated Indonesian writers whose works were recognized and read included Sutan Takdir Alisjahbana, Amir Hamzah, Chairil Anwar, Achdiat Mihardja and Pramoedya Ananta Toer. The works of these writers often carried the themes of social emancipation, individualism, politics, economics and religious thought, which gradually found resonance amongst the local literary audience.

It is against this cultural milieu of the decades after the war that we see elements of progressive ideas find expression in the works of Singapore Malay writers. Yet, while the literary response carrying reformist ideas against religious conservatism had been encapsulated in some of Ahmad Lutfi's novels, this theme did not make much headway in later decades, as there was a general aversion to criticism of religious matters. Nevertheless, Lutfi's active publication work at Qalam Press gave rise to important reading materials featuring content with engaging themes for the Malay reading public.[10] Harun Aminurrashid, regarded as the doyen of Malay literature and education in the pre-independence period, wrote several historical-themed novels that narrate the adventures of famous Malay figures of the past. These include the novel *Panglima Awang* (1958) and its sequel *Anak Panglima Awang* (1961). Although tinged with historical romanticism, his works project historical consciousness and pride, especially in the context of colonial rule, where indigenous history was afforded only a low premium. His novel *Minah Joget Moden* (1968) spoke of the plight of women forced to work as dancers in nightclubs to sustain a decent livelihood for their families. Another novel, *Simpang Perinang* (1966), provides an interesting social critique in its portrayal of a family living on the outskirts of Singapore city, struggling against poverty. While the novel does not go into the reasons for poverty being widespread, it does present a clear message that it could be addressed through education and social mobility. Without blaming the poor for their predicament, the novel comments on why attention needs to be given to the issue, a theme that until then had not appeared in Malay literature.

A similar theme of poverty and social disruption was taken up by Suratman Markasan in his debut novel *Tak Ada Jalan Keluar* (1962). Poverty and unemployment most greatly affect the women in the novel, who in desperation turn to prostitution or the entertainment industry in order to provide food for their families. It was significant for such issues to be taken up in the literary medium because, whilst these problems were acute and strikingly visible, such subjects were not deliberated in the open.

Post-separation Literary Development

After Singapore's separation from Malaysia, a few of the ASAS '50 writers remaining in the city state provided the literary and cultural leadership. Senior writers from ASAS such as Muhammad Ariff Ahmad and Masuri S.N. rose to prominence in the republic. The common literary themes taken up by them revolved around identity issues, especially anxieties felt by Malays concerning cultural erosion amidst the fast-paced development of the city state. Their critical stance on various aspects of life in the cosmopolitan city points to the significance of the Malay writers as the moral and intellectual voice of their community, particularly when other groups such as the religious elites, professionals and even the Malay teaching fraternities were no longer vocal in raising their views on the issues and challenges facing Malays in Singapore.

Prominent Malay writers adhered to an idea of literature that incorporated a sense of social commitment, and this has been popularized by other literary activists. Hence, it is no surprise that many of their works carry socio-economic and political themes. At the top of their concerns were underachievement by the Malays in education and under-representation of the community at the national level. The fact of their criticism, albeit expressed in a literary form, is significant in a milieu where there was very little space to project critical voices.

Muhammad Ariff Ahmad, one of the founding members of ASAS '50, emerged as a cultural and language expert highly respected at the national level. It was not uncommon amongst the literati that they would try to assuage readers to embrace progress and to fully participate in the development of the country in the context of community and nation-building. While refraining from direct political activism, the literati generally focused on cultural and linguistic enhancement as a ballast against foreign influences considered incompatible with the community. This, however, is not to be read as cultural conservatism. Rather, it was an assertion for Malays to adapt to the demands of a global economy while at the same time preserving the cultural and religious identity of the minority group.

Suratman Markasan rose to become lecturer at a local teacher's training college. Today he is still actively writing, on top of giving seminars and workshops. Suratman's literary repertoire is mainly concerned with the concrete issues and problems facing the Malay community. These include parental neglect, spiritual emptiness, cultural alienation, language deprivation, the plight of the poor, and the mismanagement of mosques.[11] Over the decades, Suratman's literary repertoire has expanded in terms of both form and themes. Two of his works in particular deserve mentioning here. One is his novel *Penghulu yang Hilang Segala-galanya* (1998), which narrates the lives of a family that moved from one of the Southern Islands to mainland Singapore, a phenomenon that took place in the 1970s and 80s. While the story points to the problems of maladjustment experiences among the islanders resettled on mainland Singapore, it also brings across the message of the huge social implications of displacement. This was a problem many Malay families had to face, particularly in the early period of urban resettlement from villages to the housing estates.

Masuri S.N., who had already made his name in the post-war period, emerged as a leading poet. Although Masuri's output was diverse and extensive, a theme that commonly appears in both his poems and his essays is the idea of *kemanusiaan* (humanism or sense of humanity). His repertoire is loaded with enunciations of the ideals of progress, humanity and modernity, though critical denouncements of the same are not altogether absent. This approach may be seen as a literary form of affirming societal commitment, minus any overt political assertions, which Masuri obviously shunned throughout his literary career.[12]

The Significance of Literary Humanism

Kemanusiaan became one of the hallmarks of modern Malay literature after 1965. Authors and critics of the Malay literary scene in Malaysia such as Keris Mas, Usman Awang, Shahnon Ahmad and Kassim Ahmad have been active in affirming *kemanusiaan*. Masuri and Mohamed Latiff Mohamed stand out in literary circles in affirming such values. Masuri's notion of this literary humanism is aimed at addressing the needs and challenges of society and of humanity:

> In my opinion, a creative writer must have the awareness to appreciate and give meaning critically and sensitively to the strengths and limitations that are unfolding in society and his environment, whether they pertain to matters of politics, socioeconomics, education or culture. This is important to guarantee a better life for humanity in the future. Without the need to emphasize that these critical views generated by creative writers are indeed the development of his thought and his awareness—the writers must realise their position and responsibility as human beings, who are responsible to the society they belong to.[13]

Similarly, Hadijah Rahmat—who is both a literary scholar and a creative writer—places a high premium on humanistic value in literature, and for her the role of the writer cannot be underestimated:

> The role of the writer is as the spokesperson for his society and the epoch he lives in. Especially in modern Malay society, which is facing demands and pressures of the current order, the role becomes ever more challenging. This is the responsibility that must be undertaken with earnest preparations and sacrifice, and this cannot be accomplished in a short period of time. However, as a writer, if we are able to fulfil these and to ultimately inspire and be appreciated by readers—it is indeed a grace [that we have endowed]. This is the most valuable contribution that could be made by human beings to his/her society and the larger humanity.[14]

In contrast to the universal humanism and rationalism that the Malays should embrace, Hadijah was vehemently against the kind of unthinking or sheer ignorance, or *bebalisma*, in the literary landscape, a concept coined by S.H. Alatas:

> I conclude that the elements of *bebalisma*, especially regarding the features of irrational thought, are to be found in our modern literature. Consciously or unconsciously it has resulted in negative and disappointing effects.... It reflects the limited grasp of knowledge among our writers in taking up the subject matter in their writings, often hasty to understand and to make proposals, and easily influenced by other writers, becoming emotional and uncomfortable with criticism, and averse to rational arguments. To overcome this problem, our writers should embrace the idea of increasing the quality of their writing. They should take initiatives to upgrade their knowledge, especially related to literature. They should not rush to write without a deep understanding of the issues they are embarking on. The world of literature has developed over centuries. Our writers should refer to these earlier writings, without postulating new theories that are only misleading. Most importantly, we should not be easily influenced and we should accept an idea with our soul and mind rationally and critically, without being too emotional.[15]

In sum, a high standard must be observed and maintained in the realm of literary activities. This includes the ability to read social phenomenon in a critical manner. It is also necessary to be sensitive to the pluralistic milieu and to transcend ethno-religious proclivities. Hadijah emphasized the importance for writers to be aware of and to have an empathy for social realities:

> Are we so zealous of the idea of the superiority of our culture and religion to the point we are less sensitive to other ethnic groups and religions? Such writings will not function as the social/religious bridge, and it will not contribute to recognition of our universal human values. Therefore it warrants our serious attention to the issues of race relations in our writings and to give a signal that we are equally concerned with and take responsibilities towards social welfare and national development.[16]

Indeed, in Singapore Malay literary scholarship, critical ideas are being espoused via commentary on such ideas. Sharifah Maznah and Shaharuddin Maaruf, for instance, noted:

> The consciousness of being an underprivileged minority is thinning out in the late eighties and nineties. This is because Singapore Malays are making good progress in many areas of life. Educationally they are doing better and in the economy their income level has risen. More and more Malays are starting their own business and are successful. The English-educated Malay middle class is growing. Politically, they are better represented. Malay political leaders work closely with the Malay masses to improve the conditions of their community. Self-help bodies like Mendaki and the Association of Muslim Professionals have emerged with concrete programmes to speed up Malay development. The sense of insecurity of the early years of Separation is weakening. A growing confidence can be felt. The consciousness of an underdeveloped minority is giving way to the consciousness of a progressive community. The sense of displacement and marginality as evidenced in Malay Literature of the early years can also be said to be weakening in contemporary Malay literature.[17]

While some writers see the modern city of Singapore as a threat to the preservation of Malay ideas and as a source of the moral degradation, this cosmopolitan setting is seen positively by Masuri because

> the Singapore Malay community lives in the middle of a cosmopolitan society that is plural and connected to the global culture. They, including the creative writers, are exposed to these [global] experiences, hence inspiring them to create literary works that are uniquely their own. In other words, with direct exposure to world culture and through appreciating it, there is a great possibility for the emergence of new works of Malay literature that are penetrating in their themes and styles, covering all aspects of human life.[18]

These critical and affirmative views are part of the progressive articulations in Malay cultural and literary discourse. Most importantly, the progressive view has affirmed that literary works are to be recognized beyond simply their aesthetic merit; as important social documents that reflect societal conditions, with all their human concerns, anxieties, dissent, ideals and joy. Moreover, we see writers who are in addition to their creative pieces also engaged in literary and societal issues through essays and forum pieces. The publication of reflective essays by Masuri S.N.,[19] A. Ghani Hamid,[20] Suratman Markasan,[21] Djamal Tukimin[22] and Mohamed Latiff Mohamed[23] are cases in point.

All these expressions are part of the literary humanism that is not only found in the themes and tenor of literary works and criticism but also as a paradigm that should be embraced—as enjoined by senior writers from ASAS '50 circles—especially by the younger cohort of writers. The significance of this pronouncement can be seen when we compare the clamour for "nationalistic", "Islamic" and avant-garde cosmopolitan literary expressions in the literary scene from the Nusantara region. *Kemanusiaan* in many ways is the affirmation of the literary and artistic sense of humanity and a commitment to the larger collective interest—of the need to recognize human dignity and reason, rights and duties, social justice and equality, as well as solidarity with fellow human beings in denouncing all forms of prejudice, discrimination and oppression. It obviously demands a universalistic outlook that transcends the segmented interests of ethnicity, religion, class, gender and nationality, although the tenor and intensity of *kemanusiaan* may differ from one writer to another.

Moreover, in a context where political overtures are discouraged, the clamour for *kemanusiaan* implicitly aims at overcoming inhibited voices and self-censorship among writers. Where the politics of agitation has generally been averted and ideological expressions—be they of nationalist or leftist tendencies—have taken a backseat, the fervour of *kemanusiaan* has remained the mainstay of literary ideational momentum. It is also interesting to note that while religious discourse has been lukewarm in accepting humanism as part of the critical concept of religio-intellectual engagement, it has been the literary circle that has emerged as the moral and intellectual voice, which altogether points to the fact that the literary realm is an important site for progressive ideas to be nurtured and projected.

Among the few to have taken up critical themes with some consistency has been Mohamed Latiff Mohamed. His poems are culturally iconic inasmuch as they lay bare the hypocrisy, timidity, inhumanity and poverty that have beset the community. Some of Latiff's satirical short stories contain clear political innuendoes, criticizing the leadership, the ethnic divide and exclusivism, and the underdeveloped consciousness of the public. Although Latiff's works are not free of pessimistic overtones,[24] they do demonstrate a consistent engagement with the problems and concerns facing the Malay community. His *Kota Airmata*

(1977) deals with the way we view poverty in urban Singapore, where educational underachievement and social dislocation are often blamed on those affected for their indocility and cultural deficiencies. In his poems Latiff takes a stance in particular against intellectual malaise, especially of writers who avoid the realities of life by escaping into their own literary fantasies. An example of this can be seen in his poem "Nostalgia Nusantara":

> Suradi seeks justice with dust in his way
> Rasiah dan Hadijah with their loud intellectual cry
> Entices Suratman to interpret the meaning of loss
> After his penghulu lost the island, dignity and rambutan orchard
> Masuri in search of humanism in the peak of humanity
>
> Oh artists of Singapore
> Are you all dreaming
> Frolicking on the dais of a courtier's princess
> Or peeping the fingers of Princess Gunung Ledang
> Or in love with Radin Mas
> And for longing the smells of Tun Teja's body
> On the dais of lover
> Without a map
> Without rooted in a real polity.[25]

In poetry and drama, Rafaat Hamzah emerged as a critical voice with a thematic repertoire not unlike that of Latiff, except that his tone is far more cynical and witty. Importantly, Rafaat includes many of his poetic protests in his dramatic pieces for the stage. While Latiff and Rafaat are typically vocal in their dissenting poetics, the more discursive and intellectual engagement comes from the university-trained cohorts, such as Hadijah Rahmat, Rasiah Halil, Saedah Buang, Sharifah Maznah and Isa Kamari. The first four of these—all women and graduates of the University of Singapore's Malay Studies programme—were at one point active in writing creative pieces such as poems and short stories as well as producing academic papers on Singapore Malay literature. Themes of inhumanity, prejudice, mediocrity, traditionalism and exclusivism have been some of their concerns, which in a way placed literary discussions as one of the most critical voices in the local Malay cultural and intellectual discourse.

Isa Kamari is a highly prolific writer and his work has recently gained more attention through translations, as well as his debut in writing in English.[26] His historical novels are interesting in many ways, although his novels with religious themes document very much the orientations that could be found in contemporary society. Although his works may not be "revisionist", his literary articulations of important historical episodes are of interest in the way they view history in an imaginative fashion, departing from conventional and dominant narratives. The significance of historical novels lies very much in the way they engage critically with colonial ideology, which in turn affects the way we view ourselves, others, and even our own culture and history. Given time, these are some explorations that Isa and other writers could undertake, where the historical novels truly become works of brilliant literary prose with sparkling insights into the intricacies of man, power, ideology and humanity.

The Challenge of Ideational Transmission

During the colonial period, Singapore was the cultural and intellectual capital of Malaya, where the cultural and literary intelligentsia from the Peninsula and the region congregated. Many of them worked in various journalistic, cultural, artistic and film-making sectors. There was already a strong connection with cultural and literary ideas between Malaya and Indonesia, including the political imagining of a larger *Melayu Raya* or *Indonesia Raya* by certain Malay and Indonesian nationalists. In some ways, the formation of ASAS '50 was very much inspired by the Angkatan '45 in Indonesia. It was not uncommon then for the Malay intelligentsia to be familiar with Indonesian literary works, including translations into Bahasa Indonesia of important Western cultural and literary works. There was a degree of traffic of ideas from Indonesia (primarily written in Bahasa), with the nation serving as an important intellectual, literary and even religious source for members of the Malay intelligentsia, especially for those who had received only a Malay medium education.

However, after 1965, when leading members of the Malay intelligentsia moved to Kuala Lumpur, the remaining intelligentsia, who were primarily Malay-educated teachers, inevitably took active leadership in the Malay cultural and literary affairs of Singapore. Malay was no longer the dominant working language of Singapore, with Malay schools eventually closing. In the course of time, Malay discourse has been confined to the realms of creative literature, religious instruction and the learning of Malay as a second language in public schools, which has had an impact on the extent and degree of Malay cultural and intellectual discourse and language use. The Malay teaching fraternity, including the literati, had looked to Malaysia's language and literary corpus as a standard model to be emulated. But then the Malay discourse that evolved in the post-separation decades took a different posture. With the Malay language operating mainly in the educational domain, it was no longer the linguistic medium for Malay intellectual and cultural expression.

Today, the frequency in the traffic of Indonesian ideas into the Singapore Malay discourse has been much reduced, whether they be religious, intellectual or literary works. Regular exchanges of performative arts such as dance and drama however have been maintained, including more formal literary exchanges under the auspices of MASTERA (Southeast Asia Literary Council), a body that Singapore has been a member of since 2012. With this limited cultural and intellectual exposure, local literary development has not been able to benefit from the fast-changing literary, intellectual and religious developments occurring in Indonesia, where many creative and critical writers are public intellectuals in their own right.

The Place of Cultural Planning and Vision

The emergence of progressive cultural and literary domains requires not only the poetic talent of writers but also depends to an extent on the degree of cultural and intellectual responses in mitigating aestheticism. When the latter is deemed the sole basis for literary excellence, the social functions of literature become relegated. The situation is aggravated when the main concern among writers is with how to devise new writing techniques and in exploring the latest themes based on market or global trends. The development of Malay literature is no exception. Hence, it is not surprising to find literary workshops and forums organized around these concerns, while writers are become increasingly divorced from issues like the dehumanized conditions of urban alienation, the authoritarian complex, psychological anxieties, religious utopianism, economic deprivation, social injustice, mental health, cultural levelling-down and historical romanticism.

In addition, the urban Singapore context, with all the intricacies and challenges of the current situation, does not seem to have been able to entice the interests of writers for deep reflection and analysis. Instead, it is common to encounter several writers repeating almost clichéd views that the urban environment points to moral degeneration, alongside registering pessimism and cynicism about modern living. In other words, instead of expanding on the notion of *kemanusiaan*, there is increasing literary insularity, becoming parochial in outlook, attested by the themes taken up in prose and verse. In a context where wider cultural and intellectual exposure and engagement are absent, one cannot expect a rigorous critical culture to flourish, whether this be for fictive or discursive forms.

This brings us to the need for cultural planning and vision. Simply leaving literary development to its own course is unwise. What is needed, among other things, are the following: (a) the cultural and intellectual horizons of young writers need to be expanded; (b) homegrown literary criticism, in both the public and academic spheres, needs to be cultivated; (c) translations of leading literary and reflective pieces from around the world need to be encouraged and disseminated; (d) discursive platforms where issues and problems of the day can be debated and scrutinized should be developed, and (e) writers and budding talents should be provided opportunities for creative writing residencies and for exposure to research stints.

In a context where religious interest and religious discourses are expanding within the Malay Muslim community, it is important that religious circles—whose medium of communication is primarily Malay—receive literary exposure. The participation and contribution from this group to the literary and cultural scene is still very minimal. Equally important is harnessing this group with cultural and literary interests, with organic links with the community. In other words, the literary realms, with all their universalistic and particularistic dimensions, should be important ideational resources for religious discourses to develop, as the experience in Indonesia has shown.

Conclusion

In Malay intellectual history, progressive ideas have been articulated via the literary medium, inasmuch as conservative and regressive ideas have also been expressed through a number of works too. In the absence of or with only a limited space for critical discourse to be articulated in the Malay community (so, too, in the broader Singapore society), the literary medium becomes the best site for progressive ideas to be articulated. While the religious domains for the most part focus on confessional and practical rituals, and the Malay cultural and language domains have largely emphasized the preservation of cultural identity, it becomes clear that the realm of literature and the role of the literati are ever more important. Literature, in other words, becomes an avenue for critical ideas to be articulated in the community.

The Singapore Malay literary scene, in a certain period of its history, provides a good example of progressive ideas encapsulated in literary works. It is important to note that while there are a few sparks of progressive thinking, one cannot say that the literary culture is distinctively and consistently progressive. Any study of the ideational contestations and conflicts in the community would not be complete if the literary arena is neglected or underemphasized. Being progressive not only entails ideas and values that are universal and humanistic in nature. It also refers to a kind of societal commitment to literary and artistic endeavours, including a tone of empathy and of taking the side of those who have been silenced and tormented. A cultural and societal grounding is therefore essential. A progressive dimension can also be seen when some writers not only respond to the dominant ideas within society but also react to their fellow writers who have championed certain ideas, especially those perceived as counterproductive to the community and nation.

The socio-political and cultural environment has inevitably conditioned the literary and arts scenes. Today, the infrastructure developed to support literature is extensive, with various publication grants, awards and literary competitions provided to encourage writers to continuously produce and create a robust literary ecology. But, ironically, with these incentives and support, the kind of literature produced bears witness to a departure from the earlier themes of social critique. The call to produce works for social and cultural enlightenment is muted;

instead, individual, domestic and even trivial narratives are becoming the conventional literary mode. With popular literature flooding the market, it becomes increasingly challenging for critical or progressive alternatives—resisted in some cases—to register a deep presence.

The trials and tribulations of progressive ideas are always complex and varied, but progressive voices and ideas have surfaced and evolved throughout history, making their impacts on individuals and communities. Malay literary development is no exception. The task ahead is to increase the dissemination and reception of progressive ideas in the Malay Muslim community in Singapore. The literary scene could play the role of harnessing progressive ideas, provided prominent literary doyens demonstrate the necessary leadership as men of ideas. But progressive cultural and literary realms do not exist in isolation. Indeed, intellectual and cultural insularity is the very challenge that prevents progressive ideas from developing, although often many would attribute the reason to political control and self-censorship. The dynamism of the literary environment, or the lack of it, also depends on the other sectors of religious, intellectual and political life of the community—and particularly their respective leaderships—without which, no support or encouragement would be possible.

While such an ideal deserves to be expected, the fact remains that amid the failure of these sectors to harness progressive ideas in public, it falls to the literary realm to be forthcoming or proactive in infusing progressive, emancipative and reformist ideas and values. For progressive religious and intellectual thought to be developed and sustained, the role of literature and culture as a medium for ideational transmission and engagement must be recognized, invested and expanded. This is not an impossible task, but it is one that must be taken up by the community's intelligentsia and cultural workers.

Notes

1. See Johan Jaafar, Hawa Abdullah, Mohd Thani Ahmad, Safian Hussain, and Ungku Maimuna Mohd Tahir, eds., *History of Modern Malay literature*, vols. 1–2 (Kuala Lumpur: Dewan Bahasa dan Pustaka, 1992).
2. George Lukacs, *Studies in European Realism* (London: Merlin Press, 1972), p. 17.

3. See Mana Sikana, "Wajah Sastera Melayu Singapura Selepas Perpisahan dengan Malaysia", *Sari* 27, no. 2 (2009).
4. Talib Samat, *Syed Syeikh Al-Hadi Sasterawan Progresif Melayu* (Kuala Lumpur: Dewan Bahasa dan Pustaka, 1992).
5. Talib Samat, *Ahmad Lutfi Penulis, Penerbit dan Pendakwah* (Kuala Lumpur: Dewan Bahasa dan Pustaka, 2004).
6. Khalidah Adibah Binti Haji Amin, "Ahmad Lutfi on the Education and Freedom of Women" (Academic exercise in Malay Studies, University of Malaya, Singapore, 1957).
7. Junus Amir Hamzah, *Hamka sebagai Pengarang Roman: Sebuah Studie Sastra* (Djakarta: Megabookstore, 1964).
8. Athi Sivan Mariappan, *Hamzah Hussin Sekitar Pemikiran Seni Untuk Seni* (Bangi: Penerbit Universiti Kebangsaan Malaysia, 1997).
9. Za'ba, "The Malays and Religion", in *Tamadun Islam di Malaysia* (Kuala Lumpur: Persatuan Sejarah Malaysia, 1980).
10. Hashim Ismail and Mohd Hanafi Ibrahim, *Ahmad Lutfi Pembangkit Semangat Zaman* (Kuala Lumpur: Dewan Bahasa & Pustaka, 2019).
11. Suratman Markasan, *Bangsa Melayu Singapura dalam Transformasi Budayanya* (Singapore: Anuar Othman & Associates, 2005).
12. See Azhar Ibrahim, "Masuri SN dan Nilai-nilai Islam: Menelusuri Kesalehan Sosial dan Kepenyairannya", in *Cendekiawan Pentyuluh Emansipasi* (Kuala Lumpur: SIRD, 2014).
13. Masuri S.N., *Kreativiti dan Kemanusiaan dalam Kesusasteraan* (Shah Alam: Penerbit Fajar Bakti, 1998), p. 133.

    [Saya berpendapat peranan penulis-penulis kreatif ialah mereka harus cukup peka untuk turut menghayati dan sekaligus cuba memberi makna secara kritikal dan sensitif terhadap kebaikan dan kekhilafan terhadap kelebihan dan kekurangannya yang sedang berlaku di dalam masyarakat dan lingkungannya (kehidupannya), baik dari segi politik, sosioekonomi, pendidikan, kebudayaan dan lain-lainnya untuk mendapatkan kehidupan yang lebih cerah dan baik buat umat manusia yang akan datang. Maka di sini rasanya sudah tidak perlu ditekankan, bahawa pandangan kritikal yang dibual, atau ditulis oleh seseorang penulis kreatif menerusi ciptaan karya sasteranya itu adalah merupakan perkembangan fikirannya yang menunjukkan dia cukup peka cukup peduli serta menyedari posisi dan tanggungjawabnya sebagai seorang manusia yang berwibawa di dalam kehidupan masyarakat yang dihadirinya.]

14. Hadijah Rahmat, *Sastera & Manusia Melayu Baru* (Singapore: Persatuan Wartawan Melayu Singapura, 1998), p. 159.

    [Tugas penulis sebagai jurubicara masyarakat dan zamannya ketika ini. Terutama dalam masyarakat Melayu baru yang

> sedang memenuhi tuntutan dan tekanan kehidupan semasa yang mendesak, sebenarnya memang sukar dan mencabar. Ini adalah tanggungjawab yang perlu dipenuhi dengan persiapan dan pengorbanan yang tidak dapat disudahkan dalam tempoh yang singkat. Tetapi sebagai penulis, jika kita berjaya memenuhinya sehingga mencetuskan rasa cinta pembaca terhadap alam dan kehidupan ia merupakan suatu anugerah. Yang tidak ternilai, yang dapat dihulurkan oleh seorang insan terhadap masyarakat, kemanusiaan dan kehidupan keseluruhannya.]

15. Ibid., p. 117.

> [dapat saya simpulkan bahawa unsur-unsur bebalisma, khususnya ciri-ciri pemikiran yang tidak rasional, terdapat dalam dunia kesusasteraan moden kita. Ianya secara disedari atau tidak telah menimbulkan suatu kesan yang tidak sihat dan mengecewakan. Kesemua isi yang dibincangkan memperlihatkan kecetekan pengetahuan penulisnya dalam memperkatakan subjek tersebut, sikap terburu-buru memahami dan membuat satu saranan, mudah dipengaruhi oleh pendapat penulis-penulis lain, emosional dan tidak berlapang dada dalam menerima kritikan dan juga menolak hujah dan pendapat yang rasional. Untuk mengatasi masalah ini, para penulis kita haruslah mengambil sikap baru dalam usaha mempertinggikan mutu penulisan mereka. Mereka haruslah mengambil inisiatif untuk meninggikan ilmu pengetahuan terutama berkaitan dengan hal-hal yang rapat dengan dunia penulisan. Jangan terburu-buru menulis tanpa benar-benar memahami apa yang ditulis. Dunia penulisan telah berkembang sejak ratusan tahun yang lampau. Bahan-bahan pembacaan dan perbincangan yang mahu dikemukakan mungkin sudah dibincangkan secara mendalam oleh penulis-penulis terdahulu. Tulisan-tulisan seperti ini harus dirujuk bukan membina teori-teori baru yang menyeleweng sama sekali. Yang penting sekali ialah kita jangan mudah terpengaruh, terimalah sesuatu dengan jiwa dan fikiran yang rasional dan kritikan bukan terlalu emosional.]

16. Hadijah Rahmat, "Lukisan Sastera Melayu Antara Keunggulan dan Kenyataan", in *Sastera Melayu Warisan Jati Diri dan Jagat*, edited by Mohammed Pitchay Gani Mohamed Abdul Aziz (Singapore: Angkatan Sasterawan '50/National Library Board, 2003), p. 354.

> [Mungkinkah kita terlampau taksub dengan ketinggian budaya dan agama kita sehingga kita kurang peka dengan bangsa/agama lain? Karya seperti ini tidak akan berfungsi sebagai jambatan sosial/agama dan tidak mencapai nilai kemanusiaan sejagat. Oleh itu adalah wajar agar perhatian yang lebih serius diberikan kepada isu perhubungan kaum ini dalam penulisan dan kegiatan sastera kita sebagai sumbangan dari golongan penulis dan juga sebagai isyarat bahawa kita juga turut prihatin dan bertanggungjawab terhadap kebajikan sosial dan pembangunan nasional kita.]

17. Shaharuddin Maaruf and Sharifah Maznah, "Singapore Malay Literature", in *Modern Literature of ASEAN*, edited by Budi Darm (Jakarta: ASEAN Committee on Culture and Information, 2000), p. 177.
18. Masuri, *Kreativiti dan Kemanusiaan*, p. 204.

> [Masyarakat Melayu Singapura benar-benar dan langsung hidup di tengah-tengah masyarakat kosmopolitan yang majmuk serta berhubung dengan kebudayaan dunia maka mereka (termasuk golongan penulis kreatif) akan lebih dahulu mendapat pengalaman asas untuk dijadikan bahan menghasilkan karya sastera yang tersendiri. Ertinya, dengan didedah secara langsung kepada kebudayaan dunia dan sekali gus turut menghayatinya maka berkemungkinan akan lahirlah karya sastera Melayu baru yang lebih mendalam, penting dan kuat pengucapannya, mencakupi hidupan seluruh umat manusia.]

19. Masuri S.N., *Dalam Merenung Dalam: Kumpulan Esei dan Kritikan, 1977–2005* (Singapore: ASAS '50, 2006).
20. A. Ghani Hamid, *Laluan Budaya* (Singapore: ASAS '50, 2011).
21. Suratman Markasan, *Kembali Ke Akar Melayu, Kembali Ke Akar Islam*, vol. 3, working papers 1986–2012 (Singapore: Darul Andalus, 2013).
22. Djamal Tukimin, *Sejarah Tidak Pernah Luka Kita yang Berduka* (Singapura: Pustaka Nasional, 2008).
23. Mohamed Latiff Mohamed, *Alam Kepenyairan Singapura: Pengamatan dan Penciptaan* (Singapore: Angkatan Sasterawan '50, 2012).
24. See Sharifah Maznah Syed Omar, "The Atrophy of Vision and Hope in the Poetry of Mohamed Latiff Mohamed", *Singa: Literature & the Arts in Singapore*, no. 25 (December 1992).
25. Mohamed Latiff Mohamed, "Nostalgia Nusantara", in *Bagiku Sepilah Sudah* (Singapore: Pustaka Nasional, 2002).
26. See Isa Kamari, *Tweet* (Singapore: Kitab International, 2016).

7

The Meaning and Objectives of Progressive Islam

Syed Farid Alatas

In the last three decades, frequent reference had been made to Islam in the plural. For example, some years ago a book appeared with the title *Islams and Modernities* by Aziz Al-Azmeh. Such usage confuses rather than clarifies matters. Many Muslims would be puzzled by what is meant by "Islams". From a conceptual and empirical point of view, as well, it would be wrong to refer to Islam in the plural. Muslims understand from the Qur'an that there is only one *din* or religion of Islam. By this is meant that there are certain basic beliefs and practices common to all Muslims that neither change from space to space nor time to time. This is not an ideal but a reality.

What does change, however, are the material, cultural and ideological expressions of Muslims. For example, the cuisine of Muslims, their music and dance forms, their art and literature continuously develop in different directions. So do the ideologies; that is, the Muslims' orientations to the political, economic and social worlds. The ideologies of Muslims do draw upon the sources of Islam, such as the Qur'an, the Sunnah or traditions of the Prophet Muhammad, as well as the intellectual heritage of the Muslims that developed from the early days of Islam. But they also incorporate interpretations and experiences that are space-time bound and, therefore, continuously change. We can, therefore, speak of multiplicity and plurality when we speak of Islam at these levels. The term *din* refers to Islam as revelation, while other terms such as *sabil, shari'a, tariqah* and *jama'ah* refer to Islam as interpretation and lived experience. At the level of *din*, Islam is unitary. The diversity appears at the levels of *sabil, shari'a, tariqah* and *jama'ah*. These are the historical and empirical levels at which the *din* is realized.

While there are no multiple Islams, there are a multitude of Muslim ideologies. They are often grouped under headings such as modernism, traditionalism, neo-modernism, fundamentalism and radicalism. Some Muslim ideologies are held to be in line with Islam as a religion, and some are not. Backward and extremist ideologies and orientations have always been held on to by a minority in Muslim societies. But that is enough to cause problems. As a result, the question as to what constitutes a progressive interpretation of Islam arises. When we refer to progressive Islam, we are really referring to the progressive thinking among Muslims on various issues.

The idea of progressive Islam or its variant, progressive Muslims, is generally held to be a notion that developed in the West during the early years of this century, particularly after 11 September 2001 (or 9/11). Various Islamic organizations and movements have emerged that qualify themselves as progressive. Examples are the Progressive Muslim Union of North America (New York) and Muslims for Progressive Values (Los Angeles). The idea of progressive Islam was discussed systematically by Omid Safi, an American-based Iranian scholar, about fifteen years ago. Progressive Muslim thought is associated with the UK-based journal *Critical Muslim*. Also relevant is the idea of progressive Islamic hermeneutics, advanced by the Australian-based scholar Adis Duderija. However, it has hardly been recognized that the idea of Progressive Islam actually emerged in the Malay world. It was the name of a journal founded by Syed Hussein Alatas while he was a student at the University of Amsterdam. *Progressive Islam* was published for two years (1954–55).[1]

The objectives of this paper are as follows. First it discusses the notion of Progressive Islam as conceptualized by Syed Hussein Alatas and others. The paper then turns to more practical concerns regarding the applicability of the notion to the Malaysian case. In this regard, the paper discusses in broad outline the idea of a progressive society and enumerates some of the specific traits of a progressive Islamic orientation that are compatible with such a society.

Progressive Islam: The Beginnings

Progressive Islam appeared as a monthly publication for two years, in 1954 and 1955, in Amsterdam. The editorial of the first issue of the first volume states the following:

> This monthly, which we have called *Progressive Islam*, is the realization of an attempt to formulate a serious view concerning the nature of Islam and its relation with modern thought. The condition of the Muslim people, the nature of the Islamic religion and the impact of Western thought upon the societies of the East shall be the primary concern of this monthly...
>
> The name *Progressive Islam*.
>
> The name *Progressive Islam* does not imply any dissection whatsoever as to the nature of the Islamic faith. The idea which we intend to convey is not a kind of abstraction from the totality of the Islamic religion. By calling this paper Progressive Islam we do not mean that we have extracted one part of Islam which is progressive and left the other part of Islam which is not progressive. Rather, the name *Progressive Islam* should be regarded as another way of saying that Islam is progressive.[2]

Apart from dealing with prejudices and misunderstandings about Islam in the West, the objective of *Progressive Islam* was to publish articles on various aspects of Islam "laying a great emphasis on its rational and philosophical foundation".[3] This was with a view towards dealing with some of the fundamental problems of Muslim society. The editorial of the second issue, entitled "The Regeneration of Islamic Societies", lists five fundamental problems faced by the Muslim world. They are the nature of the group in power, the lack of sound planning, unconsciousness of the vital problems of society, desultory influences from the West, and materialism and positivism.[4]

The problem of leadership was a concern that was to occupy the thoughts of Alatas for the rest of his life. In 1977 he published a book entitled *Intellectuals in Developing Societies*.[5] His numerous books and papers on corruption also highlighted the problems of vicious and irresponsible leadership. As a young student he had stated:

> It had been a deeply felt misfortune amongst the people of Islam that the group that is usually in power from amongst themselves are people who neither are inspired by the lofty, humanitarian ideals of Islam nor by any sense of proportion. These people abused the trust invested in them by the community and shamefully raped the good name of Islam by claiming to be its followers. No amount of correct thinking will convince them about the necessity of promoting the general welfare. As we all are aware, it is not merely the presence of knowledge that induces a man to do certain things. What is more important still is the proper psycho-emotional attitude in which all strivings and thinking is rooted. The only way left to us is to find adequate means to relieve this type of people from the responsibility of leadership. Signs are not wanting that the people of Islam have become conscious of this fact and are trying [their] best to change the composition of its leadership.[6]

A symptom of the predominance of bad leadership was the lack of sound planning. With reference to Ibn Khaldun, Alatas noted that the sphere of thinking and action was influenced by the social situation, which formed the background of such thought and behaviour. Sound planning was necessary in order to create adequate conditions in society such that people could live to their potential in the spheres of thought and behaviour. Of primary importance was planning for economic reforms. This is because social vices were the outcome of economic maladjustment and exploitation.[7]

Such planning, however, was not forthcoming because of the lack of awareness of the vital problems of society. This in turn was due to the absence of a group of thinkers large enough to constitute a force in the regeneration of Muslim societies. The result is that few Muslims were aware of the vital problems confronting their societies. Alatas considered it to be "a task of great magnitude to disseminate ideas and instill attitude into the minds of millions of men".[8] His interest in the role of intellectuals in Malaysia and other developing societies continued till the end of his life.

The backwardness of Muslim society, however, was not only a result of deficiencies to be found within the Muslim world. There were also the desultory influences of the West. Of particular concern to Alatas was the uncritical imitation and adoption of nationalism. His objection to nationalism was the glorification of past imperial greatness and presenting national glory in a way that subordinates ethical and moral principles to national interests. It is interesting that Alatas here also rejects the parochial attitude whereby the philosophical foundation of a state is solely derived from the history of that state, without due consideration of the history of other states.[9]

An interesting problem raised by Alatas was the tendency of Muslims to adopt materialism and positivism in their mode of thinking. He was not so much concerned with the epistemological dimensions of these orientations but rather with their political implications. He cited the views of John H. Hallowell in his *The Decline of Liberalism as an Ideology*. Hallowell's argument is that when science achieves unassailable prestige in society, the effort to study social phenomena in a manner that would yield predictability, certainty and security also becomes dominant. Such positivist notions also affected the perception of law. Law was not viewed as a product of reason but of will. Law did not embody truths and values that transcended individuals, but rather reflected the interests and desires of individuals living in a certain time and place. Furthermore, individuals submitted to the law not due to its inherent justice but due to coercion. Hallowell goes on to say:

> By logical implication, if not explicitly, the formal liberal jurists of the late nineteenth century came close to saying that law is the command of superior force. And by so saying they anticipated the brutal nihilism of National Socialism.[10]

Alatas viewed Islamic law, on the other hand, as allowing the widest limits for human action, and that its fundamental rule was liberty.[11] Regarding the method of *Progressive Islam*, Alatas had drawn from Ibn Khaldun:

> Islam, from the dawn of its history, has always been inclined to that particular mode of viewing human history and human thought which we at present call the socio-historical method. The brilliant exponent of this method was, none other than the founder of modern sociology and scientific history, Abdul Rahman Ibn Khaldun....

> Led by our desire to establish a rational and scientific framework for the Islamic faith to which reason and science were from its very birth inalienable, we have decided to adopt this socio-historical method as the manner of approach of this paper.[12]

The socio-historical method as applied to the study of Islam and Muslim societies required consideration of the following factors: (1) the culture and civilization in which a particular system was born; (2) the age in which it occurred; (3) the area to which it was related; (4) the individual or group who initiated the system; (5) the situation in which the individual or group found themselves when they commenced advocating that system; (6) the class to which this individual or group belonged, and (7) the personality of the founder.

Although Alatas attributed this approach to Ibn Khaldun, he was at the same time clearly influenced by the method of the sociology of knowledge of Karl Mannheim, whom he had also discussed in *Progressive Islam*[13] and whose writings had guided his thinking in his seminal work, *The Myth of the Lazy Native*.[14]

Characteristic of Alatas's notion of Progressive Islam, therefore, was the balanced and measured approach of appropriating from both Islamic and Western traditions, whether for the theoretical diagnosis of modern problems or the methods to be used for such diagnosis. Progressive Islam was to preserve its universal and tolerant outlook and at the same time be receptive to outside influences.[15] The last issue of *Progressive Islam* appeared as volume 2, number 5 in 1955. The editorial carried a critique of colonialism.[16]

Definition, Objectives and Methods of Progressive Islam

It was not until about fifty years later that the term and idea of Progressive Islam re-emerged. In 2003, Omid Safi, a prominent proponent of Progressive Islam, describes it in the following manner:

> Progressive Islam encompasses a number of themes: striving to realize a just and pluralistic society through a critical engagement with Islam, a relentless pursuit of social justice, an emphasis on gender equality as a foundation of human rights, and a vision of religious and ethnic pluralism.[17]

Progressive Muslims have a universal approach in that they see themselves as advocates of all human beings, not just Muslims. The concern is with subalternity in all its forms; that is, poverty, oppression and other forms of marginalization. The task of Progressive Muslims is "to give voice to the voiceless, power to the powerless, and confront the 'powers that be' who disregard the God-given human dignity of the *mustad'afun* all over this Earth".[18]

Furthermore, Progressive Muslims derive their concern with social justice both from within the classical Islamic tradition as well as from modern orientations, drawing from sources as diverse as the Qur'an and Sunnah as well as scholars and activists such as Ali Shari'ati. In addition they enthusiastically draw from non-Muslim traditions to the extent that such traditions are instrumental to the pursuit of their aims. Such external sources include the liberation theology of Leonardo Boff, Gustavo Gutiérrez and Rebecca S. Chopp, and the secular humanism of Edward Said and Noam Chomsky.[19]

Progressive Islam is, therefore, Islamic humanism, premised on the idea that "all members of the human race have this same intrinsic worth because each of us has the breath of God breathed into our being: *wa nafakhtu fihi min ruhi* (Qur'an 15:29 and 38:72)".[20]

Another proponent of Progressive Islam is Adis Duderija. He introduces what he refers to as a new concept, that is, Progressive Islamism. This is founded on a progressive Muslim interpretation of Islam that has real political implications. Progressive Islamism differs from conservative forms of Islamism in that it "embraces constitutional democracy and contemporary ideas on human rights, gender equality and vibrant civil society".[21] The leading proponents of Progressive Islam are Muslim scholars such as Abdulaziz Sachedina, Khaled Abou El Fadl, Hassan Hanafi, Nurcholish Majid, Ulil Abshar Abdalla, Abdullahi An'Naim, Ahmad Moussalli, M. Hashim Kamali, Muqtader Khan and Nader Hashemi. While there are differences among them, what makes them proponents of Progressive Islam is their efforts to seriously and critically engage Islamic tradition (*turath*) and their position that Islam is not merely a matter of private belief but has relevance for politics.[22]

A more elaborate articulation of Progressive Islam is the subject of Duderija's important work *The Imperatives of Progressive Islam*.[23] In this work, Progressive Islam is described in terms of a number of imperatives. Proponents of Progressive Islam are not uprooted from

Islamic tradition, but fruitfully engage with it with a view to bring about reform at the epistemological level.[24] Progressive Islam embraces "the idea of divinely willed religious pluralism in the context of the late modern episteme".[25] Apart from being rooted in tradition, however, Progressive Muslims are also nourished by "movements and schools of thought that are not necessarily part of the historical experience of Islam's concrete historical trajectory but which are considered as being in accordance with its overall ideals, values, objectives, and, therefore, imperatives". In terms of their methods, Progressive Muslims seek to develop "systematic and sophisticated non-patriarchal Quran-Sunna/hadith hermeneutical models which affirm gender-just interpretations of Islam ... characterized by rationalist, contextualist-driven, and holistic hermeneutics which privilege the purposive and values-based approach to the Islamic tradition, as embodied in certain values considered to form the very core and spirit of Islam such as justice, fairness, and mercy".[26]

There has been a tendency to refer to Progressive Islam as an American or Western appropriation of Islam. But, according to Safi, this is a mistaken view:

> Progressive Muslims are found everywhere in the global Muslim *umma*. When it comes to implementing a progressive understanding of Islam in Muslim communities, groups in Iran, Malaysia, and South Africa lead the United States. Many American Muslim communities—and much of the leadership represented in groups such as the Islamic Circle of North America, the Islamic Society of North America, and the Council on American-Islamic Relations—are far too uncritical of Salafi and Wahhabi tendencies that progressives oppose.[27]

Safi rightly warns against connecting the Progressive Islam movement too closely with a single national or ethnic origin and would, instead, stress the global nature of this discourse. Proponents of Progressive Islam are found everywhere and the point is not to seek "an American, an Iranian, or a South Asian ORIGIN for this discourse" but to view it as a "global discourse with fluid and cosmopolitan thinkers who benefit from each other's works".[28]

Progressive Islam does not refer to any particular orientation or school of thought. As Keersten puts it, Progressive Muslims come from various backgrounds with varying objectives and different expressions of religiosity. What they do share, however, is "an orientation towards the future informed by critical engagement with the intellectual legacy of Islam as civilization".[29]

The above are descriptions of what Progressive Islam is and its objectives. It is described in terms of its objectives and what it wants to achieve. How can we define Progressive Islam though? I propose to define Progressive Islam in terms of the concept of moderation. If moderation is the goal of Islamic life, then any conception of Islam that is progressive should lead to moderation. That being the case, Progressive Islam can be defined as an orientation in Islamic beliefs and practices that is conditioned by and results in moderation. This begs the question as to what moderation is. Moderation can be defined as belief and practice that is founded on the balance between extremes.

Islam understands itself to be a religion based on "the middle way", which is captured by the Qur'anic term *ummatan wasatan*, meaning the community of the middle way, the middle between two extremes. And it is this middle way which is the "straight path" that Muslims are told by the Qur'an to travel. Intimately related to this is the notion of justice. In Islamic discourse, the term that is usually translated as justice is *'adalah*. When we discuss the justice of God, we speak of both justice and balance. In Islamic jurisprudence, the majority view has been that *'adalah* refers to a qualification according to which one abides by the prescribed obligations and recommendations of the sharia or Islamic code of morality and conduct, and avoids what it prohibited and disapproved of.[30] A specific attribute of *'adalah* is *mizan* or balance. This is in line with the Qur'anic view of God's justice:

> And we shall set up balances (*al-muwazin*) of justice for the day of resurrection, then none will be dealt with unjustly in anything. And if there be the weight of a mustard seed, we will bring it. And sufficient are we to take account.[31]

Writing a few centuries later, Ibn Khaldun noted the treatment of earlier scholars of the social function of law. For example, he refers to the speech of the Persian priest Mobedh before King Bahram bin Bahram as related by Mas'udi:

> O king, the might of royal authority materializes only through the religious law, obedience toward God, and compliance with His

commands and prohibitions. The religious law persists only through royal authority. Mighty royal authority is accomplished only through men. Men persist only with the help of property. The only way to property is through cultivation. The only way to cultivation is through justice. Justice is a balance set up among mankind. The Lord set it up and appointed an overseer for it, and that (overseer) is the ruler.[32]

Of particular interest to us here is the statement, "justice is a balance set up among mankind" (*al-'adl al-mizan al-mansub bayn al-khaliqah*). This is in reference to human justice. If we take all three quotations above into consideration, it is clear that the concepts of *'adalah* and *mizan* refer both to God's as well as to human justice.

It is clear here that moderation or following the straight path of Islam is at the same time establishing justice, which requires setting up a balance among people. The balance is established by negotiating between extremes. Extremism exists at two ends of a continuum. For example, there are the extremes of excessive strictness and harshness in following Islamic laws, on the one hand, and excessive laxity on the other. Jamal al-Din al-Afghani defined "excess (*al-ifrat*)" as that which "challenges everything ... until nothing is stable", while languid fatalism (*tafrit*) leads to the worst form of slavery, which causes the "ignorant" to accept all that issues from fortune, chance, and circumstance.[33]

Moderation can therefore be defined as the balance set up between extremes in the various spheres of private and public life. It would then be possible for us to enumerate such spheres with reference to the relevant continua in each sphere. Several are listed and discussed below.

1. The knowledge–practice (*'ilm–'amal*) continuum. Progressive Muslims do not accept the dichotomy between intellectual work and activism. Their activities are not purely academic and they stay engaged with issues of social justice on the ground;[34] that is, they maintain a balance between *'ilm–'amal*.
2. The nativism–Orientalism continuum. Progressive Muslims are very much influenced by the critique of Orientalism and inspired by the "Edward Said-ian call to 'speak truth to the powers'".[35] At the same time, they consciously seek to avoid the distortion of nativist discourse that rejects things non-Islamic and promote Occidentalism or reverse Orientalism.

3. The internal–external continuum. Progressive Muslims are as critical of external factors that have negatively impacted on the life chances of individuals and communities in the Muslim world as they are of the local, domestic and regional factors that have similar consequences. In their assessment of the problems, there is an attempt to have a balanced perspective that weighs the relative importance of internal and external factors. For example, Progressive Muslims expose the violation of human rights in the Muslim world as well as stand up to hegemonic Western political-economic structures and cultural programmes.[36]
4. The inclusive–exclusive continuum. Moderation accepts and even celebrates diversity, but there must be a balance between preserving the integrity of Islam by not arbitrarily including every group that claims to be Muslim, on the one hand, and narrowing the definition of Islam such that historically legitimate groups are excluded. In Malaysia, state authorities tend to narrowly define Islam in terms of the Shafi'i school, thereby upsetting the balance and practising exclusivism. Progressive Muslims seek to understand and challenge exclusivist Muslim orientations of all hues and colours, from textualist Wahhabis to extremist Shi'ites.[37]
5. The tradition–modernity continuity. Progressive Muslims remain rooted in tradition intellectually and culturally while engaging with the modern world and benefiting from the intellectual and cultural resources that modernity has to offer. Progressive Muslims are not traditionalistic in the sense of clinging on to tradition when it is dysfunctional, neither are they modernistic in the sense of rejecting or repudiating tradition by writing it off as innovation (*bid'ah*). Where Progressive Muslims differ from Muslims of other orientations is in their more post-modernist attitude, their "being mindful and critical of the arrogance of modernity". This refers to the Western view that its civilization represents the telos of history; that is, a final state in which humankind has reached the limits of its social, economic and cultural development.[38]
6. The exoteric–esoteric (*zahir–batin*) continuum. The entrenchment of legalistic thinking among the ulama and people in general has led to a de-emphasis on ethics, morality, spirituality and religious experience. This constitutes the lack of balance between the need to adhere to rituals, rules and regulations (sharia) on the one

hand, and the spiritual experience of worship and other human activities on the other. Progressive Muslims reject this dichotomy and affirm the necessity of balance between the exoteric and esoteric in religious life.
7. The non-rational–rational continuum. Progressive Muslims believe in the need to establish a balance between the non-rational aspects of religious experience, such as the esoteric and mystical dimensions, with the rational and intellectual aspects.
8. The freedom–coercion continuum. In any society there is obviously a need for the state to exercise coercion over its stubborn and recalcitrant citizens. Such force, however, has to be balanced with the provision of personal and civil liberties. Progressive Muslims do not accept the policing of religious life. An example of upsetting this balance is legislation in Malaysia that allows for a fine or jail term for Muslim men who fail to attend Friday prayer more than three consecutive times.
9. The nationalist–imperialist continuum. Progressive Muslims are neither excessively nationalistic nor indifferent to imperialism. I have already mentioned above the criticism by Alatas of nationalism. Progressive Islam is also critical of global structures of oppression, including the various international institutions and regimes that make this possible.[39]
10. The this worldly–otherworldly continuum. This refers to the need to establish a balance between concern with salvation in the afterlife with interest and commitment to conditions of life on this earth, in all its dimension.

The tradition–modernity continuum is of particular interest. Progressive Islam draws from both traditional and modern ideas. Yet it is at the same time critical of both. Take, for example, the critique by Alatas of mental captivity as a modern condition in knowledge production.

Alatas originated and developed the concept of the captive mind to conceptualize the nature of scholarship in the developing world, particularly in relation to Western dominance in the social sciences and humanities. The captive mind is defined as an "uncritical and imitative mind dominated by an external source, whose thinking is deflected from an independent perspective".[40] The external source is Western social science and humanities, and the uncritical imitation influences all the constituents of scientific activity such as problem selection, conceptualization, analysis, generalization, description, explanation and interpretation.[41] Among the characteristics of the captive mind are an inability to be creative or to raise original problems, an inability to devise original analytical methods, and alienation from the main issues of indigenous societies. The captive mind is trained almost entirely in the Western sciences, reads the works of Western authors, and is taught predominantly by Western teachers, whether in the West itself or through their works available in local centres of education. Mental captivity is also found in the suggestion of solutions and policies. Furthermore, it reveals itself at the level of theoretical as well as empirical work.

Earlier, in the 1950s, Alatas referred to the "wholesale importation of ideas from the Western world to eastern societies" without due consideration of their socio-historical context as a fundamental problem of colonialism.[42] He had also suggested that the mode of thinking of colonized peoples paralleled political and economic imperialism. Hence the expression *academic imperialism*,[43] the context within which the captive mind appears.

The consumption of social science knowledge from the West arises from the belief in the superiority of such knowledge. Among the traits of this consumption that parallel the economic demonstration effect are (1) the frequency of contact with Western knowledge; (2) the weakening or erosion of local or indigenous knowledge; (3) the prestige attached to imported knowledge; and (4) that such consumption is not necessarily rational and utilitarian.[44]

Shaharuddin Maaruf has an insightful analysis that provides Progressive Muslims with a useful means of appropriating from tradition. Shaharuddin defines tradition as a cultural or value system that has been influential in moulding or shaping the world view of a given people for a significant period in their cultural history. This "cultural or value system represents the stable core that provides the basis for the society's responses to contemporary and future challenges".[45] Tradition can be a negative or positive factor in the development of a society. Speaking about the Malay world, Shaharuddin draws our attention to two opposing traditions in Malay society—the feudal and Islamic traditions. The conflict is rooted in the past but is still present in contemporary Malay society, even after the demise of the feudal polity. Malay feudal values have survived the feudal system.

Such values include (1) a servile attitude towards authority and the acceptance of arbitrary notions of power; (2) the undermining of the positive aspects of individualism and, therefore, a lack of respect for the human personality; (3) a lack of respect for the rule of law; (4) non-distinction between the public domain and personal domains of life; (5) an emphasis on grandeur and an opulent lifestyle; (6) an indifference to social justice; (7) acceptance of unfair privileges for those in a position of power; (8) an obsession with power, authority and privileges for their own sake; (9) the undervaluing of rationalism and the philosophical spirit, and an encouragement of myths that serve the interests of those in power; and (10) an emphasis on leisure and indulgence of the senses and the simultaneous undervaluing of work.[46]

These feudal values are not only at odds with the spirit and outlook of modernization but also clash with the fundamental values of Islam. As opposed to such feudal values, Islamic tradition emphasizes (1) a more rational and egalitarian conception of authority; (2) limiting arbitrary power; (3) recognition of positive individualism and respect for the human personality; (4) the rule of law; (5) a more humanistic conception of leadership; (6) ethical integrity and honesty in public office; (7) frugality; (8) social justice; (9) effort rather than unfair privileges; (10) the ideal of excellence for life on this earth; (11) rationalism and the philosophical spirit; (12) disapproval of irrational belief and superstition; and (13) dignity of labour.[47]

Shaharuddin's argument is that both feudal and Islamic values exist in a conflicting relationship in Malay tradition. The question of progress in the modern era greatly depends on the outcome of such a conflict; that is, "on which value system gains the upper hand in the conflict".[48]

With regard to the method of thinking and inquiry of Progressive Islam, we have already mentioned the discussion by Syed Hussein Alatas of the socio-historical method. According to this method, Islam and Muslim societies are studied with due recognition of the socio-historical context, which includes cultural, environmental, class and other social attributes that define the context.[49] Esack has argued that "there is no objective theory unaffected by each person's socio-historical particularity" and, therefore, "for Islam to be self-consciously grounded in praxis".[50] It is the lack of the socio-historical approach that also explains the failure, as noted by Moosa, of modernist Muslim scholars to "subject the entire corpus of historical Islamic learning to the critical gaze of the knowledge-making process (episteme) of modernity".[51] It is because of the lack of such a method that the works of apologetics yield problematic ideas. Examples cited by Moosa are Qur'anic measures to manumit slaves as penance for certain moral violations, and the Caliph Umar's prohibition of the sale of slave women whose children are fathered by their masters. These are mistakenly held up as indicating notions of freedom, the result of a failure to appreciate the socio-historical context of Qur'anic revelation.[52]

An example of the workings of the socio-historical method comes from Ottoman history. Ottoman scholars used Ibn Khaldun's socio-historical method to deal with the religious requirement that the caliphs come from the Quraysh. The Ottomans adopted Ibn Khaldun's argument that the requirement only held when the *'asabiyya* of the Quraysh was intact. The necessary condition was that the caliphate was to be in the hands of the group that possessed superior *'asabiyya*. When rule passed from the Arabs to the Turks, it was the Turks that possessed superior *'asabiyya*. The Quraysh could no longer satisfy the condition.[53]

Another example of contextual interpretation in a socio-historical mode concerns not the interpretation of Islamic law but rather the understanding of theological ideas and doctrines. The late Ottoman thinker Mehmet Şerafeddin suggested that theological ideas in a society were related to their communal form. For example, the revelation of Islam and the rejection of tribalism facilitated belief in a universal and transcendent God. After the death of the Prophet, however, political and religious disputes formed the backdrop for the emergence of multiple theological schools of thought. In pre-Islamic times, the context of tribalism meant that each tribe had its own idol. When the tribes came together for joint cultural feasts and made peace agreements during the holy months, there was the acceptance of a common, superior God alongside the other idols. Such an approach to understanding theological beliefs does not deny the reality of revelation.[54] It merely suggests that revelation does not take place in a socio-historical vacuum but interacts with specific features and characteristics of society.

Ibn Khaldun and the Good [Progressive] Madina

Alatas had a strong interest in Ibn Khaldun, as reflected in his writings in *Progressive Islam*. It was Ibn Khaldun who furnished him with the socio-historical method that he adopted for the idea of Progressive Islam. Alatas also wrote another article on Ibn Khaldun in *Progressive Islam*.[55]

What is the relevance of Ibn Khaldun for our understanding of Progressive Islam? Ibn Khaldun sought to understand the causes of the rise and decline of dynasties. He explained this in terms of the essential differences in social organization between nomadic (*badawi*) and sedentary (*hadari*) social organization. The differences between these two societal types are explained in terms of the differences in their modes of making a living (*al-ma'ash*). The *badawi* adopt agriculture or animal husbandry as their principle mode of making a living, and they live in desert areas. The principal modes of making a living for *hadari* society were commerce and trade, but also include agriculture. Sedentary people live in cities, towns and villages.[56]

The theory revolved around the term *'asabiya*, Ibn Khaldun's conceptualization of social solidarity. According to the theory, social groupings with a fortified *'asabiya* established rule over groups with a weak *'asabiya*. *'Asabiya* is a form of social solidarity founded on the belief of the members of the group that they share a common descent. Ibn Khaldun believed that *'asabiya* was more potent than other forms of social solidarity. The relatively greater degree of *'asabiya* among the nomads made them more closely knit than sedentary people. This resulted in a greater degree of mutual support and aid among them, and contributed to the fear felt for them by their enemies.[57]

The nature of pastoral nomadic societies was such that their social organization kept their *'asabiya* relatively more intact. However, even as the tribal group conquered and established its rule over the sedentary folk, settlement during the course of generations resulted in the erosion of their own *'asabiya*. They became like the dynasty they had conquered some generations ago; that is, politically and economically weak, disunited and vulnerable to conquest from the desert.

Clearly, the specifics of the theory do not apply to many modern societies that are not characterized by the *badawi–hadari* dichotomy and for which pastoral nomadism is not a significant factor in their geopolitical make-up. However, there is a way in which Ibn Khaldun is relevant to the study of modern societies. This has to do with the more normative or prescriptive discussions on the nature of a good polity or civilized society. These can be taken as prescriptions for a progressive society. Ibn Khaldun's discussions on the features and characteristics of sedentary society give us some clues as to what he considered to be the desirable traits of the political, economic and social aspects of society.

Ibn Khaldun regarded nomadic society as superior to sedentary society. Nomads were more socially cohesive, had greater moral fibre and courage and were more observant of religious law. Sedentary people on the other hand experienced a dissipation of their social cohesion, became obsessed with a life of luxury and permissiveness, and were less observant of religious law. When we speak of the good *madina* in Khaldunian terms, there is a contradiction in that the nature of the *madina*, as part of sedentary society, is such that its inhabitants were not good (*khayr*).[58]

In sedentary society the success of the management of the economy involving production, distribution, the creation of value, the determination of prices, the role of money and the nature of public finance is dependent to a great extent on the nature of kingship. *Mulk tabi'i*, or unbridled kingship, is the form that is most destructive to the political and economic life of a people. It was in dynasties dominated by *mulk tabi'i* that people were subject to arbitrary rule, frequently under threat of their property being confiscated and constantly suffering from other forms of injustice, like forced labour and the unfair imposition of duties and taxes. Ernest Gellner had pointed out that a Keynesian-type multiplier effect can be seen in Ibn Khaldun's explanation of the fall of a dynasty.[59]

However, while Keynes blamed the middle class for failing to raise aggregate demand to an adequate level, Ibn Khaldun laid the blame on the governmental propensity to save at a time when private investment was weak:

> Now, if the ruler holds on to property and revenue, or they are lost or not properly used by him, then the property in the possession of the ruler's entourage will be small. The gifts which they, in their turn, had been used to give to their entourage and people, stop, and all their expenditures are cut down. They constitute the greatest number

of people (who make expenditures), and their expenditures provide more of the substance of trade than (the expenditures of) any other (group of people). Thus (when they stop spending), business slumps and commercial profits decline because of the shortage of capital. Revenues from the land tax decrease, because the land tax and taxation (in general) depend on cultural activity, commercial transactions, business prosperity, and the people's demand for gain and profit. It is the dynasty that suffers from the situation and that has a deficit, because under these circumstances the property of the ruler decreases in consequence of the decrease in revenues from the land tax. As we have stated, the dynasty is the greatest market, the mother and base of all trade. (It is the market that provides) the substance of income and expenditures (for trade). If government business slumps and the volume of trade is small, the dependent markets will naturally show the same symptoms, and to a greater degree. Furthermore, money circulates between subjects and ruler, moving back and forth. Now, if the ruler keeps it to himself, it is lost to the subjects.[60]

As Gellner noted, this was "one of the most eloquent inflationary, expansionist, anti-Milton-Friedman pleas ever made."[61] Ibn Khaldun also explained that there is a relation between the political and economic aspects of the decline of a dynasty:

It should be known that at the beginning of the dynasty, taxation yields a large revenue from small assessments. At the end of the dynasty, taxation yields a small revenue from large assessments. The reason for this is that when the dynasty follows the ways (*sunan*) of the religion, it imposes only such taxes as are stipulated by the religious law, such as charity taxes, the land tax, and the poll tax.... When the dynasty continues in power and their rulers follow each other in succession, they become sophisticated. The Bedouin attitude and simplicity lose their significance, and the Bedouin qualities of moderation and restraint disappear. [Kingship] with its tyranny, and sedentary culture that stimulates sophistication, make their appearance. The people of the dynasty then acquire qualities of character related to cleverness. Their customs and needs become more varied because of the prosperity and luxury in which they are immersed. As a result, the individual imposts and assessments upon the subjects, agricultural laborers, farmers, and all the other taxpayers, increase. Every individual impost and assessment is greatly increased, in order to obtain a higher tax revenue.[62]

As assessments exceed the limits required by the demands of equity, there is a decrease in productive activities and tax revenues. Individual taxes are then increased to compensate for the loss. This in turn creates a disincentive for productive activity. The final result is a downturn in the production, fiscal and political cycles of the dynasty.[63] The characteristics of nomadic life that gave them the power to establish a dynasty—that is, an austere lifestyle, greater fortitude as a result of less reliance on law, and a stronger *'aṣabiya*—all diminish once the nomads become sedentarized. An irreversible process of decline is set in motion once sedentarization takes place.[64]

For Ibn Khaldun, the decline and fall of a state is not only a political or socio-psychological phenomenon. It is also an economic phenomenon, as there is an important role played by wealth.

> As for the disintegration that comes through money, it should be known that at the beginning the dynasty has a desert attitude, as was mentioned before. It has the qualities of kindness to subjects, planned moderation in expenditures, and respect for other people's property. It avoids onerous taxation and the display of cunning or shrewdness in the collection of money and the accounting (required) from officials. Nothing at this time calls for extravagant expenditures. Therefore, the dynasty does not need much money. Later comes domination and expansion. Royal authority flourishes. This calls for luxury. (Luxury) causes increased spending. The expenditures of the ruler, and of the people of the dynasty in general, grow. This (tendency) spreads to the urban population. It calls for increases in soldiers' allowances and in the salaries of the people of the dynasty. Extravagant expenditures mount. It spreads to the subjects, because people follow the religion (ways) and customs of the dynasty. The ruler, then, must impose duties on articles sold in the markets, in order to improve his revenues. (He does so,) because he sees the luxury of the urban population testifying to their prosperity, and because he needs the money for the expenditures of his government and the salaries of his soldiers. Habits of luxury, then, further increase. The customs duties no longer pay for them. The dynasty, by this time, is flourishing in its power and its forceful hold over the subjects under its control. Its hand reaches out to seize some of the property of the subjects, either through customs duties, or through commercial transactions, or, in some cases, merely by hostile acts directed against (property holdings), on some pretext or even with none. At this stage, the soldiers have already grown

bold against the dynasty, because it has become weak and senile, as far as its group feeling is concerned. (The dynasty) expects that from them, and attempts to remedy and smooth over the situation through generous allowances and much spending for (the soldiers). It cannot get around that. At this stage, the tax collectors in the dynasty have acquired much wealth, because vast revenues are in their hands and their position has widened in importance for this reason. Suspicions of having appropriated tax money, therefore, attach to them. It becomes common for one tax collector to denounce another, because of their mutual jealousy and envy. One after another is deprived of his money by confiscation and torture. Eventually, their wealth is gone, and they are ruined. The dynasty loses the pomp and magnificence it had possessed through them.[65]

The luxurious lifestyle that appears at the early stages of the dynasty necessitates increased government expenditure on salaries and allowances. Furthermore, with growing expectations of the military, the ruler has no choice but to increase taxes and duties. He also resorts to illegal means such as the confiscation of property in order to satisfy the army. As the dynasty becomes weaker in 'asabiya and the army becomes bolder in challenging the ruler, the state begins to fragment and eventually crumbles.[66]

What lessons can be drawn from Ibn Khaldun's discussions on the economy? There is a very important principle of taxation that underlies his account of the relationship between the ruler and the economy. Taxes collected should reflect an attitude of justice, fairness and equity. There should be a correspondence between the rate of taxes and the level of productivity. Taxes exacted should not exceed the ability to pay. The rule governing taxation should be strictly adhered to and preferences should not be extended to those who happen to be close to the ruler.[67] Inevitably, however, Ibn Khaldun recognized that the yield from taxation would have the same lifecycle as that of the dynasty:

> After their prosperity is destroyed, the dynasty goes farther afield and approaches its other wealthy subjects. At this stage, feebleness has already afflicted its (former) might. (The dynasty) has become too weak to retain its power and forceful hold. The policy of the ruler, at this time, is to handle matters diplomatically by spending money. He considers this more advantageous than the sword, which is of little use. His need for money grows beyond what is needed

for expenditures and soldiers' salaries. He never gets enough. Senility affects the dynasty more and more. The people of (other) regions grow bold against it. At each of these stages, the strength of the dynasty crumbles. Eventually, it reaches complete ruin. It is open to domination by (any) aggressor. Anyone who wants to attack it can take it away from those who support it. If this does not occur, it will continue to dwindle and finally disappear—like the wick of a lamp when the oil is exhausted, and it goes out.[68]

Ibn Khaldun was also very much against the rulers being involved in business and trade:

> Sometimes, the ruler himself may engage in commerce and agriculture, from desire to increase (his) revenues. He sees that merchants and farmers make (great) profits and have plenty of property. (He sees) that their gains correspond to the capital they invest. Therefore, he starts to acquire livestock and fields in order to cultivate them for profit, purchase goods, and (enter business and) expose himself to fluctuations of the market. He thinks that this will improve (his) revenues and increase (his) profits. However, this is a great error. It causes harm to the subjects in many ways. First, farmers and merchants will find it difficult to buy livestock and merchandise and to procure cheaply the things that belong to (farming and commerce). The subjects have (all) the same or approximately the same amount of wealth. Competition between them already exhausts, or comes close to exhausting, their financial resources. Now, when the ruler, who has so much more money than they, competes with them, scarcely a single one of them will (any longer) be able to obtain the things he wants, and everybody will become worried and unhappy. Furthermore, the ruler can appropriate much of (the agricultural products and the available merchandise), if it occurs to him. (He can do it) by force, or by buying things up at the cheapest possible price. Further, there may be no one who would dare to bid against him.[69]

As a result, the ruler would be able to force the seller into lowering the price. Also, the ruler may apply coercion in order to get merchants to buy agricultural products from him at higher prices, rather than rely on market conditions. This would result in the merchants and farmers exhausting their capital.[70] Even if the ruler were able to engage in profitable trade, his direct involvement in trade would result in a decline in tax revenue, as it is unlikely duties would be levied on his commercial activities.[71]

To sum up, Ibn Khaldun would argue that the direct involvement of the government in business is a key factor that leads to the decline of the state, as that would distort the market and discourage private businesses from investment and trade. The crucial role of the government lay in the area of collecting taxes at a level that did not exceed the ability of merchants and producers to pay and that gave them the incentive to engage in productive activities. Ibn Khaldun's views on the economy do not constitute an economic theory of development but rather a political economy of development. This is because his understanding of the economy and its growth is informed by the interplay of economic, political and social factors. They can be summed up in the "circle of justice". Ibn Khaldun quotes from the book, *On Politics*, attributed to Aristotle:

> The world is a garden the fence of which is the dynasty. The dynasty is an authority through which life is given to proper behavior. Proper behavior is a policy directed by the ruler. The ruler is an institution supported by the soldiers. The soldiers are helpers who are maintained by money. Money is sustenance brought together by the subjects. The subjects are servants who are protected by justice. Justice is something familiar, and through it, the world persists. The world is a garden...[72]

Here it can be seen that the economy is intimately related to the authority of the state, its judicial institutions and the military.[73]

In much of the modern world, the majority of people are sedentary, living either in cities or villages. It is not possible to reverse the historical trend and become pastoral nomads. We are in a position where we have to make the best of our social organization, the *madina*, with all its faults as described by Ibn Khaldun. The *madina* was not all bad. The problem was that there was an inevitable movement towards degeneration and decay. In the early stages of the up cycle, the *madina* functioned well in terms of its political, economic and social dimensions. It is the characteristics of the *madina* in its early stages, as delineated by Ibn Khaldun, that we may wish to consider for emulation. These characteristics are the nature of authority, the role of the government in the economy, and the nature of education. These aspects of the life of the *madina* are founded on such universal values as the rule of law, justice, accountability, responsibility and the quest for knowledge and truth. Ibn Khaldun's description of injustice highlights the vulnerability to arbitrary confiscation of money and property, and the imposition of forced labour and unfair taxes. These are exacerbated by unbridled kingship and unpredictability and inconsistency on the part of government officials. As such, Ibn Khaldun offers contemporary societies a basis for understanding and addressing inequities in contemporary systems of governance, be they local, national or global.[74]

Progressive Islam and Reform

While Progressive Muslims speak of reform, they do not advocate a Protestant-type Reformation. As Safi puts it, while it is true that the Muslim world faces serious economic, social, and political problems that need to be urgently addressed, the reform that is sought is not tantamount to "developing a 'Protestant' Islam distinct from a 'Catholic' Islam".[75] Indeed, the notion of Protestant Islam is not appropriate.

The idea of Protestant Islam should be understood in the context of intellectual imperialism. There are two prevalent explanations as to why the Muslim world is unable to catch up with the West. According to the first, the problem does not lie with Islam but rather with what is termed "Islamism", with the extremist orientations of such figures as Muhammad Ibn 'Abd al-Wahhab in the eighteenth century, Sayyid Qutb in the twentieth century, and Osama bin Laden in the twenty-first. The solution is for "moderate" Muslims to marginalize the appeal for Islamism by undertaking "Protestant-like" reforms.

The second view attributes the problems facing the Muslim world as originating from within the religion of Islam itself, and not just specific to Muslim ideologies or utopias. The religion of Islam is inherently irrational and overly politicized. Owing to its legalistic framework, it is unable to adapt to changing circumstances. Not having undergone a process of transformation like Christianity, the Muslim world is consequently stuck in its own Middle Ages. For Muslims to enter the modern world, they have to undergo a "Protestant-type" reformation. A "Protestant-like" reformation, however, is difficult to achieve because of the power of the clergy over the masses.

Progressive Muslims see both views as problematic because the basic assumptions are erroneous. The first view understands Muslim revivalist movements as having "Protestant-like"' features and imagines parallels between sixteenth century Protestant reformers and contemporary Muslim activists in terms of doctrines, institutions and practices. For example, the refusal by Muslim reformers to unquestioningly apply Islamic teachings and tenets are compared to Luther's refusal to obey the authority of the Catholic Church. What is glossed over is the considerable difference in the socio-political contexts of both religions. Muslim scholars and activists have throughout history always exhibited critical and oppositional attitudes towards political and religious authority. What they sought to reform, however, were certain beliefs and practices among Muslims, rather than Islam itself.

The second view, which attributes the problems of the Muslim world to the inherent backwardness of Islam, is equally problematic. The idea of "Islamic Protestantism" originally came from Muslims, most notably Iranian activists in the context of the Constitutional Revolution of 1905 and, later, from Ali Shari'ati in the 1960s. But they had not advocated a complete theological revolution for Islam, arguing instead for social and legal reform. Not only is there no equivalent to the papacy in Islam—and, therefore, no "church" to break away from—Progressive Muslims are also not working to create further splits within the Muslim community.[76]

As such, portraying the phenomenon of contemporary Islamic resurgence through the prism of sixteenth century Christianity is rather superficial. It is part of a larger tendency to intellectually Christianize all religions, a form of intellectual imperialism. Even though other religions such as Islam are assumed to have universal validity, a hidden cultural Christianization is at work, judging by attempts to ascribe to them characteristics specific to Christianity. There are inherent dangers to attributing Christian features to all religions, since such intellectual speculations tend to disregard the self-perception and self-actualization of the practitioners of other faiths.

While Progressive Muslims actively borrow from Western and other non-Muslim traditions, they are at the same time conscious of and reject imperialistic tendencies in knowledge production. They would argue that the quest for progressive reformation in the Muslim world does not lie in its "Protestantization" but rather in attempts to understand the real needs and concerns of Muslims.[77]

Conclusion

Progressive Islam is neither a theological or jurisprudential school of thought in Islam, nor an ideology or utopia. It would be more accurate to call it a broad orientation that encompasses diverse proponents from different theological and theoretical background, but united on a number of themes and objectives as outlined above. Above all, Progressive Islam can be said to be a way of moderation that consciously seeks to find a balance in terms of the various continua discussed above. In doing so, Progressive Islam believes in drawing not only from classical and modern Islamic tradition but also from other civilizational and religious traditions, particularly those that are critical and liberating, that speak truth to power, and that operate in a decolonial mode of knowledge.

As Alatas had said in the first issue of *Progressive Islam* in 1954, "[t]he name *Progressive Islam* does not imply any dissection whatsoever as to the nature of the Islamic faith.... By calling this paper Progressive Islam we do not mean that we have extracted one part of Islam which is progressive and left the other part of Islam which is not progressive. Rather, the name *Progressive Islam* should be regarded as another way of saying that Islam is progressive."[78] The contributors to the volume, *Progressive Muslims: On Justice, Gender and Pluralism*, on the other hand, preferred the phrase "Progressive Muslims" to "Progressive Islam" in order to draw attention to the fact that it is the responsibility of human beings, the Muslims, to be progressive.[79]

Notes

1. According to Farid Esack, the expression "progressive Islam" was initially made popular by Suroosh Irfani's *Revolutionary Islam in Iran – Popular Liberation or Religious Dictatorship* (London: Zed, 1983). See Farid Esack, "In Search of Progressive Islam beyond 9/11", in *Progressive Muslims: On Justice, Gender and Pluralism*, edited by Omid Safi (Oxford: Oneworld, 2003), pp. 78–97, 79. This, however, is true for the generation succeeding Syed Hussein Alatas. One work that did mention the monthly *Progressive Islam* is Carool Kersten's *Islam in Indonesia: The Contest for Society, Ideas and Values* (Oxford: Oxford University Press, 2015), where he notes the appearance of some articles by Mohammad Natsir, the Indonesian Muslim

scholar and politician and Indonesia's fifth prime minister (1950–51). See Kersten, *Islam in Indonesia*, p. 189.
2. Hussein Alatas, "Editorial Announcement", *Progressive Islam* 1, no. 1 (1954).
3. Alatas, "Editorial Announcement".
4. Hussein Alatas, "The Regeneration of Islamic Societies", *Progressive Islam* 1, no. 2 (1954).
5. Syed Hussein Alatas, *Intellectuals in Developing Societies* (London: Cass, 1977).
6. Alatas, "The Regeneration of Islamic Societies".
7. Ibid.
8. Ibid.
9. Ibid.
10. John H. Hallowell, *The Decline of Liberalism as an Ideology* (Berkeley: University of California Press, 1943).
11. Alatas, "Editorial Announcement".
12. Ibid.
13. Hussein Alatas, "Karl Mannheim (1894–1947)", *Progressive Islam* 1, nos. 7–8 (1955).
14. Syed Hussein Alatas, *The Myth of the Lazy Native: A Study of the Image of the Malays, Filipinos and Javanese from the 16th to the 20th century and its Function in the Ideology of Colonial Capitalism* (London: Cass, 1977).
15. Syed Hussein Alatas, "The Regeneration of Muslim Societies: The Meaning of Progressive Islam", Progressive Islam and the State in Contemporary Muslim Societies, Report on a Conference organized by the Institute of Defence and Strategic Studies (IDSS), Singapore, 7–8 March 2006, http://www.rsis.edu.sg/wp-content/uploads/2014/07/ProgressIslamConference0613.pdf (accessed 15 April 2019).
16. Full texts of issues of *Progressive Islam* are available at the Universiti Sains Malaysia repository, Repository@USM, http://eprints.usm.my/view/creators/Alatas=3ASyed_Hussein=3A=3A.html (accessed 15 April 2019). For an account of Alatas's notion of Progressive Islam and of the founding of the journal, see Mona Abaza, "The Sociology of Progressive Islam between the Middle East and Southeast Asia", in *Islam, a Motor or Challenge of Modernity* (Yearbook of the Sociology of Islam), edited by Georg Stauth (Hamburg: Lit Verlag, 1998), pp. 129–52. Another version of this appears in Mona Abaza, "Syed Hussein Alatas and Sociological Investigation in Southeast Asia", in *Debates on Islam and Knowledge in Malaysia and Egypt: Shifting Worlds* (London: RoutledgeCourzon, 2002), pp. 121–39.
17. Omid Safi, "What is Progressive Islam", *ISIM Newsletter* 13, nos. 48–49 (December 2003): 48; Omid Safi, "Introduction: The Times They Are A-Changin': A Muslim Quest for Justice, Gender Equality, and Pluralism",

in *Progressive Muslims: On Justice, Gender and Pluralism*, edited by Omid Safi (Oxford: Oneworld, 2003), pp. 10–11.
18. Safi, "What is Progressive Islam", p. 48.
19. Ibid.
20. Ibid. See also Safi, "Introduction: The Times They Are A-Changin'", p. 3.
21. Adis Duderija, "Why I am a Progressive Islamist", *ABC Religion and Ethics*, 6 September 2016, http://www.abc.net.au/religion/articles/2016/09/06/4533540.htm (accessed 15 April 2019).
22. Ibid. Duderija's use of the term "Progressive Islamist" instead of "Progressive Islam" is problematic. It has the same pitfalls as the term "Islamism". For a discussion on this, see Syed Farid Alatas, "Rejecting Islamism and the Need for Concepts from within the Islamic Tradition", in *Islamism: Contested Perspectives on Political Islam*, edited by Richard C. Martin and Abbas Barzegar (Stanford: Stanford University Press, 2010), pp. 87–92.
23. Adis Duderija, *The Imperatives of Progressive Islam* (New York: Routledge, 2017).
24. Ibid., pp. 30, 54.
25. Ibid., p. 56.
26. Ibid., p. 190.
27. Omid Safi, "Progressive Islam in America", in *A Nation of Religions: The Politics of Pluralism in Multireligious America*, edited by Stephen Prothero (Chapel Hill: The University of North Carolina Press, 2006), pp. 43–60, 44–45.
28. Personal correspondence with Omid Safi, 24 September 2017.
29. Kersten, *Islam in Indonesia*, p. 281.
30. Ibn Rushd, *The Distinguished Jurist's Primer: Bidayat al-Mujtahid wa Nihayat al-Muqtasid*, vol. 2 (Reading, 1996), p. 556. See also the Arabic original, *Bidayat al-Mujtahid wa Nihayat al-Muqtasid*, vol. 2 (Beirut: al-Ilmiah, [1418] 1997), p. 678.
31. Al-Anbiya' (21): 47.
32. Ibn Khaldun, *The Muqadimah: An Introduction to History*, vol. 1, translated by Franz Rosenthal (London, 1967), p. 80.
33. "Haqiqat al-insan wa haqiqat al-watan", *Misr*, 30 December 1877, p. 1. See also "Al-'illa al-haqiqa li-sa'adat al-insan" in the same issue of *Misr*, p. 4; "Tarbiya", *Misr*, 5 June 1879, p. 2; and "Hakim alsharq", *Misr*, 24 May 1879, pp. 1–2. All cited in Michael Ezekiel Gasper, *The Power of Representation: Publics, Peasants, and Islam in Egypt* (Stanford: Stanford University Press, 2009), p. 45.
34. Safi, "What is Progressive Islam", p. 48.
35. Ibid.
36. Safi, "Introduction: The Times They Are A-Changin'", p. 2.

37. Ibid., p. 8.
38. Ibid., p. 4.
39. Farid Esack, "Contemporary Democracy and Human Rights Project for Muslim Societies", in *Contemporary Islam – Dynamic not Static*, edited by Abdul Aziz Said, M. Abu Nimer, and M. Sharify Fumk (London: Routledge, 2006), pp. 117–29, 127; Adis Duderija, "Progressive Muslims – Defining and Delineating Identities and Ways of Being a Muslim", *Journal of Muslim Minority Affairs* 30, no. 1 (2010): 128–36, 130.
40. Syed Hussein Alatas, "The Captive Mind and Creative Development", *International Social Science Journal* 26, no. 4 (1974): 692.
41. Syed Hussein Alatas, "The Captive Mind in Development Studies", *International Social Science Journal* 24, no. 1 (1972): 11.
42. Syed Hussein Alatas, "Some Fundamental Problems of Colonialism", *Eastern World* (November 1956).
43. This was first elaborated in a lecture in 1969 on academic imperialism. See Syed Hussein Alatas, "Academic Imperialism", lecture delivered to the History Society, University of Singapore, 26 September 1969. This was expanded and published about thirty years later. See Syed Hussein Alatas, "Intellectual Imperialism: Definition, Traits and Problems", *Southeast Asian Journal of Social Science* 28, no. 1 (2000): 23–45.
44. Alatas, "The Captive Mind in Development Studies", pp. 10–11.
45. Shahruddin Maaruf, "Some Theoretical Problems Concerning Tradition and Modernization among the Malays of Southeast Asia", seminar papers, Department of Malay Studies, National University of Singapore, 2002/2003, p. 2.
46. Ibid., p. 16.
47. Ibid., p. 17.
48. Ibid., p. 17.
49. See also Duderija, "Progressive Muslims", p. 129.
50. Esack, "In Search of Progressive Islam", p. 84.
51. Ebrahim Moosa, "The Debts and Burdens of Critical Islam", in *Progressive Muslims: On Justice, Gender and Pluralism*, edited by Omid Safi (Oxford: Oneworld, 2003), pp. 111–27, 119.
52. Ibid., p. 121.
53. Syed Farid Alatas, "The Historical Sociology of Muslim Societies: Khaldunian Applications", *International Sociology* 22, no. 3 (2007): 276.
54. See M. Sait Özervarlı, "Reading Durkheim through Ottoman Lenses: Interpretations of Customary Law, Religion, and Society by the School of Gökalp", *Modern Intellectual History* 14, no. 2 (2017): 393–419.
55. Syed Hussein Alatas, "Objectivity and the Writing of History", *Progressive Islam* 1, no. 2 (1954): 2–4.

56. Ibn Khaldun, *Al-Muqaddimah*, vols. 1, 'Abd al-Salam al-Shaddadi [Abdesselam Cheddadi] (Casablanca: Bayt al-Funun wa-l-'Ulum wa-l-Adab, 2005), p. 62 [84–85]. Page numbers in square brackets refer to Rosenthal's English translation.
57. Ibn Khaldun, *Al-Muqaddimah*, vol., p. 206 [pp. 262–63].
58. Ibn Khaldun, *Al-Muqaddimah*, vol., pp. 197, 200, 203 [pp. 254, 257, 259–60].
59. Ernest Gellner, *Muslim Society* (Cambridge: Cambridge University Press, 1981), p. 34.
60. *Muqaddimah*, vol. 2, p. 79 [pp. 102–3].
61. Gellner, *Muslim Society*, pp. 34–35.
62. *Muqaddimah*, vol. 2, pp. 67–68 [pp. 89–90].
63. Ibid., p. 68 [pp. 90–91].
64. Ibid., p. 92 [p. 117].
65. Ibid., pp. 97–98 [pp. 122–24].
66. Ibid., p. 98 [p. 124].
67. Suphan Andic, "A Fourteenth Century Sociology of Public Finance", *Public Finance* 22, nos. 1–2 (1965): 33–34.
68. *Muqaddimah*, vol. 2, p. 98 [p. 124].
69. Ibid., p. 71 [p. 94].
70. Ibid.
71. Ibid.
72. *Muqaddimah*, vol. 1, pp. 58–59 [pp. 81–82].
73. Ibn Khaldun did not regard this as constituting a thorough analysis of the political economy. While he did not find the ideas expressed in the "circle of justice" erroneous, he did state that such ideas lacked thoroughness and were expressed at too general a level. His goal was to provide a more exhaustive treatment of the topic based on explanation, proof and demonstrations. See *Muqaddimah*, vol. 1, p. 59 [p. 82].
74. See Syed Farid Alatas, "Ibn Khaldun and the Good *Madina*", *Islam and Civilizational Renewal* 4, no. 4 (2013): 530–s47.
75. Safi, "What is Progressive Islam", p. 49.
76. Safi, "Introduction: The Times They Are A-Changin'", p. 16.
77. For a more detailed discussion, see Syed Farid Alatas, "Contemporary Muslim Revival: The Case of 'Protestant Islam'", *Muslim World* 97, no. 3 (2007): 112–32.
78. Hussein Alatas, "Editorial Announcement", *Progressive Islam* 1, no. 1 (1954).
79. Safi, "Introduction: The Times They Are A-Changin'", p. 18.

8

Mainstreaming Alternative Islamic Voices in Malaysia

Norshahril Saat

Judging from the behaviour of ordinary Muslims, as well as the rulings issued by the religious elite (ulama), observers have expressed concerns about the rise of Islamic conservatism in Malaysia. They also note the rise of "Arabization" among the Malay/Muslims—their preference for Arabic culture, lifestyle and ideas at the expense of Malay culture, heritage and intellectual tradition. They also worry that there are groups promoting Saudi Arabian puritan Islamic ideology—namely, Salafi-Wahhabism—which counters Malaysia's Shafii School of jurisprudence and Sufi leanings.[1] Not totally unrelated to these broad observations, some have complained that officials in the religious bureaucracy—particularly those bending towards conservatism—have been becoming more powerful since the turn of the millennium. These officials restrict the circulation of different viewpoints in public. Islamic NGOs, academics and politicians promoting alternative views complain about the extensive reach of federal religious institution JAKIM (Department of Islamic Development Malaysia). The institution has the power to decide who has authority to speak on Islam, to define what the "correct" version of Islam is and to clamp down on progressive groups.

This chapter highlights the challenges facing groups promoting progressive Islamic discourse in Malaysia and examines how these groups have been marginalized. It also analyses the issues that the religious authorities seek to restrict from being discussed in public. The basis for these restrictions goes beyond theological differences, but includes power play as well. While most of the examples here cover issues from during the Barisan Nasional (National Front) government—the Abdullah Badawi government (2003–9) and the Najib Razak government (2009–18)—the chapter also analyses issues discussed during the Pakatan Harapan (Coalition of Hope) government. At the general election of 9 May 2018 (GE14), former prime minister Dr Mahathir Mohamad led the Pakatan Harapan coalition to topple the six-decade-old Barisan Nasional government.

Is there room for progressive voices to be aired in contemporary Malaysia? Can the Pakatan Harapan government undo the Barisan Nasional's policies and approaches to the progressives and ensure the religious bureaucracy does not overstep its role? In the following, a conceptual definition of progressivism will be provided. This will be followed by a discussion of the role of JAKIM and the muftis (official ulama) as religious authority in the country. The article will then examine how the state bureaucracy has responded to three different groups who hold alternative ideas from that promoted by the state: they include individuals such as academic Dr Faizal Musa; groups such as the feminist Sisters in Islam (SIS), Islamic Renaissance Front (IRF) and G25 (Group of 25 Prominent Individuals); and foreign speakers such as Ulil Abshar Abdallah and Dr Muním Sirry.

Defining Progressive Islam

How can the term *progressive* be objectively defined? To be sure, a progressive as defined by one group could be a conservative, revivalist or Islamist by another (noting that these terms, too, need to be unpacked). The term *progressive* connotes a positive value. Azhar Ibrahim explicates the term as "a positive movement of ideas, not necessarily in chronological historical order, but a persistency of human search for and refinement of truth".[2] Progressives are direct opposites of traditionalists or conservatives. According to Towler, traditionalism is the blind, emotional adherence to selected traditions transmitted from the past, reflecting a non-questioning attitude towards what is passed to them by their teachers and mentors. Traditionalists cannot explain what is believed, but could mainly recite or quote a verse from sacred texts. Towler states that "traditionalism as a type of religious attitude is marked by a certainty which is unquestioning. It is not only certain, it is delighted by its certainty, for the stable and secure order which it knows is something to guard and cherish."[3] Unlike the progressive, traditionalists believe that ideas cannot be questioned, and views of savants of the past are fixed and immutable.

Azhar highlights three traits of progressivism: the language of appreciation; the language of critiques, and the language of possibilities and hope.[4] Progressives generally appreciate the richness of intellectual history. A progressive mind is one that is not passive, is discerning in accepting views, does not dwell on nostalgia for the glorious past (in the Muslim world, the constant hyping of returning to the time of the Prophet Mohammad fourteen centuries ago), and asks critical questions. To appreciate is also to understand diversity of views within the Islamic tradition. To adopt the language of critique is to understand the dialectical processes underlying a certain viewpoint. According to Azhar, the reading of certain scriptures "cannot be devoid of its historical, cultural and social background", and appreciating an alternative viewpoint is by no means attacking the religion.[5] Lastly, progressives are always hopeful that they can generate change in society. They are imaginative and committed towards social transformation, as opposed to being passive, uncritical and timid, to use Azhar's terms. They also exhibit a greater appreciation of social reality when discussing issues, and do not deal in illusive or utopian ideas.

Progressive is a trait that one does not ascribe to oneself. Today, slogans are used and applied rather loosely to individuals, groups and nations, particularly in the post-9/11 context. There is greater scrutiny by governments towards terrorists and radicals, including in Southeast Asia, where some are attracted to and have even joined international terrorist networks such as al-Qaeda, Jemaah Islamiah (JI) and Islamic State in Iraq and Syria (ISIS). To counter these radical groups, states and leaders have coined terms such as *Islam Hadhari* (Civilizational Islam), *Islam Berkemajuan* (Modern Islam), *Islam Wasatiyyah* (Moderate Islam), *Islam Nusantara* (Archipelagic Islam) and *maqasid syariah* (the purpose of Islamic laws). These moderate labels have been used to describe individuals, theologians and politicians who condemn terrorists. Yet, if we apply Azhar's definition of progressive, the act of condemning terrorism does not necessarily mean the person or group can be classed as progressive. The person may condemn terror, and perhaps be actively involved in counselling radicalized individuals, but could be close-minded when it comes to issues of rituals, respect for religious minorities, and appreciating alternative religious viewpoints. For example, a religious cleric may condemn terrorism but at the same time remain silent about hate speech towards Shias. Non-progressives also do not appreciate the diversity of viewpoints regarding secularism or its merits when applied to the Malaysian context, seeing it simply as a Western import and not in line with Islamic principles.

Are there examples of progressive Muslims in Malaysia? Some of the personalities who meet the criteria that Azhar suggests are trained in theology. But there are non-theologians too, and they are academics who teach at Malaysian universities. The ones highlighted below are the prominent ones, and this should not discount the fact that some ordinary religious teachers and scholar also exist in Malaysia, though they are not pushed into the limelight. One academic who meets the above criteria is Dr Chandra Muzaffar, the Director of JUST, the International Movement for a Just world. His writings mainly examine the humanistic aspects of Islam and how they should be practised in the modern world. A political scientist by training and a student of the late prominent sociologist Professor Syed Hussein Alatas, Chandra is a strong critic of corruption and a champion of human rights. He is also concerned about Islamic reforms, the struggle for a compassionate Islam and a fair global world order. His important work on this topic is *Rights, Religion, Reform*, which is a compilation of his articles.[6] His views have at times clashed with those of the religious authorities. Though not a theologian by training, his writings reflect empathy for Islam. He has also written works that are critical of Islamic resurgence. Though his writings do not challenge matters of theology, they talk about the impact of theological ideas on multiracial Malaysia. Chandra is one of many reformers to be identified in Malaysia, while others include experts in the legal field such as Hashim Kamali and Shad Faruqi.

Malaysian Islamic Institutions

The Malaysian Constitution states that Islam is the religion of the federation; other religions are free to be practised. What is prohibited is evangelism that outwardly seeks to convert Muslims out of their faith. The constitution also indicates that Islam is a state matter, and not a federal one. The religion is mainly under the authority of the Malay Rulers, and in the case of states that do not have rulers, Islam falls under the jurisdiction of the King (Yang di-Pertuan Agong).

JAKIM was officially formed on 1 January 1997. It was largely an expansion of the Islamic affairs Department called BAHEIS. Its role centres mainly on coordinating relations between the different state Islamic Religious Councils. It is a body that does not issue fatwas or religious rulings, but it mainly acts as the secretariat to the formal meetings of all state muftis. In addition, JAKIM organizes conferences and seminars and communicates religious rulings to the masses. It also coordinates with NGOs and civil society in clamping down on "deviant" teachings. By and large, JAKIM functions as a religious bureaucracy, though lately it has been seen as overstepping its role and the constitutional provision that Islam is a matter for the state. The institute has the backing of the federal government, and it is allocated a huge budget every year. It also runs the Internet portal that streamlines the functions of all the state religious councils. JAKIM also oversees halal certification and issues its logo to products, which signals whether a consumable conforms to Islamic teachings. It also manages the religious programmes to be featured on national television.

JAKIM generally works closely with the ministries, especially on enforcement matters. For instance, JAKIM would provide recommendations to the Home Affairs Ministry on publications and films as to whether they are in line with the country's Sunni Islam. Since JAKIM does not issue fatwas, its rulings and opinions cannot be enforced as law. For fatwas to carry enforcement weight, they have to be passed by the state religious council and published in the state's gazette. This requires the endorsement of the Malay Rulers of the state. In some states the religious councils have issued fatwas to declare some sects as deviant. For example, those religious councils to have gazetted the anti-Shia fatwa include the Federal Territories (1997), Negeri Sembilan (1998), Melaka (1997), Pulau Pinang (1997) and

Kedah (2013).[7] The fatwa means that Shias are not allowed to openly practise their faith and they have had to stop the circulation of any materials containing Shia teachings. In 2014 a fatwa was issued by the Selangor religious council declaring the organization Sisters in Islam (SIS) as promoting liberalism and that all publications associated with the ideology are unlawful and are to be confiscated. SIS was active in struggling for gender equality for women and it is an internationally renowned organization made up of academics, human rights activists and lawyers. The matter is currently being brought to the federal court to seek a verdict as to whether the accusations are constitutional.

State's Response to Alternative Discourses

The following section will explore how progressive speakers have been denied the opportunity to speak or to raise important issues that could have a significant impact on society. Some of these methods include banning books, public shaming, and the denial or retraction of a permit to speak in public. It will discuss groups, individuals and foreign speakers. The section will briefly showcase some of the ideas promoted by these actors before detailing the ways religious authorities have sought to deny them their voices. The section mostly covers examples from during the Najib Razak government (2009–18). The Najib government was defeated by the Pakatan Harapan led by former prime minister Mahathir Mohamad in GE14. So far, while the new Mahathir government has made attempts to reverse the policies of the Najib administration, it has faced several setbacks resulting from the generally conservative Malaysian society and an inability to change the attitude of public administrators and the world views of the current cabinet ministers.

Locals

During the Najib Razak administration, several individuals were targeted by the official religious elites. Those targeted were seen by state officials as promoting a form of Islam that had deviated from the "mainstream". Generally, Shias and liberal Muslims were targeted. The officials had not only failed to understand the diversity within these denominations but they had also formed biased and prejudiced opinions of them. They also failed to understand the long history these groups have established for themselves in Malaysia. How progressive debates have been articulated in neighbouring Indonesia and Singapore, as well as in other parts of the Islamic world, were also not appreciated.

One significant personality targeted by the official ulama is Mohd Faizal Musa, a novelist and academic who is popularly known as Faizal Tehrani. He is a research fellow at the Institute of the Malay World and Civilization (ATMA), National University of Malaysia (UKM). He has won many accolades, both in Malaysia and internationally, and some of his works of fiction have been translated into English. During the Najib administration, seven of Faizal's novels were banned by the Ministry of Home Affairs. The reasons for the bans were not clear, but Faizal was publicly dubbed as a Shia and some believed he was promoting the sect in his works. As an academic, he has also published on the plight of Shias in internationally refereed academic journals, but these academic works were not targeted.

The declaration of Shias as deviant by the religious elites was a fairly recent development in modern Malaysia's history. The religious elites acted mainly on the basis of a legal ruling made by the JKF-MKI (National Fatwa Committee) in 1996, which declared Shiism a deviant sect. This was not the case previously, with the group, though a minority, being regarded as part of mainstream Islam. The fatwa issued by the JKF-MKI was not legally binding in Malaysia, though it was the result of consensus among all the muftis (Islamic religious scholars from the various states). However, it became legally binding after the respective religious councils in the states agreed to gazette the fatwa, with this being endorsed by the Malay rulers of those states.

Ulama from the establishment are wary of ideas that challenge their authority or counter their discourse. In their sermons, the state ulama are concerned not only with ideas that theologically contradict the Sunni version of Islam but also with ideas they deem inspired by the West. Here they are concerned about feminism and liberalism. These two terms have come to have negative connotations. Two groups to receive the brunt of the ire of the religious elite are Sisters in Islam (SIS) and the Islamic Renaissance Front (IRF). The official ulama's engagement with these two groups has not been at the level of discourse or intellectual debate. The way they have gone about trying to silence these groups has been by denying them permits to hold talks, by issuing fatwas to declare them as illegal or deviant, and by harassing members through public shaming.

SIS as an organization was initiated by prominent lawyers in Malaysia who were keen to study the impact of the 1984 Islamic Family Laws, particularly on women. In 1987 a group of lawyers, academics, journalists and civil rights activists came together to set up a sharia committee within the Association of Women Lawyers (AWL).[8] The organization was officially registered in 1993. Admission to membership is by invitation only.[9] The organization conducts programmes, including legal clinics, research, training and public lectures, and conducts advocacy work. It also has a help line for legal counselling.[10]

The ideas SIS promotes are not in sync with those of the official ulama, including a hermeneutical interpretation of the Qur'an. SIS has also called for a contextual reading of religious texts and for understanding the values underlying certain rules and regulations promoted by scholars of the past. For example, SIS is unhappy with the view that says a man's testimony is equal to that of two women, which is extended to the duality of understanding gender roles as witnesses. A recent controversy involving the religious elite and SIS occured during the formation of the Musawwah project in 2009, where some religious elites condemned the project. SIS was prominent in voicing the plight of women, particularly with regard to three issues: the Kartika Sari case, the conversion of minors through the conversion of one parent, and the caning of three women for adultery in 2010.

In 2014 the Islamic Religious Council of Selangor declared that SIS was a "deviant" group. The fatwa was gazetted by the Islamic religious council of Selangor, which means it can be enforced as law, as it received the approval by the Selangor Sultan. The fatwa also means that any publications that contain elements of liberalism or pluralism are considered un-Islamic and they may be seized by the Islamic religious authorities of the state. The youth wing of PAS also supported the move for the organization to be banned. The matter later became a legal battle in the Malaysian courts. SIS asked for a judicial review against the deviant fatwa. In 2016 the High Court dismissed the legal challenge by SIS. The matter is currently being discussed at Malaysia's apex court, the federal court.[11]

Another organization the religious authorities are uncomfortable with is the IRF, which was established in 2009. Members of the IRF claim to drive intellectual discourse in order to empower Malaysian Muslims. Subjects the organization discusses through forums and publications include democracy, liberty and social justice. The IRF is run by Dr Mohd Farouk Musa with the assistance of many young graduates and activists. Its main focus is organizing seminars involving many progressive thinkers. It also often invites speakers from other Malaysian NGOs such as SIS.

When it was first formed, the IRF did not get into much trouble with the religious elites. At that time the organization mainly discussed the works of thinkers whom the religious elites consider to uphold mainstream Islamic teachings, such as the modernist, former Egyptian Grand Shaykh of Al-Azhar Muhammad Abduh (b.1949–d.1905). Mohd Farouk was able to organize conferences freely without interference from the religious elites or the state.

Things changed however for the IRF from 2012. The religious authorities began subtly to try to influence whom the IRF could invite and what topics it could discuss. In 2012 the IRF co-organized a forum on women's rights with ISTAC (Islamic Institute of Thought and Civilisation), an academic research institute housed at IIUM (International Islamic University of Malaysia). JAKIM was upset that no JAKIM speaker was invited to speak at the session. JAKIM also objected to some of the speakers that had been invited and they wanted them to be dropped. There was also a rumour that IIUM also wanted one of the speakers, the Perlis mufti Dr Mohd Asri Zainul Abidin, to be dropped. As a form of compromise, the organizers invited some of the religious elite speakers approved by JAKIM to speak, including Uthman El Muhammady and Md Asham (from IKIM, Institute of Islamic Understanding in Malaysia). In the end, the programme was permitted to go ahead with the following speakers: Zainah Anwar (SIS), Uthman El Muhammady, and academic Farish A. Noor.[12]

The approach taken by the religious authorities to the women's forum is considered soft compared to later incidents in which the religious authorities have tried to intervene directly to stop IRF events. As will be discussed shortly, the IRF was again sanctioned by the religious authorities for bringing in foreign speakers. The authorities have elected to take a more hands-on approach to deny liberal and progressive thinkers from speaking in the country.

Another group to have faced sanctions by the Najib Razak government was the loose affiliation of individuals calling themselves the G25 (Group of 25 Prominent Individuals). The group was made up of former civil servants, professionals and members of civil society. On 7 December 2014, twenty-five individuals publicly expressed their unhappiness with the ongoing debate over the application of Islamic laws in Malaysia. They wrote an open letter to the prime minister asking him to show greater leadership in discussing problems associated with Islamic conservatism. The group grew in size—though retaining the name G25—and in 2016 collected a series of articles together into a book entitled *Breaking the Silence, Voices of Moderation: Islam in a Constitutional Democracy*.[13] The book features articles by the progressives Chandra Muzaffar, Azmi Sharom, Syed Farid Alatas and Zainah Anwar. In July 2017 the Home Affairs Ministry banned the book on the grounds that it could disrupt public order.

Foreign Speakers

In September 2017, Mustafa Akyol, a progressive Turkish scholar, was barred from speaking at a forum organized by the IRF. He was questioned by the religious authorities and told to return to his country. Dr Farouk was called in by the Federal Territories Religious Department (JAWI) for issuing the invitation. Akyol was supposed to speak on freedom of conscience, which is in line with Islamic values. The religious authorities claimed that Akyol had not obtained proper accreditation. Akyol claimed that the religious authorities did not like the proposed topic of his talk, on the commonalities between Islam, Judaism and Christianity, and took issue with his book *The Islamic Jesus: How the King of the Jews Became a Prophet of the Muslims*. He also added that it was only after former Turkish president Abdullah Gul intervened with a member of the Malaysian royalty that he was released.[14]

JAKIM had earlier expressed its discomfort with liberal Muslims, regarding them as deviant. Liberals are equated with groups promoting secularism and with those who have obtained a Western education. The traits they perceive as defining liberalism include promoting secularization and secularism, religious pluralism, critical readings of Islamic texts or religious traditions, applying hermeneutics, and Islamic feminism. Such labels do not consider the diversity within the group and they do not differentiate among those who have empathy for Islam—showing commitment to Islamic traditions (including the Qur'an and Sunnah) and contextualized traditions with the modern world—and those who have no such empathy. The religious elites consider liberals as promoting "foreign" teachings and of using less authoritative sources. They also question the morality of their liberal opponents, instead of engaging with their discourse intellectually. Some Indonesian thinkers are associated with liberalism because they received their training from Western universities and because they apply Western philosophy that the religious elites deem to not be Islamic.

One such Indonesian group to have been prevented from speaking in Malaysia is Jaringan Islam Liberal (JIL). Whilst some Indonesian Muslims also have differences with the organization, the group receives a following in the country. Activist Ulil Abshar Abdalla of JIL was prevented from speaking at a seminar in Malaysia in October 2014 on the grounds that his views were not in line with mainstream Islam. The seminar was organized by the IRF. There were reports that Ulil had been blacklisted by Malaysian immigration.[15] Clearly, banning speakers from entering Malaysia is an outmoded way of preventing foreign ideas coming into the country. In the age of social media, ideas move across borders without the need to bring in a person physically. In the end, Ulil managed to speak at the forum via a video Skype call from Indonesia.

The Ulil case might be one that was picked up by the media. Yet, keen observers of Islamic discourse in Malaysia know that Indonesian thinkers do not have much following in the country. For instance, internationally renowned modernist thinkers such as Azyumardi Azra, Nurcholis Madjid and Amin Abdullah are rarely featured in the mainstream media. The religious elites also publicly shame personalities who provide alternative views. They have taken steps to ban speakers and to charge organizers. In 2017 the IRF organized a forum inviting Indonesian scholar Dr Munim Sirry to speak at a forum called "Moderation in the Quran". The forum was co-organized with G25. JAKIM was quick to accuse the IRF and G25 of promoting deviant discourses in Malaysia.[16] There is also a lack of discussion between scholars from the two countries.

On the flipside, controversial foreign speakers are allowed to preach in Malaysia, and they have a significant following. One example is Indian preacher Zakir Naik. He is a wanted man in his home country for money laundering and hate speech, although he has denied breaking any laws. There is a YouTube clip of Zakir declaring that if Osama bin Laden "is terrorising America the terrorist, the biggest terrorist, I am with him".[17] Several countries have banned him, including Britain, yet he is allowed to come to Malaysia. A number of groups demanded that the government deport Zakir, but it refused to do so. The Mahathir government said that Zakir had abided by Malaysian laws and hence he could stay. Mahathir even granted him an audience at the prime minister's office.

Similarly, the religious authorities in Malaysia have not taken any issue with Middle East preachers. It is publicly known that some preachers from the Middle East are inclined to the puritan understanding of the religion known as Salafism-Wahhabism and that their messages are not in sync with how mainstream Muslims in Malaysia and the Malay world practise Islam, which is more Sufi oriented. The issue is not whether Malaysia should prevent Middle East scholars from entering Malaysia on account of their theological inclinations; however, if the country wants to uphold diversity of opinions, then the same judgement should also be given to Indonesian scholars. It is also clear that some politicians show their affection for influential preachers. For example, prime-minister-in-waiting Anwar Ibrahim is known to be close to controversial ulama Yusof Al-Qaradawi, an ideologue affiliated with the Muslim Brotherhood, an organization banned in many Middle Eastern countries. In 2005, Qaradawi suggested that some circumstances permitted suicide bombing, particularly for Muslims being oppressed in Palestine and Iraq.[18]

Reforms under Pakatan Harapan

Before GE14, critics of the Najib Razak government's handling of Islamic affairs were optimistic that should Pakatan Harapan come to power it would reverse the policies of the Barisan Nasional government. While many can understand that it could take years to reverse the policies of the previous government, one can observe whether the Pakatan Harapan government is starting on the right footing to reform the religious sector. Two factors will prove crucial for whether change can eventually take place. The first is Mahathir's leadership. The second is the pool of reformist ministers appointed to the cabinet. While one can remain optimistic that change can take place, the pace of change—given the current crop of leaders and their backgrounds—is proving to be a challenge for Mahathir's reform agenda.

One has to go back in history to understand Mahathir's views on Islam. Mahathir come to power in 1981, when the Islamic resurgence movement was taking root. There was a lot of excitement in the Islamic world about how a return to the glory days of Islam—by which they meant implementing policies grounded in the Qur'an and Sunnah—would lead to progress and development. This project proposed by the resurgence entailed the greater Islamization of state and society. This was when the drive to Islamize all aspects of modern life originated: to Islamize the economy, the law, instruments of the state, politics, consumption, and fashion. The activists driving Islamization then are now the main political actors in Malaysia and Indonesia, and they are mentoring the current crop of young leaders. As already mentioned, since the 1980s we have also witnessed in Malaysia an expansion of the religious bureaucracy and of Islamic civil society, which has championed revivalist issues that can slow down attempts at reforms. Mahathir had to respond to a resurgent PAS (Islamic Party of Malaysia), which has seen a significant revival with the ulama faction taking leadership of the party. In the 1970s, PAS joined the Barisan Nasional, but after four years it decided to go its own way again. As a result of this partnership, PAS lost control of its stronghold state Kelantan to the Barisan Nasional. The ulama then took control and changed the inner workings of the party. They were inspired by what they witnessed in the Iranian revolution, where the cleric Ayatollah Khomeini returned from exile to lead a revolution that toppled the US ally the Shah of Iran.

In order to control the demands made by the Islamic resurgence movement, Mahathir introduced Islamic policies and co-opted Islamic leaders into the party. He established the Islamic University, featured more Islam in the government machinery, and co-opted Anwar Ibrahim into the government. In a way, Mahathir leveraged on the mood for

Islamization to restrict the influence of PAS (except for the east coast states of Peninsula Malaysia—Kelantan and Terengganu—and some parts of Kedah). But Mahathir's authoritarian tendencies had managed to keep Islamization in check, even within the bureaucracies that he created or expanded. For instance, the role of JAKIM expanded under his rule but Mahathir was clear about his disagreement over *hudud* laws and the exclusive behaviour of the religious bureaucrats. By creating and expanding Islamic institutions at the federal level, it set them in competition with Islamic institutions at the state level, which are under the purview of the Malay rulers and the Yang di-Pertuan Agong. The muftis also towed the line of the Mahathir government, and the fatwa that led to the banning of the Darul Arqam movement in 1994 serves as a case in point.

It leaves one to wonder whether Mahathir's second government can still control the religious elites and bureaucrats in the country. To be sure, the powers of the religious elites were strengthened under the Abdullah Badawi and Najib Razak governments. Both leaders played on the Islamic card for popular support and gave the religious elites more say in the public sphere. The religious elites have also captured and controlled some parts of the government machinery, and this is not only limited to the religious department. The U-turn by the Mahathir government over the ICERD (International Convention on the Elimination of All Forms of Racial Discrimination) serves as a case in point. The earlier suggestion by Mahathir to ratify the United Nation's ICERD was met with unhappiness by conservatives, which led to the government backing down and not pursuing the matter. The muftis also weighed in on the debate and supported the move against ratifying the convention.

The focus on tackling Islamic conservatism should not rest on veteran Prime Minister Mahathir alone, but also on his cabinet ministers. Thus, the backgrounds and modes of thinking of his cabinet ministers deserve some scrutiny. In the Pakatan Harapan cabinet, the Malay-Muslim ministers are mainly from three parties: Amanah (National Trust Party), PKR (People's Justice Party) and PBBM (Malaysian United Indigenous Party). Most of the members in Amanah are former PAS members, though they are often described by analysts as progressives, or Anwarinas (close to Anwar Ibrahim). The Amanah members were also deemed to be from the "professionals" camp within PAS. Key

Amanah leaders Mohamad Sabu, Khalid Samad, Dr Dzulfefly Ahmad and Mujahid Rawa were appointed in the first Pakatan Harapan cabinet. Mujahid, who is the son of former PAS president Yusof Rawa, oversees the religious affairs as a minister in the Prime Minister's Office. While Mujahid has been described as a progressive, the question remains as to whether he will be firm enough to take on the conservatives. For example, since being in power Mujahid has been confronted with the LGBT issue. While he has made some progress to speak to some activists and members of the community to address discrimination, he has also made several questionable moves, such as calling for the removal of portraits of LGBT activists Nisha Ayub and Pang Khee Teik from the George Town Festival. He admitted ordering the Penang government to remove the pictures, as he claimed he was not in favour of promoting LGBT rights. Mujahid's view was controversial because the pictures were meant to reflect patriotism.[19]

A second incident to test Pakatan Harapan's resolve to counter the religious elites was on the permissibility of *khalwat* raids. *Khalwat* raids were common in Malaysia, where religious police would conduct random checks of hotel rooms to catch unmarried Muslim couples being together behind closed doors. Critics have argued that such raids are an invasion of privacy. The media quoted Mujahid in an interview saying the *khalwat* raids should end as the government has no business knowing what happens behind closed doors.[20] Muslim conservatives were unhappy with Mujahid's comments and Anwar Ibrahim came to his defence saying that Mujahid merely wanted the issue of *khalwat* to be enforced more efficiently.[21] Clarifying the issue a few days later, Mujahid stood by his comments and said he merely wanted the procedure of conducting the raids to be in line with Islam and that they should not embarrass those involved. This means that Mujahid agreed that *khalwat* raids should continue, even though this is not practised in many Islamic societies or was even done during the Prophet's time.

A further issue to test Pakatan Harapan's resolve was to do with academic freedom. In this case, education minister Dr Maszlee Malik was put to test. The first controversy surrounded the announcement he would be appointed as IIUM president. This went against Pakatan Harapan's manifesto to not appoint politicians to manage universities, and it created unhappiness among students. Dr Maszlee had previously been a lecturer at the university. He became president on 5 September 2018, but he agreed to step down by the end of November that year.[22] Civil society groups were also unhappy with the habit of universities cancelling academic talks by critical scholars or activists. In November 2018, political activist Hishamuddin Rais had his proposed lecture cancelled by UKM. Before that, Professor Syed Farid Alatas from the National University of Singapore had his scheduled lecture at University Sains Islam Malaysia (USIM) cancelled.[23] This went against Dr Maszlee's pledge for academic freedom. Though the minister condemned the move by the universities, it was not enough to tackle the conservative and exclusivist groups placed in power by the previous government.

Conclusion

The behaviour of Malaysian politicians, religious elites and society has to be understood in the context of the Islamic resurgence movement in the 1980s. Student leaders championing the Islamization of state and society on university campuses back then are now the current crop of leaders in Malaysia, if not mentoring younger politicians.

The religious bureaucracy has been active in preventing progressive views from being aired in seminars, and we see some continuity with the current government. Pakatan Harapan may argue that this is a work in progress, given the policies undertaken by the previous Barisan Nasional government. The way forward for the progressives is to continue engaging with the conservatives. They must also work to convince the increasingly conservative masses of new ideas. This is the only way for the regeneration of progressive voices in the country. Here, civil society has to work closely with the government, and civil engagement should be conducted with the religious elites, and there should be less confrontation.

Universities also play a part in reforming society. Here there must be a conscious effort to get good academics to teach in the universities, and subjects should not revolve solely on theology. Familiarity with the social sciences is also necessary to understand the wide corpus of knowledge, and to also encourage students to understand different modes of thinking in society.

Notes

1. Salafism refers to the move to return to the practices of the Prophet's time and of the period of the three generations after him. While Salafism is not necessarily conservative, the Wahabbi brand of Salafism (hence Wahabbi-Salafi) adopts a more puritan approach that frowns upon such Sufi practices as visiting the graves of pious Muslims, the mass recitation of prayers, and celebrating the Prophet's birthday.
2. Azhar Ibrahim, "The Making of Progressive Religion", in *Islam, Religion and Progress: Critical Perspectives* (Singapore: The Reading Group, 2006), p. 2.
3. Robert Towler, *The Need for Certainty: A Sociological Study of Conventional Religion* (London: Routledge, 1986), pp. 90–91.
4. Azhar Ibrahim, "The Making of Progressive Religion", p. 3.
5. Ibid.
6. Chandra Muzaffar, *Rights, Religion and Reform: Enhancing Human Dignity through Spiritual and Moral Transformation* (London: Routledge, 2002).
7. Norshahril Saat, "Deviant' Muslims: The Plight of Shias in Contemporary Malaysia", in *Religious Diversity in Muslim-Majority States in Southeast Asia: Areas of Toleration and Conflict*, edited by Bernhard Platzdasch and Johan Saravanamuttu (Singapore: Institute of Southeast Asian Studies, 2014), pp. 359–78.
8. Sisters in Islam website, http://www.sistersinislam.org.my/page.php?35 (accessed 14 September 2017).
9. Azza Basarudin, *Humanizing the Sacred: Sisters in Islam and the Struggle for Gender Justice in Malaysia* (Seattle: University of Washington Press, 2016), p. 12.
10. Ibid., p. 13.
11. Ida Lim, "Mais Gets Court's Nod to Continue Bid to Stop SIS's 'Deviant' Fatwa Challenge", *Malay Mail*, 11 July 2017, http://www.themalaymailonline.com/malaysia/article/mais-gets-courts-nod-to-continue-bid-to-stop-siss-deviant-fatwa-challenge#KVH4ttWXBaYzJeCL.97 (accessed 23 October 2017).
12. IRFront.net, "Penganjur: Pihak atasan agensi agama 'haling' forum hak wanita", 8 April 2012, http://irfront.net/print_version/160.html (accessed 15 April 2019).
13. G25, *Breaking the Silence, Voices of Moderation: Islam in a Constitutional Democracy* (Singapore: Marshall Cavendish, 2016).
14. "Mustafa Akyol: Jawi Didn't Like My Talk on Commonalities between Islam, Christianity", *Malay Mail*, 28 September 2017, https://www.malaymail.com/s/1475433/mustafa-akyol-jawi-didnt-like-my-talk-on-commonalities-between-islam-christ (accessed 15 April 2019).

15. "Dianggap Menyesatkan Umat Islam Ulii Malaysia", *Republika*, 13 October 2014.
16. Boo Su-Lyn, "Called Deviant, Muslim Scholar Says Was Just Challenging Orthodox View", http://www.themalaymailonline.com/malaysia/article/called-deviant-muslim-scholar-says-was-just-challenging-orthodox-view-on-qu#uTEi1Fxg7BidMIk8.97 (accessed 23 October 2017).
17. "Wanted in India, Zakir Naik Resurfaces in Perlis to Deliver Speech", *New Straits Times*, 2 December 2018.
18. Antony Barnett, "Suicide Bombs Are a Duty, says Islamic scholar", *The Guardian*, 28 August 2005, https://www.theguardian.com/politics/2005/aug/28/uk.terrorism (accessed 15 April 2019).
19. Loshana K. Shagar, "Mujahid: Portraits of LGBT Activists Removed from George Town Festival on My Orders", *The Star*, 8 August 2018.
20. Zakiah Koya, "No More Night Khalwat Raids or Intrusion into Muslim's Private Lives Says Mujahid", *Nation*, 6 October 2018.
21. "Mujahid Not Encouraging Vice, Says Anwar", *Nation*, 8 October 2018.
22. "Maszlee Confirms Stepping Down as IIUM President End of This Month", *The Star Online*, 12 November 2018.
23. "Gerak Condemns UKM for Barring Hishamuddin Rais, Overhaul of Leadership in Public Universities Needed", *The Star Online*, 22 November 2018.

Challenges Facing Alternative Voices

9

Democracy and the "Conservative Turn" in Indonesia

Zainal Abidin Bagir and Azis Anwar Fachrudin

Discourse on Islam in Indonesia has focused on the question of a "conservative turn" or rising intolerance. The question seems to be more pertinent in the wake of the 2 December 2016 rally called Defending Islam Act ("Aksi Bela Islam", or more popularly the 212 rally) against the then governor of Jakarta, Basuki Tjahaja Purnama (Ahok), for allegedly committing blasphemy. More recently, the appointment by President Joko Widodo (Jokowi) of the Indonesian Ulama Council (MUI) general chairman Ma'ruf Amin as his running mate for the 2019 presidential election has made this question even more pressing.[1] Ma'ruf was the one who signed MUI's "religious stance" stating that Ahok's remarks (he was Jokowi's vice governor in 2012–14) constituted blasphemy. He was also one of the expert witnesses during the trial, contributing to the judge's decision to imprison Ahok for two years. Unlike Ahok, Jokowi is a Muslim. He was still concerned however that the 2019 election would be about which candidate is more Islamic. He seems to have been vindicated in this regard by the issues raised during the campaign.[2] Recent events have amplified the polarization within Indonesian society, which in many cases boils down to competition between pro-Jokowi and anti-Jokowi groups.

It is ironic that Indonesia's conservative turn occurred during the post-1998 democratization phase. It has also, directly or indirectly, caused many setbacks to the process. These setbacks can be seen in two forms: the agenda of the conservatives on the one hand, and the government's reaction to them, such as the move to limit their freedom, on the other. In a sense, there is a tension between maintaining pluralism as a rival to the conservative agenda and democracy. While this chapter looks at recent events taking place in Indonesia, including the issues raised during the 2019 presidential election campaign, the issue about the tension between pluralism, conservatism and democracy is not unique to today's Indonesia, but is also an issue even for established democracies.

This chapter begins with the question of how to characterize the situation of Indonesian Islam today. Has it become more conservative or intolerant? While the perception of increased religious conservatism is valid, this article argues for a nuanced understanding of what is now happening in Indonesia. Characterizing the present situation beyond conservatism or intolerance, especially if the two terms are understood as mostly referring to discursive competition, this chapter suggests that paying more attention to the political dynamics—including, more narrowly, the electoral dynamics—would provide a better understanding of the situation. In this way it looks at what kind of interventions, by the state as well as civil society, may influence the current situation towards a more inclusive democracy.

The Changing Religious-Political Landscape

The discourse on the "conservative turn"—at least if it is defined as drawing primarily from a turning point in Indonesian religious discourse that happened in 2005—is not primarily about the changing modes of religiosity among average Muslims, but is rather more about the changing landscape within elite circles of major Muslim organizations. Greg Fealy, in an essay titled "A Conservative Turn", referred to the forced closure of unregistered churches, attacks on "heretical sects", the election of conservative figures to the national boards of Nahdlatul Ulama (NU) and Muhammadiyah, and the introduction of local "sharia" regulations (*perda syariah*) as confirming the turn.³ However, in response to those blaming only the rising influence of puritanical forms of Islam for this conservative turn, Fealy argued that the confrontational attitude of liberal Muslim groups is a major contributing factor.

In so far as NU and Muhammadiyah are concerned, the tide has turned the other way in later elections. Said Aqil Siradj, who is more inclined to the Gusdurian strand within NU (referring to followers of former president Abdurrahman Wahid, who was NU chairman), was elected in 2010 and re-elected in 2015 as NU's executive (*tanfidziyyah*) general chairman. Haedar Nashir, who was more progressive in comparison to the other strong candidates in the organization, was elected as Muhammadiyah's general chairman in 2015. Indeed, in 2015 Ma'ruf Amin became NU's supreme leader (*rais aam syuriyah*), but this happened only after Mustofa Bisri (Gus Mus), who was proposed initially by the Ahlul Halli wal Aqdi (lit. those with authority to free and bind), composed of the nine most senior NU ulama for being the *rais aam*, retreated. Similar to Aqil Siradj, Gus Mus is also from NU's progressive camp. Noteworthy also is that during the 2015 NU congress the political tone of the organization was palpable, with the National Awakening Party (PKB, which was founded by NU leaders) being seen to have penetrated to the NU leadership. Many PKB politicians later came to hold key positions in NU's national board as a result of the congress. Ma'ruf Amin was also a former PKB politician.⁴ His holding of NU's highest position cannot therefore be regarded simply as signifying NU's move towards more conservatism (cf. Arifianto and Wanto 2015), but more as an accident that later benefitted PKB in the 2019 election.

Martin van Bruinessen's edited volume has contributed to popularizing the term "conservative turn". He uses different indicators though when describing the phenomenon. "The clearest expression of the conservative turn", he says, "was perhaps given by a number of controversial *fatwa*, authoritative opinions, issued by MUI."⁵ These *fatwas* included a declaration about the incompatibility of secularism, pluralism and liberalism with Islam; condemnation of the practice of interreligious prayers and interreligious marriage; and declaring Ahmadis as non-Muslims, even calling on the government to restrict their activities. More generally, the "conservative turn" was about (a) the increased prominence of conservative figures in major Indonesian Muslim organizations as the influence of liberal and modernist views waned, and (b) the contested authority of the established Muslim organizations as democratization opened the door for the mushrooming of new Muslim organizations (with some of them being transnational in scope).

In more recent writings on the issue, "the rise of conservative Islam" is vindicated in Jokowi's choice of Ma'ruf Amin as his vice-presidential running mate for the 2019 presidential election.[6] And conservatism, in one way or another, leads to the retreat of democracy[7] if it leads to the "institutionalizing [of] intolerance though discriminatory laws, policies and practices".[8]

However, at this point we need to scrutinize conservatism or the conservative turn by looking at the context the phenomenon derived from. In the above analysis, the conservative turn is not simply a description of a religious trend but also an explanation for a group of events, ranging from hostility towards non-Muslims or non-mainstream Muslims, the assertion of Islamic identity in local laws, and the marginalization of liberal/modernist Muslims in the Islamic discourse. As an explanation, it focuses on a particular strand of Islamic thought or attitudes (the conservative) and pays less attention to the conditions of its emergence and the political structure that enables it.

While the emergence and strengthening of conservative Muslim organizations does take place, the view that they are dominant may have resulted from selective attention given to them. The fact is that progressive groups are still holding the fort, and remain influential, but the arena in which they are competing with the conservatives has changed considerably. In other words, what we clearly see is that the spectrum of groups contributing to the face of Indonesian Islam has become significantly more diverse, with competition between the progressives and the conservatives becoming more pronounced. Further, this competition has taken on a heightened form during some elections.

Elections and Intolerance

In general, participants in electoral politics will not necessarily play the religion card, but they may be tempted to do so when elections become more competitive.⁹ This is what we see in a small number of local elections in Indonesia, but most strikingly in the Jakarta gubernatorial election of 2017, which saw the defeat of the Christian Chinese Ahok; in the 2014 presidential electoral competition between Joko Widodo and Prabowo Subianto; as well as the 2019 presidential election campaign.

Elections, and power dynamics more generally within the state, turn out to be quite a significant factor for the so-called "conservative turn". This is well argued by Buehler in the case of the enactment of local sharia laws.¹⁰ In the democratizing Indonesia, where there are now hundreds of elections (at the national, provincial and district levels), such a "conservative turn" may emerge time and again in different places, but it may not necessarily be stable or long-lasting. When the electoral competition takes place in Jakarta the impact may be more significant. But even in Jakarta, as we will discuss later, we see that the two "reunions" of the 212 activists who had brought down Ahok, showed that sentiments mobilized during elections may not remain over time.

The question, then, may be as much about the new political arena in which the competition between the progressives and the conservatives takes place; how the new political structure, marked mostly by the democratization after 1998, enables the events described as indicating the "conservative turn". This includes consideration of overall policies on matters of religion enacted by particular regimes, especially the period in which the suggested conservative turn was taking place, i.e., the ten years of rule by Susilo Bambang Yudhoyono (2004–14) followed by those of Jokowi, as well as to the micro-political contexts of the conservative mobilizations, especially in times of elections.

This viewpoint has been taken up recently by researchers addressing the question of the causes and effects of the 2016 anti-Ahok Islamist mobilization. In this regard, Mietzner and Muhtadi provide some surprising insights from measurements of intolerance over the years. In their research, intolerance and conservatism are measured by attitudes towards religious events by non-Muslims, towards non-Muslim places of worship, and to non-Muslims holding public office (mayors, regents, governors or president). Based on polling data on religious intolerance from 2010, 2011 and 2016, Mietzner and Muhtadi conclude that while there is indeed significant support for conservative views among Indonesian Muslims, "the data show considerable *decline* in conservative and radical attitudes between 2010 and 2016" (italics in the original).[11] The 212 rally, which many see as further entrenchment of the conservative turn among Indonesian Muslims, was actually not driven by the rise of intolerance and conservatism but rather took place despite its decline.

What then was the main driver of the 2016 Islamist mobilizations? Mietzner, Muhtadi and Halida point out that while Muslim grievances (particularly against the government and the existing political order) and religious beliefs are necessary, they needed "religio-political entrepreneurs" to generate such a large mobilization.[12] The part played by these entrepreneurs was so effective that—based on a comparison of multi-year polling data for prior to and after the 2016 Islamist mobilizations—the level of intolerance had increased after the mobilizations *specifically* on the issue of non-Muslims holding leadership positions (ranging from mayor to president) and had declined on the issue of non-Muslim religious ceremonies and building houses of worship in neighbourhoods. Mietzner, Muhtadi and Halida thus conclude that the hardening of these Islamist sentiments "was not the *cause*, but the *effect* of the mobilisation" (italics in the original).[13]

The more challenging question therefore is not whether Indonesian Muslims have become increasingly conservative but rather what has made the religio-political entrepreneurs (particularly in regard to the coalition with FPI and other Muslim organizations which, on other issues, do not go along) so successful in organizing the mobilization that they managed to effectively influence Muslims' attitudes towards non-Muslims. Another fact they found was the shift in the core constituency of conservative Muslims, from those with a lower level of educational and economic background to those of the educated middle class with a better organizational capacity. Part of the explanation is attributed to the state's accommodation of Islamic conservatives during Susilo Bambang Yudhoyono's rule, which enabled and consequently strengthened their political consolidation in elite circles.[14]

The Yudhoyono administration tended to accommodate Islamic conservatism by, among other things, endorsing and accelerating the deliberation of the anti-pornography bill in 2008; tolerating attacks by FPI and other conservative Muslim groups on minorities and unorthodox groups; and by improving the political standing of MUI soon after assuming office by appointing MUI's then head of fatwa council Ma'ruf Amin as a member of the Presidential Advisory Board and providing an annual stipend to MUI.[15] This accommodation ended in 2014, as Yudhoyono could not run again. Jokowi, coming from the Indonesian Democratic Party of Struggle (Partai Demokrasi Indonesia Perjuangan, PDIP), was seen as increasingly excluding conservative Muslim groups from the formal political arena, making the Internet and the street their remaining recourse. In 2016, after Jokowi's initial success in neutralizing political parties opposing him in parliament, the challenge came from these "street parliaments".[16] Only after December 2016 did Jokowi pay more attention to Muslims and to clearly try to accommodate some Muslim groups (mostly NU), while repressing others. The so-called "conservative turn" as observed after December 2016 was more an issue of power dynamics within the state as opposed to the discursive power of conservative groups.

The entrepreneurs of grievance behind the Islamist mobilization that led to the perception of increased conservatism are not as unified and cohesive as they seem to be. The conservatives within the 212 movements are composed of groups that in normal conditions would be at each other's throats; one example being that FPI's traditional practices are deemed heretical by the Salafis. And recent developments show that the groups behind 212 have split.

In addition to past disputes between members of the Alumni Brotherhood of 212 (Persaudaraan Alumni 212) over which politician they would back or which candidate they would support in regional elections, and whether the group should be politically principled or more pragmatic,[17] developments in the lead-up to the 212 reunion in December 2018 showed that some leading members had left the group. They were concerned the group had largely become a vessel for political campaigning (not necessarily for Prabowo, but clearly against Jokowi). They included Kapitra Ampera, the former lawyer of Rizieq Shihab and now a PDIP candidate; and Usama Hisyam, chairman of the Persaudaraan Muslimin Indonesia/Parmusi. Other leading figures such as Bachtiar Nasir have voiced the same concern, though they have not left the group yet. Their concerns turned out to be true, as the political tone of the 2018 reunion was palpable. A major reason for the rally attracting far more attendees than the 2017 reunion was very likely due to the momentum for the coming presidential election.[18]

In sum, in seeking to understand the situation in Indonesia it is more productive to look at how the changing political landscape has paved the way for conservatives to gain support and political prominence. The development is therefore not one generated by conservatism per se but rather one triggered by political parties and other patrons. This is why referring to the movement that uses Islamic jargon to oppose Jokowi and to institutionalize what they understand as Islamic values as "conservative" may not be fully appropriate.

Pancasila vs. Islamists, Again?

The Jokowi administration's approach to dealing with the 212 movement reflected a mix of accommodation and repression. Two groups were accommodated. One is the Islamists themselves. Positions have been given to former Islamist critics of the government who were willing to moderate; for example, Kapitra Ampera, who joined Jokowi's party (PDI-P), Ali Mochtar Ngabalin, who was appointed as a member of the Presidential Staff Office, TGB Zainul Majid, who joined the Golkar party, and, more recently, Yuzril Ihza Mahendra, chairman of the Crescent Star Party (Partai Bulan Bintang/PBB), who was appointed as Jokowi's lawyer. Jokowi also welcomed two important figures who were central to the 2 December 2016 demonstration, Bachtiar Nasir and Zaytun Rasmin, to his palace in 2017. In contrast, others—most prominently Rizieq Shihab—have been repressed by multiple criminal charges, ranging from blasphemy, insulting national ideology, to pornography. In addition, Jokowi has clearly become more careful on topics important to Islamic conservative groups, such as investigation of the 1965 massacre (which involved NU) and LGBT issues.

At the same time, Jokowi has bolstered his Islamic credentials by appealing to NU and accepting many of its demands, signalling that he takes the side of moderate Muslims. One such step has been by disbanding Hizbut Tahrir Indonesia (HTI) via the 2017 Regulation in

Lieu of Law on Mass Organisations (Peraturan Pemerintah Pengganti Undang-Undang/Perppu Ormas), a political move with little risk, as HTI was only a small fraction within the 212 movement, though one with strong symbolism. The appointment of Ma'ruf Amin as Jokowi's running mate—pressed by PKB with the threat that NU would retreat from its support of Jokowi—can be read as Jokowi's fear of losing NU's backing. Prior to this, Jokowi had already courted the PKB-dominated NU personally (by visiting *pesantren* and inviting NU ulama to hold religious ceremonies in state palaces), materially (giving funding to *pesantren* and making NU a key beneficiary of his land redistribution programme), and institutionally (by accepting NU's proposal for the bill on Religious Education).[19]

Another strategy, which is no less significant, is the provision of an ideological counter-narrative to the Islamists through the national ideology, Pancasila. The year 2017 can arguably be seen as the most important year in the history of Pancasila after the 1998 Reformasi. Several key Pancasila-related events in 2017 included: (1) commemoration of the birthday of Pancasila on 1 June celebrated for the first time as a national day; (2) the government holding the so-called "Pancasila Week" events; (3) the establishment of the Presidential Working Unit on the Reinforcement of Pancasila Ideology; and, most importantly, (4) the dissolution, as mentioned above, of HTI on the grounds, among others, that the Islamist organization's ideological campaigns contravened Pancasila. In addition, some major events were organized at the societal level, such as Universitas Gadjah Mada's declaration as a university of Pancasila and the founding of the Front Penggerak Pancasila by thousands of members of NU.

As the Perppu has been approved by parliament and is part of the revised law on mass organizations, the ruling may have a long-lasting effect. A number of civil society organizations working on pluralism (with NU becoming the vanguard) had been concerned about the threat of Islamist organizations such as HTI to the very foundation of the republic, so they supported the government's decision. Several pro-democracy and human rights activists however have criticized the move as reducing freedom of expression.

There are three significant differences between the Perppu Ormas and the 2013 law that it revises. First, there is the removal of the lengthy procedures (which could take at least six months) required to gain court approval before disbanding an organization. Removing this requirement undermined the democratic value of checks and balances on executive power of the government. Second, is the introduction of criminal penalties simply for being a member of an organization whose activities are deemed illegal by the Perppu, which include promoting an ideology that contradicts Pancasila. And third, while the 2013 Law stated that the ideologies contravening Pancasila are atheism and communism/Marxism-Leninism, the Perppu adds to this "and other ideologies that aim to change or replace Pancasila and the 1945 Constitution". This addition can be seen to have been made intentionally to apply to HTI.[20]

Pancasila can be interpreted in such a way that can delegitimize the compatibility of HTI's ultimate goal of establishing a caliphate with Indonesia's national fabric. It indeed originated from a political compromise between the nationalists and the Islamists during the founding era in 1945. The compromise was intended to make Pancasila more inclusive towards diverse religions. However, using Pancasila as a legal-political tool to restrict freedom of expression and association has its own drawbacks.

History has shown that there are variations in how the Pancasila has been understood. Interpretations have been contested, and some have contradicted each other, unlike the popular discourse that treats Pancasila as though it is self-evident, even univocal, in its meaning. The history of how the Pancasila has been interpreted since the 1950s to the present—with influences from Islam, Marxism and democracy—and how it has been implemented, clearly demonstrates how its equivocal and malleable nature leaves it prone to legal-political instrumentalization that can erode democratic values.[21] One of the best examples we can draw here concerns the first principle of Pancasila: Belief in God ("Ketuhanan Yang Maha Esa"). The principle may simply be interpreted as recognition of religion's foundational role in the national fabric. However, post-Reformasi development shows how the principle has been interpreted so as to permeate Indonesian laws such that they must not contradict religious values. Some Islamist groups embrace the second understanding, as reflected in the debate on the pornography bill in the middle of the last decade, the (un)constitutionality of the 1965 law on defamation of religion, and arguments for expanding the definition of *zina* (to include not only adultery but also fornication) in the Constitutional Court in 2017. The supreme leader of FPI, Rizieq Shihab, has his own interpretation of this principle; for him this means that religion is the very basis of the republic. As such, religion should be protected by the state (for example through the blasphemy law that prohibits the defamation of religion); this also means that his idea of "*NKRI Bersyariah*" (the Unitary State of the Republic of Indonesia Based on Sharia) is in accordance with Pancasila.

The equivocality of Pancasila should have made it insufficient to meet the legal principle of *lex certa*; that is, something has to be unambiguous and precisely clear to be a criterion for criminal prosecution. While the discourse on recognizing Pancasila as an "open ideology" (meaning that it is open to various interpretations) was relatively prominent among Indonesian intellectuals in the last decade, the recent use of Pancasila to disband an organization has closed it. Concerns that some government in the future may use it in undemocratic ways for undemocratic purposes are justifiable, as the same thing has happened to the law on defamation of religion, whose target has expanded beyond its original addressees to include non-mainstream sects within Indonesia's recognized religions. Pancasila, albeit having certain shortcomings, will be an "open ideology" as long as it is treated along the lines of its *raison d'être*; namely, as a platform for political compromise among competing political groups, be they religious or secular, not as a legal-political tool.

How Can Democracy Deal with Conservatism?

Indonesia has faced a similar dilemma related to (conservative) religion and democracy throughout its history. The 2019 presidential election was but the latest expression of this, partly reflected in the competition between the rival candidates. After Jokowi's victory, the question remains: are his undemocratic means to curb potential threats to democracy acceptable? Have they worked? The most recent worrying trend is that in his efforts to garner wider support—for the election as well as for after—Jokowi has also had to court the conservatives and to cater to their demands. How much further would he be prepared to do this, especially now that he has Ma'ruf Amin as his vice president?

The concern of this chapter is not only about Jokowi or the recent election, but it is a good example of the broader question about how a democratic state like Indonesia faces a dilemma between democracy and pluralism. The developments of the past few years towards increased conservatism show that the issue is not simply ideological or religious but is heavily linked with contestation of power and competition of political patronage. The changing political landscape from Yudhoyono (accommodating conservatives) and Jokowi (perceived to have excluded conservatives), coupled with less centralized distribution of power brought by democratization, has given rise and prominence to religious expressions and movements that may erode democratic values. The most difficult question here is how to deal with these anti-pluralist groups.

Some of the recent moves made by the government to prosecute key conservative leaders on petty charges and to disband an Islamist organization may easily be regarded as undemocratic. Though these steps were made in the name of Pancasila, it is difficult to avoid the impression they were for short-term political gain. In particular, the case of disbanding HTI by removing an essential feature of democracy—the check and balance on executive power—could hardly be defended. No wonder that the revision of the law on mass organizations is reminiscent of what the New Order regime did in the 1980s when the government turned Pancasila from simply a "state ideology" into a legal tool for repression.

However, concerns that letting these conservatives flourish and gain further access to state resources that could undermine democracy cannot be ruled out. Referring to the debate on the "inclusion-moderation" thesis, we are posed with a dilemma: on one hand, as the thesis goes, democratic political accommodation can bring extreme or conservative groups to moderation (which, as scholars have argued, has worked in the case of the Prosperous Justice Party or Partai Keadilan Sejahtera/ PKS); on the other hand, accommodation can be worrying, as these conservatives pursue goals that may undermine democratic values.

While several scholars have suggested that repression can be part of a strategy to defend democracy against populist threats,[22] cases such as Egypt show that decades of repression instead made the Muslim Brotherhood a populist party that won by a landslide after the toppling of Mubarak. There is a strong likelihood that for the Indonesian case more repression will, in the long-term, only fuel the victimization narratives of the Islamists.

In the case of today's Indonesia, the dilemma between democracy and pluralism (or anti-conservatism, understood as a threat to equal citizenship) may not be genuine. As van Bruinessen suggests, if this line of thinking is followed we may come to the unproductive conclusion "that liberal Islamic thought could only flourish when it is patronized by an authoritarian regime".[23] There are two reasons to suggest that this should not be the case.

First, the problem may lie in the coupling of the conservative turn with a retreat of democracy, which seems to assume a certain understanding about a "proper" democracy—that is, liberal, secular democracy. The evaluation and pessimism (such as in Lindsey[24]) seems to stand on the expectation that the democratization that started in 1998 and strengthened the following year—including in the amendment of the constitution, which, among other things, inserted a new comprehensive, wide-ranging chapter on human rights—would lead to a solid *liberal* democracy. That expectation has indeed gone unfulfilled, but from the beginning it was an unrealistic one. As a number of scholars have argued, the kind of democracy that Indonesia is likely to have would not share all the characteristics of democracies in the United States or Europe (which themselves exhibit different types of democracy).[25] The issue of democracy and conservative religion is not unique to Indonesia; it is even experienced by a country with an established democracy such as the United States.[26] This is the challenge Indonesia is facing: how to nurture a democracy and promote equal citizenship but at the same time accommodate the religious aspirations of its citizens—a segment of whom may be conservative.[27]

Second, conservatism and intolerance are not simply the predisposition of certain Muslim groups mobilized by political entrepreneurs, but they have found outlets in a number of current laws and regulations. In other words, the structure of the state in terms of its management of religion to some extent nurtures intolerance. This is true with regard to the 1965 blasphemy law, which has become much more popular after 1998; the institution of Bakor Pakem, which was founded in 1952 and is still active today; or the regulation regarding houses of worship, which has been used as a legal way to express intolerance. Also, the law and institution of religious education promoted by the state does not help, to say the least, to nurture tolerance; in some cases it has even been used to promote intolerance. In other words, even within the state there are policies that have been used by intolerant groups. Changing these policies would constitute a significant long-term improvement, but this has not been seriously attempted. As an example, the government could already do so much with regard to the difficult issue of the blasphemy law, even without revoking it (which would be difficult, for historical-political reasons related supposedly to the place of religion in the Indonesian state), by simply implementing it in accordance with what is required by the law and by raising the standard of evidence required in blasphemy cases.[28] With regard to HTI, the previous law provided a more democratic (albeit longer) process to disband an organization, but this was not even tried by the government.

These examples show that had the government been serious about the potential threat to democracy posed by intolerant groups, there were already democratic means at its disposal. Also, rather than using an abstract ideology such as Pancasila as a weapon to repress intolerant groups, there are many more principled and democratic avenues that may be attempted to improve the situation. Indeed, while this is surely not an easy task, it is doable. While the existing legal framework may not be sufficient to completely achieve democracy, sufficient political will to improve things through gradual change could lead to a different picture for Indonesia. The difficulty in imagining that a conservative Indonesia could be democratic does not seem to come from a principled reasoning about foundational questions such as the relationship between the state and religion, but from the government's weak—and, most of the time, late—response to acts that attempt to dominate the public space. Otherwise, a conservative turn may not be a serious threat to democracy.

Notes

1. Alexander Arifianto, "'Conservative Turn' Will Continue in Indonesian Presidential Election Next Year", *The Conversation*, 13 August 2018, https://theconversation.com/conservative-turn-will-continue-in-indonesian-presidential-election-next-year-101032 (accessed 15 April 2019); Tim Lindsey, "The Rise of Conservative Islam in Indonesia", *Australian Institute of International Affairs*, 22 August 2018, http://www.internationalaffairs.org.

au/australianoutlook/jokowis-deputy-pick-confirms-rise-of-conservative-islam-in-indonesia/ (accessed 15 April 2019).
2. Menchik doubted that Jokowi, as a Muslim, would be the target of an anti-Islam accusation. It has now become clear however that it is not simply an issue of Islam versus non-Islam but of how Islamic or how willing the candidate would be to support vocal Muslim organizations. Jeremy Menchik, "Ahok is not Jokowi", *New Mandala*, 8 May 2017, https://www.newmandala.org/ahok-not-jokowi/ (accessed 15 April 2019).
3. Greg Fealy, "A Conservative Turn", *Inside Indonesia*, 15 July 2007, https://www.insideindonesia.org/a-conservative-turn.
4. Greg Fealy, "Nahdlatul Ulama and the Politics Trap", *New Mandala*, 11 July 2018, https://www.newmandala.org/nahdlatul-ulama-politics-trap/; Greg Fealy, "Politics and Principle at the NU Congress", *Jakarta Post*, 8 August 2015, https://www.thejakartapost.com/news/2015/08/08/politics-and-principle-nu-congress.html (accessed 15 April 2019).
5. Martin van Bruinessen, ed., *Contemporary Developments in Indonesian Islam: Explaining the "Conservative Turn"* (Singapore: Institute of Southeast Asian Studies, 2013), p. 3.
6. Arifianto, "'Conservative Turn' Will Continue"; Lindsey, "The Rise of Conservative Islam".
7. Tim Lindsey, "Retreat from Democracy? The Rise of Islam and the Challenge for Indonesia", *Australian Foreign Affairs* (July 2018), pp. 69–92.
8. Ibid., p. 79.
9. Sana Jaffrey and Ihsan Ali-Fauzi, "Street Power and Electoral Politics in Indonesia", *New Mandala*, 5 April 2016, http://www.newmandala.org/street-power-and-electoral-politics-in-indonesia/ (accessed 15 April 2019).
10. Michael Buehler, *The Politics of Shari'a Law: Islamist Activists and the State in Democratizing Indonesia* (Cambridge: Cambridge University Press, 2016).
11. Marcus Mietzner and Burhanuddin Muhtadi, "Explaining the 2016 Islamist Mobilisation in Indonesia: Religious Intolerance, Militant Groups and the Politics of Accommodation", *Asian Studies Review*, 42, no. 3 (2018): 42–43.
12. Marcus Mietzner, Burhanuddin Muhtadi, and Rizka Halida, "Entrepreneurs of Grievance: Drivers and Effects of Indonesia's Islamist Mobilization", *Bijdragen Tot De Taal-, Land- En Volkenkunde* 174, nos. 2/3 (2018).
13. Ibid., p. 183.
14. Mietzner and Muhtadi, "Explaining the 2016 Islamist Mobilisation", pp. 42–43.
15. M.C. Ricklefs, "Religious Elites and the State in Indonesia and Elsewhere: Why Takeovers Are So Difficult and Usually Don't Work", in *Encountering Islam: The Politics of Religious Identities in Southeast Asia*, edited by Hui Yew-Foong (Singapore: Institute of Southeast Asian Studies 2013), pp. 17–46;

Robin Bush. "Religious Politics and Minority Rights during the Yudhoyono Administration", in *The Yudhoyono Presidency: Indonesia's Decade of Stability and Stagnation*, edited by Edward Aspinall, Marcus Mietzner, and Dirk Tomsa (Singapore: Institute of Southeast Asian Studies, 2015), pp. 239–57.

16. Priyambudi Sulistiyanto, "Indonesia in 2017: Jokowi's Supremacy and His Next Political Battles", *Southeast Asian Affairs* 2018 (Singapore: ISEAS – Yusof Ishak Institute, 2018), pp. 153–66; Dirk Tomsa, "Indonesia in 2016: Jokowi Consolidates Power", *Southeast Asian Affairs* 2017 (Singapore: ISEAS – Yusof Ishak Institute, 2017), pp. 149–62.
17. The stories about the changing leaders among the 212 activists are dramatic, involving the changing loyalties of some of the activists, Gerindra's objection to back the candidacy of one of the 212 activists in a regional election, etc. See the report by the Institute for Policy Analysis and Conflict, *After Ahok: The Islamist Agenda in Indonesia* (Institute for Policy Analysis of Conflict, 2018), pp. 20–22.
18. Azis Anwar Fachrudin, "Notes on 212 in 2018: More Politics Less Unity", *New Mandala*, 10 December 2018, https://www.newmandala.org/notes-on-212-in-2018-more-politics-less-unity/ (accessed 15 April 2019).
19. Greg Fealy, "Nahdlatul Ulama and the Politics Trap", *New Mandala*, 11 July 2018, https://www.newmandala.org/nahdlatul-ulama-politics-trap/ (accessed 15 April 2019).
20. Usman Hamid and Liam Gammon, "Jokowi Forges a Tool of Repression", *New Mandala*, 13 July 2017, https://www.newmandala.org/jokowi-forges-tool-repression/ (accessed 15 April 2019).
21. Azis Anwar Fachrudin, *Polemik Tafsir Pancasila* (Yogyakarta: Program Studi Agama dan Lintas Budaya, Universitas Gadjah Mada, 2018), https://crcs.ugm.ac.id/news/12353/laporan-crcs-pancasila.html. For a summary in English, see "The Equivocality and Malleability of Pancasila", https://crcs.ugm.ac.id/wednesday-forum-report/13535/the-equivocality-and-malleability-of-pancasila.html (accessed 15 April 2019).
22. Stefan Rummens and Koen Abts, "Defending Democracy: The Concentric Containment of Political Extremism", *Political Studies* 58 (2010): 649–65.
23. Martin van Bruinessen, ed., *Contemporary Developments in Indonesian Islam: Explaining the "Conservative Turn"* (Singapore: Institute of Southeast Asian Studies, 2013), p. 5.
24. Lindsey, "Retreat from Democracy?"
25. Alfred Stepan, "The Multiple Secularisms of Modern Democratic and Non-democratic Regimes", in *Rethinking Secularism*, edited by Craig Calhoun, Mark Juergensmeyer, and Jonathan VanAntwerpen (Oxford University Press, 2011), pp. 114–44.

26. Jeff Spinner-Halev, *Surviving Diversity – Religion and Democratic Citizenship* (Baltimore, MD: Johns Hopkins University Press, 2000).
27. Zainal Abidin Bagir, "Democracy, Pluralism and Conservative Religion", in *On World Religions: Diversity, Not Dissension*, edited by Anindita Balslev (New Delhi: Sage, 2014).
28. Zainal Abidin Bagir, *Kerukunan dan Penodaan Agama: Alternatif Penyelesaian Masalah* [Blasphemy law in Indonesia: An alternative dispute resolution approach] (Yogyakarta: Program Studi Agama dan Lintas Budaya, Universitas Gadjah Mada, 2018), http://crcs.ugm.ac.id/news/11963/laporan-crcs-penanganan-penodaan-agama.html.

10

Sunni-Shia Reconciliation in Malaysia

Mohd Faizal Musa

It is never easy to define Shiism as a collective category. There are the Zaidiyyahs, Isma'ilis, and the Imamis (Twelvers).[1] The Shias in Iran, Iraq, Saudi Arabia, Lebanon, Indo-Pakistan and Southeast Asia differ significantly.[2] With all the diversity within Shiism itself, I will have to go back to the basic definition of Shiism. Fundamentally, the Shias believe in the succession of Ali ibn Abi Thalib after the demise of Prophet Muhammad and in 'Adl, or Divine Justice:

> The Imamate or wilayah is the very basic principle; 'Shiism, however, concentrating on the question of wilayah and insisting on the esoteric content of the prophetic message, saw in Ali and the Household of the Prophet (ahl al-bayt), in its Shi'ite sense, the sole channel through which the original message of Islam was transmitted, although, paradoxically enough the majority of the descendants of the Prophet belonged to Sunnism and continue to do so until today.[3]

On the principle of divine justice, in Asha'arism (Sunnism) there is "an emphasis upon the will of God, whatever God wills is just, precisely because it is willed by God; and intelligence ('Aql) is in a sense subordinated to this will and to the voluntarism which characterizes this form of theology'". Nasr further stated that rationality played a crucial role in Shiism and that this distinctive belief helps to define the Shias:

> In Shiism, however, the quality of justice is considered as innate to the Divine Nature. God cannot act in an unjust manner because it is His Nature to be just. For Him to be unjust would violate His own Nature, which is impossible. Intelligence can judge the justness or unjustness of an act and this judgement is not completely suspended in favour of a pure voluntarism on the part of God. Hence there is a greater emphasis upon intelligence ('aql) in Shi'ite theology and a greater emphasis upon will (iradah) in Scorn kalam, or theology, at least in the predominant Ash'arite school.[4]

Sunnis and Shias agree on three basic principles: divine unity (monotheism), *nubuwwah* or prophecy and *Ma'ad* or resurrection. Thus, the basic differences between Sunnis and Shias are historical and philosophical.

There are also other significant differences that put adherents from both schools in a difficult situation.[5] First, some Sunnis treat Islam as a public right, while others treated it as a personal matter; "religion among the Sunni is not simply a personal matter; it is a public right that cannot be forfeited by individual whims."[6] The Sunnis are keen to manipulate the law, in this case the Sharia, and employ "coercion to enforce religious (public) order", while the other sects "manipulate moral control".[7] After the 1979 Islamic Revolution in Iran, Shiism has been perceived in almost the same manner—as controlling the public through legal means. In Iran, Wilayatul Faqih gives the state space to adopt the same approach (this applies only in the case of Iran and not necessarily to the whole Shia diaspora).

The Islamic Revolution in Iran adopted one of Imam Khomeini's famous works entitled "Islamic Government: Governance of the Jurist (Wilayat al-Faqih)". Khomeini's central argument was not to wait any longer for the return of the twelfth Imam (the hidden Imam Mahdi), and that during the Occultation, religious sages should take the rule of government into their own hands. According to Khomeini the reign should be in accordance with the model of the Prophet Muhammad—a combination of religious and political leader at one and the same time.

In other words, there should be no separation between religion and the state.⁸

The relationship between Sunnis and Shias is not a straightforward one, on account of the latter's characteristic of rebelliousness: "all sects in Islam initially emerged as groups in rebellion against the established Sunni dogma and/or authority and developed later into routinized religious systems. Among some groups, such as the Shia, rebelliousness continued as a ritualistic exercise, thus continuously reinforcing the collective consciousness of the sect."⁹ While the Sunnis treated other sects as "religious phenomena", therefore "historical realities", the other sects—including the Shias—did not see themselves as "historical accidents", but rather as "eternally ordained manifestations of divinity", as expressed in their rich literature.¹⁰

The Shias in Malaysia, as with other Shia diaspora, accept themselves as a "religious minority". As a minority they cannot behave as a sect, thus they have dropped their rebellious character and have effectively learnt to adapt to "centralized Sunni authority", to "work out an accommodative formula accepting the ideology of Sunni rule".¹¹ This is one reason why we can find many Shia elements expressed in Malay culture, and even in Sunni literature. And it is the sole reason why Shia have been off the radar in Malaysia for so long. Applying Khouri's position that "sects could turn into minorities and minorities into sects", we can understand how Malaysian Shias prior to the 1979 Islamic Revolution managed to "adapt differently to different sectarian orientations".¹² They have conformed with Sunnism, and this can be easily and effectively done as Shiism allows dissimulation (concealment of faith or *taqiyyah*).

However, new converts to Shiism, Shias born after the 1979 Revolution, or Shias who were former Sunnis have been caught up with the Iranian Wilayatul Faqih, where they continue to be amazed with the "enforcement of religious order", just like in Sunnism. Their admiration of Shiism did not necessarily begin with the essence of Shiism, but rather with its ability to apply Islam to the state. No similar arrangement has been found anywhere else since the fall of the Ottoman Empire, considered to be the last Islamic caliphate. In Malaysia in the 1980s and 1990s, many Sunni academics, political activists, Islamists and admirers of the Muslim Brotherhood became attracted to Shiism. The friction between Sunnis and Shias in Malaysia occurred with post-1979

Shias. Unfortunately, those who had all along been Shias (hereditary Shias) were victimized and caught in between.

After GE14

To rectify what the new Pakatan Harapan government believe to be the wrongdoings of Najib's Barisan Nasional administration, Prime Minister Mahathir Mohamad announced the establishment of a Council of Eminent Persons (CEP). The responsibility of this council is to advise the Pakatan Harapan administration to identify, correct and reform any seismic problems affecting the economy, finance, business, law, education, arts, electoral systems or Islamic affairs, among others. In sum, the main agenda of the CEP is to help the government shape policies and programmes in order to fulfil the government's hundred-day promise to the people. The CEP is headed by a former finance minister from Mahathir's previous administration, Daim Zainuddin. The CEP was given a hundred days to complete this enormous task, with a deadline of 22 August 2018. Other members are former Bank Negara governor Zeti Akhtar Aziz, former president and CEO of Petronas Hassan Merican, Malaysian billionaire residing in China Robert Kuok and prominent economist Professor Dr Jomo Kwame Sundaram.[13]

The CEP later founded two other groups—the Institutional Reforms Committee (IRC) and the Committee for Islamic Institutional Reforms—to help them collect and listen to proposals and suggestions to reach their objectives. The IRC comprises retired Court of Appeal judge KC Vohrah, commissioner of the National Human Rights Council and retired judge Mah Weng Kwai Mah, president of the National Human Rights Society Ambiga Sreenevasan, and constitutional law expert Professor Dr Shad Saleem Faruqi.[14] The Committee for Islamic Institutional Reforms is headed by current Perlis mufti Mohd Asri Zainal Abidin. However, a number of relatively "unknown" religious scholars are also part of this committee, and their names have not been disclosed to the public.

There is another committee for Islamic institutional reform, with this one not coming under the CEP. The Conference of Rulers approved the formation of a new special committee for improving federal Islamic institutions in Malaysia, called the High-level Committee on Federal Institutions of Islamic Affairs. This committee under the Malay Rulers only began its work on 9 August 2018.[15]

I have been summoned twice to the CEP: first on 27 June 2018 and again on 9 August 2018. My topics of discussion have mainly been about the criminalization of certain faiths in Malaysia and the reform of Islamic institutions.[16] Many other subjects were brought up during the CEP meeting, but my focus here will be on issues pertaining to Shiism in Malaysia.[17]

The criminalization of faith and beliefs, in this context the Shias, began around two decades ago, during Mahathir's previous administration. The root of the problem lies in the fatwa (legal opinion) passed in 1996. The National Fatwa Council (NFC) introduced a fatwa or edict entitled "Shia di Malaysia" (Shias in Malaysia) in 1996. At a special *muzakarah* (conference) organized to discuss the Shia "problem", the NFC passed several resolutions, which were subsequently reflected in the fatwa that was issued. The first was to reaffirm an earlier decision, made at an NFC *muzakarah* in 1984, that two Shia sects that the government had recognized previously—the Zaidiyyahs and Jaafariyyahs—were no longer acceptable. Second, as far as matters of creed, religious laws and ethics were concerned, Muslims in the country could only abide by "the teachings of Islam based on the doctrine of the Ahl al-Sunnah wa al-Jama'ah [Sunni]". This definition of "official" Islam was to be written into the federal and state constitutions, and all religious laws would be amended to reflect this decision.

Third, "the propagation of any teachings other than that of the Ahl al-Sunnah wa al-Jama'ah [would be] prohibited". Accordingly, the "publication, broadcasting and distribution of any books, leaflets, films, videos, and others relating to the teachings of Islam that contradict with the doctrine of the Ahl al-Sunnah wa al-Jama'ah [was also] prohibited and unlawful (haram)." This passage from the fatwa was the main reason for the banning of my books. On 10 January 2018, the Court of Appeal quashed the banning of four of my books, citing the right to freedom of speech and expression of the Federal Constitution. A three-man panel comprising Tengku Maimun Tuan Mat, Ahmadi Asnawi and Zaleha Yusof decided that the banning of the books restricted my fundamental right, and that citing the fatwa was not sufficient to prove my works were likely to be prejudicial to public order or security.[18]

However, until today, seven of my books are still listed as banned by the Malaysian Home Ministry.

The 1996 fatwa was a pivotal turning point that paved the way for subsequent efforts at "othering" the Shia minority, and through this to discredit and deny them their human rights. That the fatwa was a federal initiative—rather than a state one—ought to have raised warning bells about the central government overstepping its boundaries and encroaching on to the jurisdiction state governments had over Islam. Instead, most states—except Sabah and Sarawak—took their cue from the centre and eventually passed variations of this fatwa, mostly keeping to what the NFC had prescribed.

Unlike elsewhere in the Muslim world, where fatwas are considered mere legal opinions, in Malaysia they have been given the force of law upon being gazetted. Contravening them could potentially lead to a maximum penalty of 5,000 ringgit and/or three years jail time—not hefty in the larger scheme of things but enough to compel many Muslims into conforming to, or at least not questioning, the state-endorsed version of Islam.

The Fear Towards Shias in 1996

The causes of fear towards Shiism are manifold, and the Shias are partly to be blamed. By this I am referring to the newly converted Shias after the 1979 Iranian Revolution, and not to the hereditary Shias.[19] In general, the Shias are widely accepted culturally and even theologically by the Sunnis. Malay Shias have practised various cultural rituals that are clearly Shia in nature. Remnants of Shiism among Malays can be seen in the *Dondang Siti Fatimah*,[20] a lullaby, the *Hikayat Hasan Husin* (Tale of Hasan and Husin) and the *Hikayat Muhammad Hanafiyyah*[21] (Tale of Muhammad Hanafiyyah), which are part of Malay literature. Other examples include the acceptance of the concept of the Imam Mahdi in the classical text *'Al-Mukhtasar fi'Alamah al-Mahdi al Muntazar* by Syeikh Muhammad Arsyad al-Banjari,[22] praise of Imam Ali,[23] and many other traces of Shiism that cannot be denied.[24]

Previously, Sunnis and Shias had lived peacefully together in Malaysia. In 1934 the Qadi of Johor allowed the marriage of a Shia man with a Sunni woman;[25] and the Mufti of Johor, Sheikh Habib Alawi (1934–61), gave permission to transmit hadith (Prophetic tradition) to Ayatullah Mar'ashi Najafi.[26] Meanwhile, the Ismaili Bohra (Sevener) society was allowed to live in the state of Selangor in 1984. Although there were a few incidents of sectarianism, they were very remote and small. At least two vestiges of sectarianism can be traced in Malaya (before the separation of Singapore from Malaysia in 1965); namely, the commotion in Singapore in 1907,[27] and the opinions of Burhanuddin al Helmy and Za'ba, two highly regarded Malay figures, about the dissensions between different sects (*mazhab*) in the 1950s and 1960s.[28]

However, it is the "post 1979 Shias" that have caused Malaysian society to fear and detest them on account of their obsession with the Islamic Revolution in Iran. Records in parliament's Hansard since 1982 highlight my point. The first issue concerning local Shias, which came up during a parliamentary debate in 1982, demonstrates how the fear of Shias in Malaysia is less about Shiism and more about the fear of exporting the Iranian Revolution to the country. Senator Othman Abdullah raised the matter.[29] The debate in the Senate on 11 January 1983 was obviously about how to regulate elements of extremism arising from competition between political parties along the east coast. The debate also raised the issue of freedom of religion, the power given to religious authorities, and mechanisms to restore harmony, with the cases of Northern Ireland and India being cited. The debate touched on deviant teachings, mentioning the Qadianis (Ahmadis) and subsequently the Shias.[30]

The debate touched on the historical differences between the Sunnis and the Shias, or, as I stated in the introduction, "sects being treated as religious phenomenon", and it resulted in a tremendous bias against the Shias. The focus of the whole debate was very much on deviancy and potential extreme teachings, and it came from a single individual—Abdul Razak Hussain. And all the Shiias, including the hereditary ones, were unfortunately lumped into one basket.

This narrative of Shiia deviancy, extremism and the potential to destabilize society grew consistently until 1985 when member of parliament Ibrahim Azmi Hassan from Kuala Nerus complained during a debate in the House of Representatives that Shiism was gaining many followers and asked whether the authorities were going to curb its teachings. Interestingly, Mohamad Yusof Haji Mohammad Noor, the minister in-charge of Islamic affairs, assured him that not all Shias are deviant and that the hereditary Shias, the Zaidiyyahs and Jaafariyyahs, are recognized by the authorities.[31] However, Mohamad Yusof came under pressure from some legislators to stop Shia teachings. In 1987 the status of Shias was raised repeatedly during parliamentary debates, and again Yusof as minister of Islamic affairs responded by saying that the increases in the numbers of Shias were relatively small and were limited to the urban areas, occurring particularly among academics. Later that year, in response to a question from Mohammad Subky Abdul Raof from Balik Pulau, Yusof emphasized the government was aware of the groups propagating Shiism and how it was going about regulating them. He also noted that the government would not hesitate to take any necessary legal action against them if they began to have a structured movement.[32] This was the first direct step in intervention by the Malaysian government. The debate appeared to make no distinction between post-1979 Shias and hereditary Shias, or of the many factions of Shias. This resulted in a single framework generalizing all Shias.

By 1993 the narrative that the Shia community was a risk to Malaysian Muslim society had been widely accepted, as reflected in a debate in the Senate between parliamentary secretary in the Prime Minister's Office Othman Abdul, Senator Ghazali Embong and Senator Zaleha Hussin. The discussion was about a group of local academics (post-1979 Shias) propagating Shiism and sending students to Iran. Othman told the Senate that the state religious departments had been galvanized to take stern action against the Shias.[33]

Confusion about local Shias, about who they were, about what rituals they practised and whether they had a political agenda were subjects of concern for the establishment. In response to a question from MP Awang Jabar in 1993, foreign minister Abdullah Fadzil Che Wan commented that the Malaysian version of Shiism is practically the same as its Iranian counterpart, since the later exported its teachings to other countries. He noted how this version of Shiism is associated with "the revolution", although he also noted positive measures taken by the Iranian government to minimize differences between Sunnis and the Shias in order to unify the Muslim ummah.[34] This response by the foreign minister accentuated misconceptions about local Shias and Shiism. Shiism had been widely accepted in Malaysia even prior to 1979, with there being many Indo-Pakistani Shias long before the country's independence in 1957. And the government continued to make no distinction between hereditary and newly converted Shias.

On 2–3 May 1996, during a meeting of the National Fatwa Committee in Langkawi, the council introduced the "Shia di Malaysia" fatwa banning Shiism and recognizing only Sunnism. The move emboldened anti-Shia activities. In 1997 there were calls from MP Mohd Zuki Kamaluddin to detain Shias under the Internal Security Act (ISA).[35] In October of that year, ten individuals were detained under the ISA. The 2003 parliamentary Hansard records that the ten Shias were detained because they represented a threat to national security and because their teachings allowed, among other things, self-flagellation.[36] Those who were released early were told to renounce their faith and "revert" to Sunni Islam as a pre-condition for their release.[37] In August 1998, the detained Shias were forced to participate in a counselling camp in Kamunting, Perak.[38] In 2000, six people were detained from 20 October until 5 January the following year.[39] Another case occurred in March 2001, with a Shia adherent being arrested and serving a two-year detention order. The Malaysian government made it a point to remind everyone that in addition to the ISA, it could use the Sedition and Public Order Act of 1959, or the Emergency Public Order Ordinance 1969 to arrest anyone misusing the term "Islam" to spread "deviationist" teachings.[40]

The victimization of Shias under the ISA is not well known about, but it came to light after one Shia, Abdullah Hassan (detained from 2 October 1997 to 31 December 1999), filed a complaint with the Human Rights Commission of Malaysia (SUHAKAM) about the conditions he was subjected to under detention.[41]

It is important to note here that Kelantan banned Shiism before the 1996 fatwa, on 30 May 1995.[42] Then, right after the 1996 fatwa was issued at the federal level, the federal territories of Kuala Lumpur and Labuan gazetted the banning of Shiism on 3 April 1997.[43] Terengganu gazetted the banning of Shiism on 2 September 1997. Selangor gazetted the fatwa on 24 September 1998.[44] Sabah issued a similar edict banning Shiism on 26 July 1996 and Sarawak following on 23 November 1996, although neither of these two states have gazetted the fatwa.[45]

Although there was pressure on them as a result of the 1996 fatwa, Malaysian Shias under Abdullah Badawi's administration (2003–9) experienced a temporary peaceful era. Abdullah's administration maintained good relations with Iran, and the prime minister twice visited the country. Mahmoud Ahmadinejad, the Iranian president, also visited Malaysia.[46] Abdullah's stand is important to note, since at this time Iran was facing pressure about its nuclear programme. During Abdullah's tenure, Malaysia also participated in two international meetings that reaffirmed that the Muslim world recognized Islam's diverse branches, including the two Shia sects—the Zaidiyyahs and Jaafariyyahs—that the National Fatwa Committee had ceased to recognize back in 1984. The first meeting was the signing of the Amman Message of 2005 in Jordan, where Malaysia was represented by Abdullah himself, as well as by Abdul Hamid Othman, the de facto minister of Islamic affairs. The second meeting was the 34th Session of the Islamic Conference of Foreign Ministers, held in May 2007. As with the Amman Message, Malaysia, through its foreign minister Syed Hamid Albar, signed the outcome document of this meeting, the Islamabad Declaration, which proclaimed:

> No Muslim whether he or she is Shi'ite or Sunni, may be subject to murder or any harm, intimidation, terrorisation, or aggression on his property; incitement thereto; or forcible displacement, deportation, or kidnapping. All Muslims to refrain seriously from any provocation of sensitivities or sectarian or ethnic strife, as well as any name-calling, abuse, prejudice or vilification and invectives.[47]

This move by Abdullah's administration explains why the 1996 anti-Shia fatwa, although issued at the national level, was not gazetted in all states.

After Najib Abdul Razak came to power in 2008, both the Amman Message and the Islamabad Declaration appear to have been conveniently forgotten. Eight other states in Malaysia gazetted the 1996 fatwa during Najib's time in power. Pahang gazetted it on 30 December 2011. Perak gazetted it on 4 January 2012[48] and Johore on 9 January 2012. Perlis gazetted the fatwa on 20 February 2012—while other states stated that following Shiism led to deviancy and contradicted Sunnism, Perlis further declared that Shias could be excommunicated from Islam.[49] Negeri Sembilan gazetted the fatwa on 7 November 2013,[50] followed by Penang on 27 March 2014[51] and Malacca on 24 September 2015.[52] Kedah was the most recent state to gazette it, on 10 November 2016.[53]

Shias under Najib Razak

Under the administration of Najib Razak (2009–18), Malaysia had been leaning towards Saudi Arabia and had allowed hard-line Islam to shape the government. Najib prioritized warmer relations with Saudi Arabia over other states in the Middle East, a nation known not only for exporting the intolerant Wahhabi-Salafi strand of Islam but also for repressing its Shia minority. Malaysia became a strategic ally of the oil-rich kingdom to the extent that the Saudi government disbursed "an additional cash profit of USD8.15 million to the 1Malaysia Development Berhad" in March 2011. It appeared the Malaysian government reciprocated this gesture by endorsing the Gulf Cooperation Council's actions against the 2011 people's uprising in Bahrain (where most Bahrainis are Shias). Najib also went the extra mile to label those in the uprising as terrorists and accused them of undermining "the stability and security of the country".[54]

Under the Najib administration, Wahhabism surreptitiously and gradually infiltrated government agencies, universities, schools and religious departments. Some followers even held ministerial posts in the previous and current administrations.[55] Since the 1996 fatwa, all Shias, be they hereditary or newly converted, have been treated in the same manner. Historically, Shias have been targeted by Wahhabis. Wahhabi teachings first reached the Malay archipelago in 1803, in the form of the Padri movement. Started by Tuanku Nan Tua to reform certain activities in Minang society in Sumatra, it was then radicalized by three pilgrims returning from the hajj. The movement began to enforce Islam in daily life. In order to do so, killings in the name of Islam were carried out. Then, due to Salafization in Johor Riau in 1845, strict laws forbade Malay people from exchanging *pantuns* (traditional poetry) or playing the lute during the rule of the young Sultan Ali. Although they belonged to the Shafi'i mazhab, they were also stirred by the rashness of laws resembling the Hanbali school of thought, the jurisprudential school of the Salafists or Wahhabists.[56] For the first time, the Malays were exposed to religious extremism.[57]

Ill treatment of the Shias under the Najib administration had been clear even by the country's second Universal Periodic Report in 2013, and nothing has changed since then.[58] There has also been an alleged case of enforced disappearance involving a Shia activist, as mentioned during a National Human Rights inquiry looking into the abduction of Amri Che Mat. Amri disappeared on 24 November 2016 while driving near his home in Kangar, Perlis. Amri's wife, Norhayati Mohd Ariffin, believes her husband's disappearance is related to a speech made by a high-ranking police officer, DCP Awaludin, on 6 November 2016, where the officer claimed that the "Shia enemy" and Christian preachers are more dangerous than the terrorist group the Islamic State.[59]

Possible Remedies and Challenges

During my meeting with the CEP, I shared how Malaysia's Islamic institutions need to be reformed. The following are my recommendations.

First, the country needs to return to secularism. I believe Islam can flourish better in a secular environment, where all faiths, beliefs, streams and schools of thought are celebrated. The Indira Gandhi case judgement by the Court of Appeals clearly states that Malaysia is a secular state.[60] Paragraphs 24 and 25 of the judgement make it clear that the constitution is above all, and that for a number of reasons—including protecting the rights of minorities—amendments cannot be tolerated. Paragraph 71 points out that the Islam recognized in the constitution has a secular "definition". Judge Zainun Ali cited the judgement in the Federal Court in the case of Che Omar Che Soh versus the Public Prosecutor in 1988, recounting that "after tracing the history of British intervention in the Malay States", judge Salleh Abas "summarised the notion of Islam as understood by the framers of the Constitution" as being restricted merely to the "narrow confinement of the law of marriage, divorce and inheritance only".[61]

Second, society must adopt the principle of "your fatwa does not apply here". The crux of the matter is how fatwas are passed in Malaysia. A mufti is not a lawmaker and a fatwa is merely an opinion. The power to enact laws for the peace, order and good governance must and can only be vested in the parliament and state assemblies. The legislative powers of the Federation shall be vested in the parliament, which shall consist of the monarch (Yang di-Pertuan Agong) and the two legislative houses (House of Representatives and the Senate). However, the fatwa on the Shias has influenced the debate in both houses at the federal level. And at the state level, once gazetted, a fatwa becomes a force of law.

The Administration of Islamic Law enactments in various Malaysian states have provided the Islamic institutions—such as the fatwa committee or office of the mufti—powers to make legislation (delegated legislation) for the betterment of the Malay-Muslim majority.[62] The legislation provides that any verdict issued by a fatwa committee and published in the Gazette shall be binding, both on individuals and on the government.[63] It is in fact a crime under the Sharia Criminal Offences Act to violate, disobey or fail to recognize any gazetted fatwa. The Act provides that:

> Any person who acts in contempt of religious authority or defies, disobeys or disputes the orders or directions of the Yang di-Pertuan Agong as the Head of the religion of Islam, the Majlis or the Mufti, expressed or given by way of fatwa, shall be guilty of an offence and shall on conviction be liable to a fine not exceeding three thousand ringgit or to imprisonment for a term not exceeding two years or to both.[64]

Similarly, the act also criminalizes the communication of an opinion or view that is contrary to the gazetted fatwa. Thus, "any person who gives, propagates or disseminates any opinion concerning Islamic teachings, Islamic Law or any issue, contrary to any fatwa for the time being in force in the Federal Territories shall be guilty of an offence and shall on conviction be liable to a fine not exceeding three thousand ringgit or to imprisonment for a term not exceeding two years or to both".[65]

Furthermore, a provision in the act criminalizes the distribution or possession of any view issued contrary to Islamic law.[66] Therefore, by implication, the act prohibits any kind of disagreement (oral or written) to a fatwa issued in Malaysia; including aiding and abetting anything that would lead to the dissemination of information contrary to the fatwa. The 1996 fatwa against the Shias, for instance, caused so many human rights violations. I am, for example, affected by the fatwa. It directly impinged on my right to freedom of expression. In fact, the judgement by the Court of Appeal to lift the ban on four of my books clearly addressed this:

What we want to stress here is where is the part that could create public disorder and would threaten national security, except for those few lines mentioned earlier, which we agree with learned counsel for the appellant, are not evidence of prejudice to public order and security? Merely stating that the respondent was following the decision of Jawatankuasa Fatwa in our view is not sufficient to prove that the 4 books are likely to be prejudicial to public order and security as Jawatankuasa Fatwa's decision has not mentioned the 4 books. To state that the prohibition is on the recommendation of Bahagian Kawalan Penerbitan dan Teks Al Quran and on advise [sic] of experts from JAKIM without showing more is also in our view not enough to show that the 4 books are likely to be prejudicial to public order and security.[67]

... We also find that the order is indeed a restriction on the appellant's constitutional and fundamental right to freedom of expression.[68]

Third, Malaysia needs to adopt a human rights approach for Islamic institutions. By a human rights approach, I am not referring to the Cairo Declaration (1990), which is culturally relative, but to the universal one—the Universal Declaration of Human Rights of 1948. The previous Barisan Nasional government refused to ratify the International Covenant on Civil and Political Rights (ICCR) with the excuse that "some items in the ICCPR, particularly on religion,... can cause discomfort among the races".[69] There are many international covenants that Malaysia has not adopted or ratified. The covenants that need to be ratified are the International Convention Against All Forms of Racial Discrimination; the Covenant on Civil and Political Rights; the UN Convention against Torture and Other Cruel, Inhuman or Degrading Treatment or Punishment; the International Covenant on Economic, Social and Cultural Rights; the International Convention on the Protection of Migrant Workers and Members of their Families; and the International Convention for the Protection of All Persons from Enforced Disappearance. The new Pakatan Harapan government has made it public that Malaysia is willing to ratify six human rights covenants.[70] Having these covenants ratified and adopted by parliament will surely result in many changes, in particularly for Shias.

Adopting a human rights approach will also discipline religious leaders and clerics from propagating hate speech in the name of *dakwah*. For instance, Malaysia should surely implement "The Rabat

Plan of Action on the Prohibition of Advocacy of National, Racial or Religious Hatred that Constitutes Incitement to Discrimination, Hostility or Violence".[71] The plan was developed through a series of international expert workshops organized by the Office of the United Nations High Commissioner for Human Rights (OHCHR). The plan was officially published on 13 February 2013, in Geneva, Switzerland. It was designed to be a series of practical steps to use legislation, jurisprudence and executive policies to achieve the implementation of Article 20 of the International Covenant on Civil and Political Rights, which includes a clause that reads: "any advocacy of national, racial or religious hatred that constitutes incitement to discrimination, hostility or violence shall be prohibited by law".

Under international human rights standards, "hate speech" can be restricted on different grounds, including respect for the rights of others, public order, or even sometimes national security. States are also obliged to "prohibit" expression that amounts to "incitement" to discrimination, hostility or violence. The plan concludes with a series of recommendations for states, the United Nations and other stakeholders. For example, it explains that any limits on speech must meet threshold requirements of legality, proportionality and necessity—all state restrictions on speech must be provided by law, be narrowly defined to serve a legitimate societal interest, be necessary in a democratic society to protect that interest, and be proportionate so that the benefit to the stated interest outweighs the harm to the freedom of expression.

The plan formulated six factors to determine which expressions could be criminally prohibited:

1. context—placing the speech act in the socio-political context it was made and disseminated to assess whether it was likely to "incite";
2. speaker—considering the speaker's standing in relation to the target audience of the speech;
3. intent—determining whether or not the speaker intended the speech act to cause incitement, excluding from limitations those cases arising from negligence or recklessness;
4. content or form—analysing the content of the speech for its level of provocation, looking at the form of arguments deployed;

5. extent of speech—looking at the reach of the speech act, analysing its level of publicity and magnitude, the amount and extent of communication; and
6. likelihood—determining whether or not there was a reasonable probability the speech would incite harm and identifying the degree of risk of that resulting harm.

If adopted, the Rabat Plan of Action would censure any associated fatwa that incites hatred against Shias.

The plan also lays out steps for civil society involvement. It encourages the media to be aware that they are often the vehicles for perpetuating negative stereotypes and they should thus avoid reference to unnecessary group characteristics that could promote intolerance. The plan urges journalists to properly contextualize their reporting while ensuring that acts of discrimination are brought to the attention of the public. It also says that the media need to play an active role in giving different groups a voice in the national conversation.

For civil society generally, the plan recommends that NGOs and other civil society groups create and support mechanisms to encourage cultural exchanges and dialogue among different communities, and it calls for political parties to establish and enforce strong ethical guidelines for their representatives, especially with regard to public speech.

There are many challenges ahead to reconcile Sunnis and Shias after more than two decades of demonization of Shias, but one major challenge is confronting religious traditionalists. Traditional Islamists do not accord with the idea of a more open and democratic country. They do not believe in equality in politics. They believe that the ulama know better, that it is better for men to lead, and that it is better for Muslims to be ministers. Traditional Islamists also believe that laws or fatwa based on religious sources are divine and should therefore not be questioned.

As I have stated earlier, religious commandments should not be turned into law. In recent years, Malaysian policymakers have been embroiled in controversy over sharia law in relation to civil law and over which of the two should take precedence, particularly in relation to family matters involving non-Muslim partners in marriage. The Indira Gandhi case judgement has nailed the issue.

However, will Malaysian Muslims be ready to embrace and be open to reformist Islam? By reformist Islam, I refer to the following. First, proponents of reformist Islam reject discrimination based on religion, gender, race or ideology and perceive no difference between different schools of law in Islam, between Muslims and non-Muslims, men or women, or between religious scholars and non-clerics in the public sphere. Second, they hold that all people possess freedom of belief and religion, and that no one should be compelled to accept a particular belief or religion. Third, social responsibility and fulfilment of religious commitments should occur with the consent of others; the propagation of religion should be based on convincing others of the superiority of religious solutions over non-religious ones, and people should be free to make their own choices. Fourth, religious precepts that are respected by believers are still open to discussion, criticism and questioning. Fifth, articulations of Islam in the current context should adhere to three requirements: they must be just, reasonable (open to intellectual debate), and superior to alternative solutions. Sixth, reformist Islam believes that Islam provides general principles that allow space for human experience, collective human wisdom and initiatives relevant to various temporal and locational circumstances.

How will Malaysian Muslims—already accustomed to traditional Islam, jurisprudential Islam and institutionalized Islam—reform so that their religious understanding can be compatible with reality, modernity and the contemporary world? If Sunnis and Shias in Malaysia willingly adopt reformist Islam, then Sunni and Shia reconciliation can succeed. This means that the Sunnis must be willing to tolerate the Shias, including the newly converted and the hereditary Shias. The local Shias however need to drop their behaviour as a sect and to remain as a religious minority so that they can blend in with the Sunnis, as they did before 1979. In other words, the Shias need to drop their obsession with Wilayatul Faqih, which generated the fear that led to the 1996 fatwa.

Conclusion

The 1996 fatwa against Malaysian Shias had the unintended consequence of causing sectarian apartheid. What is happening in Malaysia with the Shia community is like what took place in South Africa under apartheid rule. However, instead of being based on the colour of a person's skin, discrimination and persecution is taking place against a minority group based on their religious beliefs. Culturally, the Sunni-Shia adherents have lived peacefully side by side for ages, but the situation and context gradually changed after 1979, caused, among other things, by the newly converted Shias and by the Wahhabization of Islamic institutions in Malaysia.

"Reconciliation" of the Malaysian Sunnis and Shias is in the hands of the Pakatan Harapan government. The adoption of a human rights framework and the reformation of Islamic institutions are essential to put these two factions of Muslims together. If not, the hard-line Muslims will again hijack the long-lost camaraderie.

Notes

1. Existing research on Shiism has covered the origins and evolution of the religion; its theology and philosophy; laws, rites and rituals; relations between Shia followers and the state; and Shiism and artistic expression.
2. To start with, I would suggest the four volumes of Shiism edited by Paul Luft and Colin Turner, *Shi'ism: Critical Concepts in Islamic Studies* (Routledge: New York, 2008). Farhad Daftary has also contributed a lot through his works. See Farhad Daftary, *A History of Shi'i Islam* (London: Tauris and the Institute of Ismaili Studies, 2013). In order to understand the Shias in Iran, I would like to suggest Pedram Khosronejad, *Iranian Shi'ism* (New York: Tauris, 2012), although I have to say the presentation of essays are mainly on how Shiism is being expressed in the arts. Meanwhile, the book by Faleh A. Jabar, *The Shi'ite Movement in Iraq* (London: Saqi, 2003), is still in my view the best book to explain Iraqi Shias. The Saudi Shias may be observed in Fouad Ibrahim, *The Shi'is of Saudi Arabia* (London: Saqi, 2006). The only collective work I can recommend for understanding the mysterious Southeast Asian Shias, since studies of their histories and survival are still underdeveloped, is a book edited by Dicky Sofjan, *Sejarah dan Budaya Syiah di Asia Tenggara* (Jogjakarta: Penerbit Universitas Gadjah Mada, 2013). The contributions to this edited volume are from the Shias themselves or from people who have worked on them for a long time in the field. The Daudi Bohras may be understood from Jonah Blank, *Mullahs on the Mainframe: Islam and Modernity among the Daudi Bohras* (Chicago: University of Chicago, 2001).

3. Sayyid Husayn Nasr, *Preface: A Series of Islam and Shia* (Qom: Ansariyan Publications, 2007), p. 27
4. Ibid., p. 26.
5. I have often been asked in Malaysia, what is wrong with Shiism that the Shias cannot live in peace with the Sunnis?" And my answer will be, "You are looking into the wrong premise. All other sects in Islam should be asking the Sunnis, what is wrong with Sunnism that the Sunnis cannot live in peace with the others." Perhaps Fuad I. Khouri explains it best in his book, Fuad I. Khouri, *Imams and Emirs: State, Religion and Sects in Islam* (London: Saqi, 1990).
6. Ibid., p. 19.
7. Ibid., p. 20.
8. Ali Siyar Rezai, "Velayat-e Faqih: Innovation or Within Tradition" (Master's Thesis, Arizona State University, 2016), https://repository.asu.edu/attachments/170651/content/Rezai_asu_0010N_15994.pdf.
9. Khouri, *Imams and Emirs*, p. 19.
10. Ibid., p. 20.
11. Ibid., p. 22.
12. Ibid., p. 23.
13. "Tun M Announces 'Council of Elders'", *New Straits Times*, 12 May 2018, https://www.nst.com.my/news/politics/2018/05/368729/tun-m-announces-council-elders (accessed 15 April 2019).
14. Yuen Mei Keng, "Reform Committee Identifies Key Institutions on Its List", *The Star Online*, 17 May 2018, https://www.thestar.com.my/news/nation/2018/05/17/reform-committee-identifies-key-institutions-on-its-list/#hktSO1MThlyMpU2S.99 (accessed 15 April 2019).
15. Vinodh Pillai and Nur Hasliza Mohd Salleh, "Okay to Task 2 Groups to Reform Islamic Bodies, Says Don", *Free Malaysia Today*, 9 August 2018, http://www.freemalaysiatoday.com/category/nation/2018/08/09/kay-to-task-2-groups-to-reform-islamic-bodies-says-don/ (accessed 15 April 2019).
16. See Sheith Khidhir Bin Abu Bakar and Ho Kit Yen, "Islamic Bodies Need Advisers, Banned Author Tells Putrajaya Council", *Free Malaysia Today*, 27 June 2018, http://www.freemalaysiatoday.com/category/nation/2018/06/27/islamic-bodies-need-advisers-banned-author-tells-putrajaya-council/ (accessed 15 April 2019). See also Vinodh Pillai and Nur Hasliza Mohd Salleh, "Fatwas Violated My Right As an Author, Says Faisal Tehrani", *Free Malaysia Today*, 9 August 2018, http://www.freemalaysiatoday.com/category/nation/2018/08/09/fatwas-violated-my-right-as-an-author-says-faisal-tehrani/ (accessed 15 April 2019).

17. 'Mohd Faizal Musa, 'The Malaysian Shi'a: A Preliminary Study of Their History, Oppression, and Denied Rights", *Journal of Shi'a Islamic Studies* 6, no. 4 (Autumn 2013): 411–62; Mohd Faizal Musa, "Religious Freedom in Malaysia: The Reading of Qur'an 2:256", in *The Qur'an in the Malay-Indonesian World*, edited by Majid Daneshgar, Peter Riddell, and Andrew Rippin (New York: Routledge, 2016), pp. 177–97; and Mohd Faizal Musa, "State-Backed Discrimination against Shia Muslims in Malaysia", *Critical Asian Studies* 49, no. 3 (2013): 308–29.
18. "Court of Appeal Quashes Ban on Faisal Tehrani's Books", *Free Malaysia Today*, 10 January 2018, http://www.freemalaysiatoday.com/category/nation/2018/01/10/court-of-appeal-quashes-ban-on-faisal-tehranis-books/ (accessed 15 April 2019).
19. I have written extensively on the existence of hereditary Shias in the Malay world prior to 1979. See Mohd Faizal Musa, "The Malaysian Shi'a".
20. See Faisal Tehrani, "Dondang Siti Fatimah", *Free Malaysia Today*, 8 March 2018, http://www.freemalaysiatoday.com/category/opinion/2018/03/08/dondang-siti-fatimah (accessed 15 April 2019).
21. Mohd Faizal Musa, "Sayyidina Husein Dalam Teks Klasik Melayu", in *Sejarah dan Budaya Syiah di Asia Tenggara*, edited by Dicky Sofian (Universitas Gadjah Mada, 2013), pp. 153–72.
22. Faisal Tehrani, "Imam Mahdi Dalam Teks Melayu", *Malaysiakini*, 27 April 2018.
23. See Faisal Tehrani, "Imam Ali, sebelum jabatan agama", *Free Malaysia Today*, 29 March 2018, http://www.freemalaysiatoday.com/category/opinion/2018/03/29/imam-ali-sebelum-jabatan-agama/ (accessed 15 April 2019).
24. See Mohd Faizal Musa, "The Malaysian Shi'a".
25. Letter from Johore Kadhi 2 30 (34), dated 24 March 1934, subject 82/34 Perkahwinan Sah, Johore State Archive Department.
26. Habib Alawi bin Tahir al-Haddad (1884–1962) was a prominent mufti of Johor from 1934 to 1961. He demonstrated his openness by granting permission (*ijazah*) to transmit hadith (sayings of the Prophet Muhammad) to senior Iranian Shia cleric Ayatullah Mar'ashi Najafi. See Syed Farid Alatas, "Salafism and the Persecution of Shi'ites in Malaysia", Middle East Institute, 30 July 2014, http://www.mei.edu/content/map/salafism-and-persecution-shi%E2%80%98ites-malaysia (accessed 15 April 2019).
27. An Arab Muslim named Sayyid Muhammad al-'Aqil al-Hadrami said that cursing Mu'awiyah, the first Umayyad caliph, was "meritorious". Sayyid Muhammad al-'Aqil al-Hadrami was a local Shia from the Arab community in Singapore. See Mohd Faizal Musa, "The Malaysian Shi'a".

28. Though it is difficult to trace Shia practice throughout the nineteenth and twentieth centuries, there are many indications of its existence. In 1960 a prominent politician, the former president of the Pan-Malayan Islamic Party (later known as Parti Islam Se-Malaysia), Burhanuddin al-Helmi, mentioned in his opening speech at a symposium on Sufism that the Shia-Sunni conflict in society should be resolved and that the conflict was only instigated by greedy rulers. Years before, in 1953, a well-known linguist, writer and religious figure, Za'ba, mentioned in an article that Shiism should be tolerated and that Malay Muslims should be more open to pluralistic ideas coming from various schools of thought. The works of Za'ba were banned in the state of Perak and he was accused of disseminating Mu'tazilite doctrines. Thus, sectarian awareness was already present among Muslims in Malaysia, and this suggests that Shia practice never truly ceased among the Malays. See Mohd Faizal Musa, 'The Malaysian Shi'a".
29. Othman Abdullah, Parliamentary Debates, Senate, Sixth Parliament, First Session, vol. 1 (2), 9 December 1982, p. 106:

> Begitu juga dengan Revolusi Islam, dengan fahaman Syiah. Setiap yang berkata Islam itu adalah Islam dan di Malaysia ini orang Melayu Islam, itu Islam; serupa macam itu sehingga kita confused mengatakan apa yang berlaku di sana itu Islam, inilah Islam. Maka kita perlu meminta penjelasan daripada Kerajaan apakah bentuk, apakah sikap kita terhadap Mazhab Syiah yang mengelolai dan mengetuai sebuah Kerajaan revolusi. Kita mengetahui di dalam Perlembagaan tiap-tiap buah negeri dalam negara kita mengatakan bahawa Islam ialah ugama rasmi negara dan Mazhabnya ialah Mazhab Shafie, kecuali negeri Perlis yang mengatakan mazhab tidak pakai, dia Ahli Sunnah Waljamaah selain daripada itu semua mazhab Shafie. Mazhab Shafie bukan mazhab Syiah. Sekarang kita hendak membawa satu fahaman daripada satu negara yang fahamannya Syiah. Ataukah ulamak-ulamak Syiah ini yang dimaksudkan di dalam Titah Ucapan ini antara ulamak dan umarak? Adakah ulamak yang dimaksudkan ini ulamak Syiah atau ulamak ini dimaksudkan ulamak ahli sunnah wal jumaah? Apakah sikap ulamak-ulamak kita.

30. Abdul Razak Hussain, Parliamentary Debates, Senate, Sixth Parliament, First Session, vol. 1 (19), 11 January 1983, pp. 2177–79:

> Kita semua tahu bahawasanya ia lebih kiblat kepada Ali radhia'llahu'anhu. Apabila dia selepas membaca bang,

minta izin, Tuan Pengerusi, sebahagian daripada bang itu. "Muhammada rasulullah, Ali yalalqalam, Al radhia'llah", dia sebut begitu. Kalau siapa yang pernah berjemaah dengan orang Iran, dia mesti sebutkan "Ali" itu. Pada kita Ali ialah sahabat Nabi, yang akhir Muhammad. Kita pada masa itu macam mana fikiran kita, adakah kita bersekutu dengannya ataupun kita mufarikkan sembahyang kita, bahawa dia bukan Islam, kita yang Islam. Kita tidak boleh kata dia bukan Islam sebab undang-undang ini mengatakan kita tidak boleh mengatakan seseorang itu bukan Islam jikalau tidak cukup syarat-syaratnya. Tetapi kenyataannya sudah ada. Tuan Pengerusi, sebagaimana kita semua maklum, Iran berbalah dengan Imam yang empat selepas Nabi kita wafat, bukan kerana hukum tetapi kerana "ummamah", kepimpinan, sebab mengikut selepas daripada Nabi wafat, Iran mesti menegakkan bahawa Ali lah yang menjadi kalifah yang pertama. Orang Iran yang syiah ini tidak akan mengakui bahawa Abu Bakar itulah yang pertama dan sampai sekarang ini pun, itulah yang saya katakan tadi selepas daripada bang menyebut, "Asyhadu anlaa ilaaha illallah Muhammadar rasulullah" mesti sebutkap Ali kalamullah atau Ali radhia'allah, sebaliknya dan kita tidak ada lagi. Selain daripada itu, sehingga sekarang pertandingan perebutan antara Iran dengan negeri Arab ini bukan pertandingan mengesahkan kufur tetapi mengesahkan "ummamah" selepas Nabi wafat. Hingga sekarang orang Iran tidak akan mengakui bahawa pengikut Abu Bakar, pengikut Othman, pengikut Omar kecuali Ali. Menangislah mereka itu di kubur Madinah dan Mekah umpamanya dengan secara sungguh-sungguh kasih sayang mereka kepada Ali sedangkan Ali terbiar tercampak sedangkan Ali ialah menantu Rasulullah, Alilah yang berhak menjadi khalifah yang pertama pada masa itu. Adakah orang ini yang kita mahu katakan dia Islam atau tidak Islam. Kalau kita katakan dia bukan Islam, kita akan sendiri menarik diri kita ke dalam jel dan Kerajaan boleh bertindak seperti itu. Saya minta bertanya Yang Berhormat Menteri yang bijaksana macammana kedudukan saya supaya saya terang dan menerangkan kepada yang lain.

31. Mohamad Yusof Mohammad Noor, Parliamentary Debates, House of Representatives, Sixth Parliament, Third Session, vol. 3 (22), 24 July 1985, pp. 4098–99:

> Bukan semua aliran Syiah itu terkeluar dari akidah Islamiah. Di Malaysia umpamanya, Majlis Muzakarah Mufti-mufti mengakui aliran Syiah Jaafariah dan Zaidiah tidak terkeluar dari akidah Islamiah. Walau bagaimanapun dalam usaha untuk mengukuhkan akidah Islamiah kepada penganut- penganut Islam di Malaysia, Kerajaan dengan agensi-agensi dan institusi-institusi keugamaan yang ada sentiasa mengawasi pengaruh Syiaah yang tidak diiktiraf keislamannya terus meresap kepada penganut Islam di sini.

32. Mohamad Yusof Mohammad Noor, Parliamentary Debates, House of Representatives, Seventh Parliament, First Session, vol. 1 (56), 30 June 1987, pp. 9067–68. See also Mohamad Yusof Mohammad Noor, Parliamentary Debates, House of Representatives, Seventh Parliament, First Session, vol. 1 (76), 28 October 1987, pp. 12659–660.
33. Othman Abdul, Parliamentary Debates, Senate, Eighth Parliament, Third Session, vol. 3 (9), 4 August 1993, pp. 1307–9.
34. Abdullah Fadzil Che Wan, Parliamentary Debates, House of Representatives, Eighth Parliament, Third Session, vol. 3 (1), 27 April 1993, pp. 137–38.

> Mengikut maklumat yang ada pada pihak kerajaan, tidak terdapat perbezaan di antara Syiah di Iran dengan Syiah yang terdapat di Malaysia kerana penyebaran fahaman gerakan Syiah di Malaysia merupakan lanjutan daripada dasar luar negara Iran yang ada hubungannya dengan revolusi di negara tersebut. Walau bagaimanapun, sudah terdapat usaha-usaha positif kerajaan Iran untuk memperdekatkan fahaman di antara golongan Syiah dengan Sunni demi menjaga perpaduan ummah.

35. Mohd Tajol Rosli Mohd Ghazali, Parliamentary Debates, Senate, Ninth Parliament, Third Session (31), 10 December 1997, pp. 15–16.
36. Abdul Kadir Annuar, Noh Omar, Mohd Apandi Mohamad, and Mohamad Aziz, Parliamentary Debates, 1 October 2003, pp. 12–13.
37. One of those held—Lutpi Ibrahim, a former professor at University Malaya's Academy for Islamic Studies—confirmed this in a conversation with the author on 13 June 2015.
38. Engku Ahmad Zaki, *Ajaran Sesat di Sebalik Lipatan Sejarah Islam* (Selangor: Mustread, 2013), p. 132.
39. Leong Kar Yen, "Use of ISA against Shia Followers Unislamic and Unconstitutional", *Malaysiakini*, 18 June 2001, http://www.malaysiakini.com/news/3500 (accessed 14 May 2010).

40. Suaram (Suara Rakyat Malaysia), *Malaysian Human Rights Report 2001: Civil and Political Rights* (Petaling Jaya: Suaram Komunikasi, 2002), p. 5.
41. Abdullah had been accused of "receiving secret funds, distributing pamphlets, and sponsoring secret meetings ... and certain activities on teachings deviating from the teachings of Islam that may cause confusion and disunity among the Muslims in Malaysia". Cited in Leong, "Use of ISA against Shia".
42. Sharifah Nor Ainnul Khairiyah Syed Abdul Rahman and Mohd al Adib Samuri, "Fatwa Sebagai Mekanisme Mengawal Ajaran Syiah: Satu Tinjauan Literatur", in *Prosiding Kolokium Siswazah Syariah Peringkat Kebangsaan 2014*, edited by Anwar Fakhri bin Omar Muhammad Adib Samsudin Ahmad Dahlan Salleh (Jabatan Syariah, Fakulti Pengajian Islam, UKM, 2014), pp. 83–95.
43. http://efatwa.muftiwp.gov.my/fatwa/24f1d9a2e68003e1054a26bba4ff462b.
44. http://www.muftiselangor.gov.my/soalan-lazim/85-fatwa/akidah/59-fatwa-tentang-fahaman-syiah.
45. Sharifah Nor Ainnul and Mohd al Adib, *Fatwa Sebagai Mekanisme Mengawal*.
46. "Iranian President Ahmadinejad Meets Malaysian Prime Minister Abdullah Ahmad Badawi in Tehran", United Press International (UPI), http://www.upi.com/News_Photos/view/upi/826125b99975120671f218fc584467f4/Iranian-President-Ahmadinejad-meets-Malaysian-Prime-Minister-Abdullah-Ahmad-Badawi-in-Tehran/#ixzz3JNuUROpd (accessed 25 December 2008). See "Iran's Ahmadinejad Arrives for Visit to Malaysia", Bernama, 1 March 2006, https://www.kln.gov.my/archieve/content.php?t=4&articled=16600 (accessed 12 February 2014).
47. A/61/981 S/2007/656, "Islamabad Declaration", The Thirty-Fourth Session of the Islamic Conference of Foreign Ministers Session of Peace, Progress and Harmony, Resolution No. 28/34-Pol on Strengthening Islamic Unity, pp. 91–93.
48. Sharifah Nor Ainnul and Mohd al Adib, *Fatwa Sebagai Mekanisme Mengawal*.
49. Ibid.
50. http://www.muftins.gov.my/index.php/arkib2/himpunan-fatwa/169-fatwa-mufti-negeri-sembilan/867-penyelewengan-ajaran-taslim-qadiani-syiah (accessed 15 April 2019).
51. http://mufti.penang.gov.my/index.php/index.php/2014-11-12-02-37-08/2014-11-12-03-34-32/2014-11-12-06-39-56 (accessed 15 April 2019).
52. http://www.muftimelaka.gov.my/jmm/index.php/en/perkhidmatan/fatwa-warta/aqidah/267-pengukuhan-fatwa-pengharaman-ajaran-syiah (accessed 15 April 2019).
53. Alias Azhar and Mohd Shauki Muhammad Baderuddin, "Kesalahan Ajaran Sesat Dalam Kerangka Perundangan Dan Fatwa Di Negeri Kedah: Satu

Tinjauan", *Journal of Humanities, Language, Culture and Business* 2, no. 8 (2018): 1–16.
54. "Malaysia Supports Saudi Arabia and GCC's Peace Initiatives In Bahrain", Bernama, 22 March 2011, http://web6.bernama.com/bernama/v3/news_lite.php?id=572665 (accessed 1 April 2011); Liew Chin Tong, "Troops to Bahrain: Worst Idea Ever for Our Armed Forces", Media Statement, 15 May 2011, http://dapmalaysia.org/english/2011/may11/bul/bul4575.htm (accessed 15 May 2011). During the recent earthquake in the state of Sabah, Najib's absence from the country was conspicuous. He claimed this was unavoidable because he had to meet the new Saudi king, King Salman. See Mohd Farhan Darwis, "Important Bilateral Ties with Saudis Kept Me from Sabah, Says Najib", *Malaysian Insider*, 9 June 2015, http://www.themalaysianinsider.com/malaysia/article/important-bilateral-ties-with-saudis-kept-me-from-sabah-saysnajib (accessed 9 June 2015).
55. See Lee Shi-Ian, "Rise of Salafism Cause of Controversial Fatwas, Says Sociologist", *Malaysian Insider*, 18 October 2014, http://www.themalaysianinsider.com/malaysia/article/rise-of-salafism-in-malaysia-cause-ofcontroversial-fatwas-says-sociologist#sthash.m0avn5dn.dpuf (accessed 19 October 2014). See also "The Wahhabi Threat to Southeast Asia", *Malaysian Insider*, 30 March 2015, http://www.themalaysianinsider.com/sideviews/article/the-wahhabi-threat-to-southeast-asia-dennis-ignatius (accessed 2 April 2015); "Wahhabism Has No Place in Malaysia", *Malaysiakini*, 16 August 2004, http://www.malaysiakini.com/letters/29193 (accessed 16 August 2004).
56. Michael Cook, *Commanding Right and Forbidding Wrong in Islamic Thought* (New Jersey: Princeton University, 2001).
57. In Barbara Watson Andaya, "Gender, Islam and the Bugis Diaspora in Nineteenth and Twentieth-Century Riau", *Sari* 21 (2003): 85–86, the notable historian wrote:

> Raja Ali was particularly concerned with social reform in accordance with stricter interpretations of Islamic law. He ordered women to be veiled, for instance, and forbade activities that "led to loose behaviour between men and women, and those who sang and crooned pantun with veiled invitations to adultery. On occasion he sent people to confiscate the lutes played by those who were serenading near the homes of decent folk." Observation of the obligatory prayers was enforced, and like the Wahhabis in Mecca Raja Ali even instituted a dawn watch to ensure that people rose for the morning prayer.

58. The Coalition of Malaysian NGOs in the UPR Process (COMANGO), "Stakeholder Report on Malaysia for the 17th Session in the 2nd Cycle of the HRC's Universal Periodic Review in 2013", https://uprdoc.ohchr.org/uprweb/downloadfile.aspx?filename=181&file=EnglishTranslation (accessed 15 April 2019). The human rights report discussing the situation of the Shias was based on a report by Liz Gooch, "In a Muslim State, Fear Sends Some Worship Underground", *New York Times*, 27 January 2011, https://www.nytimes.com/2011/01/28/world/asia/28iht-malay28.html?pagewanted=all&_r=0. See also Patrick Lim, "Malaysian Shiites Face Growing Persecution", *Free Malaysia Today*, 14 January 2012, http://www.freemalaysiatoday.com/category/nation/2012/01/14/malaysian-shiites-face-growing-persecution/ (accessed 15 April 2019).
59. Norhayati Mohd Ariffin and Susanna Liew, "Open letter to PM from the Wives of Raymond Koh and Amri Che Mat", *Malaysiakini*, 12 June 2018, https://www.malaysiakini.com/news/429417 (accessed 15 April 2019).
60. Zainun Ali, Federal Court of Malaysia, Appellate Jurisdiction, Civil Appeal No. 01(f)-17-06/2016 (A), Indira Gandhi A/P Mutho vs Pengarah Jabatan Agama Islam Perak, Pendaftar Mualaf and Kerajaan Negeri Perak, 29 January 2018, pp. 13–14, http://ejudgment.kehakiman.gov.my/ks_builtin/file_dispatcher_pub.php?id=1636&key=86f4ee0d71846f2c19db3068d46cd10d (accessed 15 April 2019).
61. Ibid.
62. See Article 32 of the Administration of the Religion of Islam Enactment (Federal Territories) Act 505, 1993. The article provides:

    (1) The Yang di-Pertuan Agong may, on the advice of the Minister, after consulting the Majlis, appoint fit and proper persons to be the Mufti and the Deputy Mufti for the Federal Territories.

    (2) Upon the commencement of this section, any person who immediately before the commencement, was the Mufti of the Federal Territories appointed under the Enactment shall be deemed to have been duly appointed under this section to be the Mufti of the Federal Territories and shall hold office as such.

63. See Section 34 of the Administration of the Religion of Islam Enactment (Federal Territories) Act 505, 1993. The Article provides:

    (1) The Mufti shall, on the direction of the Yang di-Pertuan Agong, and may, on his own initiative or on the request of any person made by letter addressed to the Mufti, make and publish in the Gazette, a fatwa or ruling on any unsettled or controversial question of or relating to Islamic Law.

(2) No statement made by the Mufti shall be taken to be a fatwa unless and until it is published in the Gazette pursuant to subsection (1).

(3) Upon publication in the Gazette, a fatwa shall be binding on every Muslim resident in the Federal Territories as a dictate of his religion and it shall be his religious duty to abide by and uphold the fatwa, unless he is permitted by Islamic Law to depart from the fatwa in matters of personal observance, belief, or opinion.

(4) A fatwa shall be recognized by all Courts in the Federal Territories as authoritative of all matters laid down therein."

64. Section 9 of the Shari'ah Criminal Offences Act 1997.
65. Section 12 of the Shari'ah Criminal Offences Act 1997.
66. Section 13 of the Shari'ah Criminal Offences Act 1997, the section provides:

(1) Any person who: (a) prints, publishes, produces, records, distributes or in any other manner disseminates any book, pamphlet, document or any form of recording containing anything which is contrary to Islamic Law; or (b) has in his possession any such book, pamphlet, document or recording, shall be guilty of an offence and shall on conviction be liable to a fine not exceeding three thousand ringgit or to imprisonment for a term not exceeding two years or to both.

67. Tengku Maimun Tuan Mat, Ahmadi Asnawi, and Zaleha Yusof, Court of Appeal, Civil Appeal No. W-01(A)-336-08/2016, Mohd Faizal Bin Musa vs Menteri Keselamatan Dalam Negeri, 10 January 2018, pp. 34–35.
68. Ibid.
69. Martin Carvalho, "Deputy Minister: Malaysia Will Sign ICCPR Only If Beneficial to Nation, *The Star Online*, 3 December 2013, https://www.thestar.com.my/news/nation/2013/12/03/malaysia-iccpr-signatory/#KXAwLRgiVyYG4LB6.99.
70. Martin Carvalho, "Saifuddin Pledges to Push for Ratification of Six International Human Rights Conventions, *The Star Online*, 2 July 2018, https://www.thestar.com.my/news/nation/2018/07/02/saifuddin-pledges-to-push-for-ratification-of-six-international-human-rights-conventions/#t21O vLHLJp9usb1G.99 (accessed 15 April 2019).
71. United Nations, "Report of the United Nations High Commissioner for Human Rights on the Expert Workshops on the Prohibition of Incitement to National, Racial or Religious Hatred", A/HRC/22/17/Add.4, 11 January 2013, Human Rights Council Twenty-second Session, https://www.ohchr.org/EN/Issues/FreedomReligion/Pages/RabatPlanOfAction.aspx (accessed 15 April 2019).

11

Contemporary Human Rights Issues in Indonesia

Ahmad Suaedy

In post-*reformasi* Indonesia, we have not seen much progress in the attention given to minority rights, to groups holding "alternative" beliefs, or to small sects.[1] Various cases of violence against and expulsions of minority sects—such as the Shias in Sampang, Madura (East Java) and the Ahmadis in Lombok—attest to this. Also lacking has been any protection for or rehabilitation of victims of violence and expulsions.[2] And to the further detriment of some of these groups, rights that they had been accorded in the past have now been reduced. A case in point is that of the Ahmadiyah. Under the Susilo Bambang Yudhoyono administration (2004–9), three joint ministerial decrees were passed that limit the activities of the sect.[3] Two bills—the Religious Harmony Bill and the Penal Code Bill—that had reached the draft stage are no longer being actively discussed in parliament. From what is known about them so far though, should the laws be passed the situation would potentially be more discriminatory towards these groups than the status quo.

In the case of economic rights for the poor and marginalized groups and for the victims of political violence under the New Order government (1966–98), whilst there has been little in the way of substantive progress, discussions about them in the public sphere at least have been robust. And some inroads have been made, with the introduction of new laws such as the Special Autonomy Law for Aceh and Papua—the two regions subject to the greatest repression during the New Order—providing affected groups some form of rights. With the passing of a new Village Law (Undang-undang Desa, UU No 6/2014), economic distribution to indigenous communities and villages affected by the decentralization exercise witnessed significant improvements.[4] Conversely, the Constitutional Court's 2017 decision has not received adequate follow-up by the government of President Joko Widodo (Jokowi). The decision ordered that groups falling under the categories of "Aliran Kepercayaan" or "Aliran Kebatinan" (local beliefs) be accorded recognition similar to that received by the six "official religions" (Islam, Protestant Christianity, Roman Catholic Christianity, Hinduism, Buddhism, and Confucianism).[5] The government remains hesitant in listening to mainstream Muslim voices calling for improvements on this aspect, but has instead allowed counter narrative voices to be dominant in the public sphere.[6] The government should carry out the decision of the Constitutional Court and grant services and rights of protection to minorities as full citizens.

This chapter examines the various dynamics of the collective rights of minorities and marginalized groups in Indonesia. It also looks at how the Jokowi government has responded to these groups, analysing the level of progress it has made in alleviating their concerns, and at the challenges it faces. Even though claims have been made about resolving human rights issues, the situation remains stagnant and has not been fully resolved.[7] These cases have even led to stigmatization against communism and atheism.

Political Identity and Populism

Indonesia, without exception, has become part of the current phenomenon of rising identity politics and populism, with politicians using religion, ethnicity and nationalism as a means to mobilize support and to sway public opinion.[8] Brexit in the United Kingdom and the election of Donald Trump as President of the United States demonstrate how playing up anti-immigrant sentiments can achieve political results. The political, economic and cultural openness of the post-reformation period in Indonesia has allowed rival political parties to restrict if not violently suppress minority groups in their attempts to dominate the political sphere.[9] They have benefitted from the openness of democracy as a means of achieving nefarious goals.[10] This has been the irony of the successful transition to democracy in the country since the fall of Suharto in 1998.

The political coalition that won the 2014 general election may not be able to follow through with its promises of openness and protection of communities that are marginalized and discriminated against. This is because employing the tactics of political identity and populism—using religion, ethnicity, or narrow nationalistic sentiments—is seen as a vehicle of political mobilization. And in this transitional democracy, there are limitations on civil society's ability to address the problem. So it is government intervention that is necessary. But in reality there are no guarantees that reforms of the economy or of the political system will raise the status of or secure legal guarantees for minority groups. By minorities, I am not just referring to classification by relative numbers but also to those who adopt different traditions and beliefs from the mainstream and who as a result have been discriminated against and oppressed. For many, there is a need for their identity to be recognized, preserved and transmitted to the next generation.[11]

The commitment to justice and equity expressed by the current Jokowi government has not significantly affected religious minorities and those sects within the official religions, including atheists and collective cultural rights. Minority groups and collective identities have been ignored in the thinking and planning of government officials.

In a plural society such as Indonesia, which accommodates many religions, ethnicities and beliefs across the scattered archipelago, it is not sufficient to classify collective and minority groups as "indigenous peoples" in the same manner as they are classified in the international discourse.[12] Respect for diversity should also incorporate minority sects within religions and local belief systems, as well as modern social movements defined by collective identities such as LGBT (lesbians, gays, bisexuals and transgender). Indigenous peoples, who have been internationally accepted as collective identities in the human rights discourse,[13] must also be included.[14] This discourse is related to the rights of the classic nation state.¹⁵ This pertains to a social and cultural group that has its own government, laws and system of governance, including a claim to ancestral land, asserting that it is part of their traditions and beliefs. Such groups tend to be marginalized in the formation of a nation state and imagined communities, and their desire to be part of the larger community are very much circumscribed.¹⁶ These groups demand changes to the centralized concept of the modern nation state, and they have requested autonomy in order to safeguard social and cultural cohesion, indigenous laws and the traditional or sub-national government. This means "shifting from such national to sub and transnational collectivities in human rights".¹⁷ As Matthias Koening puts it, this will gradually contribute to the delegitimization of the classical nation-state model and the institutionalization of multicultural citizenship".¹⁸

Constitutionally, Indonesia's reformation period provided the foundation for human rights. The movement in theory aims to respect, protect and to serve collective and minority rights of religions, beliefs and cultures. Article 28 of the amendment to the 1945 constitution provides the basis for such protection, in line with international human rights, complementing the guarantees for religious freedom as mentioned in the first two paragraphs of article 29. The first two clauses of article 18B provide a strong foundation for the existence of traditional groups and customary law, even if these groups have occupancy claims on ancestral lands and models of government or customary laws of their own.

Nevertheless, there are some deficiencies to the post-amendment process of the 1945 constitution. First, there is an absence of steps to synchronize the substance of the laws or any other existing rules towards the spirit and substance of the articles in the amended constitution. Second, this lack of synchronization has led to parallel laws and regulations, although they substantially contradict the spirit and content of the amended constitution. Third, the passing of new laws and regulations contradicts the spirit of the amended constitution, as they are based on earlier versions of laws or regulations that appear in the 1945 amended constitution.

Lastly, as the Constitutional Court reinstated the enactment of Presidential Decree No. 1/PNPS/1965, later called the 1965 PNPS Act, article 156A of the Penal Code on blasphemy remains the main source of discriminatory laws forming the basis for human rights violations.[19] In some cases, such as with the Interreligious Harmony Bill and the Penal Code Bill, which touches on religion, the amended constitution has virtually abandoned the substance and spirit of humanity by reconstructing various laws and regulations passed previously.[20] Moreover, the discourse of collective human rights is not part of the government agenda towards change.

The Role of the State in Freedom of Religion and Collective Rights

Along with the change in emphasis from individual rights to collective rights, it is necessary to alter the role of the state with respect to religious freedom. When it comes to individual rights, the ideal is for the government to remain impartial. However, in the development of recent human rights discourse, the state is required to be more assertive and active in providing defence and protection for the collective identity of minority groups.[21] In a plural nation like Indonesia, collective rights approaches are needed because, while many minority groups have been oppressed and excluded, local governments, politicians, intellectuals and human rights activists have not given enough attention to their plight.[22]

This does not mean that individual rights should be abandoned, but rather that this is the first step forward, especially when individual rights approaches have thus far left super-minority groups behind.[23] Because there is no law or regulation that explicitly protects religious minority groups, other discriminatory laws and regulations from prior to the constitutional amendments have been applied.[24] These laws have then become the foundation for the creation of new laws and regulations that affirm discrimination and ignore the spirit of the constitution.

The affirmation and enforcement of *bineka* (diversity) citizenship (taken from *Bhinneka Tunggal Ika*)[25] or multicultural citizenship[26] and cultural citizenship[27] are necessary for the protection of collective human rights. That is, a stance of equality for all citizens without exception, providing for minority collective rights no matter how small the community, with each culture claiming a legacy distinct from the majority. The affirmation of tradition and culture is important to show respect not only for individuals but also for their collective identity. As Koening points out, in the recent development of international human rights discourse, multicultural citizenship belongs to minority collective rights, and it has become the duty of the state that it

> ... should no longer merely tolerate, but actively promote religious diversity. National identities with strong religious or secularists are thus delegitimized. Characteristically, states with secularist conceptions of religious freedom, such as France, have been increasingly criticized by international human rights bodies.[28]

Koening further notes that the direction of post–Cold War globalization has led international human rights advocates to acknowledge the rights of minorities with collective peculiarities. Further interpretation of the ICCPR by international and regional human rights bodies, such as the European Council of the EU, emphasize the collective dimension and collective ownership of individual rights for minorities. Koening provides an example from the *Declaration on the Rights of Persons Belonging to National or Ethnic, Religious and Linguistic Minorities* adopted by the UN General Assembly in 1992. The declaration requires "obliging states to protect the identity of minorities"[29] and stresses "that equality and non-discrimination of members of minorities can only be guaranteed by the active promotion of the collective identity".[30]

Koening demonstrates the importance of multicultural citizenship to encourage respect for the identity of collective morality. He further writes:

> ... the changing content of human rights in international law suggest that the classical model of national statehood and citizenship has become successively deinstitutionalized. Sub- and transnational collectivities have become highly legitimated through international human rights discourse. The emerging model of 'multiculturalism' citizenship, amounting to the decoupling of state membership, individual rights and national identity, provides new repertoires of contestation of groups engaged in struggles for recognition and formulates new obligations and public functions of modern state.[31]

The spirit of the 1945 constitution and its subsequent amendments, in particular articles 28 and 18B, provide an opportunity for the formation of collective minority guarantees. Yet, the House of Representatives, the government and the Constitutional Court have neglected them, and have even intensified disharmony by re-enacting the 1965 PNPS Act in 2009 and in 2017.[32] Indeed, there is no statement in the Indonesian constitution on the existence of official or unofficial religions. Nor is there any statement about any hierarchy between religious adherents, believers of faith, or indigenous people. However, with the passing and re-enactment of the 1965 PNPS Act (which was passed within a specific context, to be discussed shortly), the focus of the government has been redirected towards policies supporting discrimination, distinction and hierarchy, which are against the constitution.

So far, article 18B of the amended 1945 constitution has been used for the elaboration and implementation of the Special Autonomy Law of Aceh no. 18/2001 (later changed to no. 11/2006) and the Special Autonomy of Papua Law no. 21/2001. It includes rules that guarantee certain peculiarities of local governments and the right to enforce local customary laws. Article 18B has also been translated into Law No. 6/2014 on villages and indigenous communities and applied to the enforcement of customary law within the scope of villages for indigenous communities.

However, none of the aforementioned laws outline the basis for protection of religious belief or sects, either within the scope of the administrative territory, for those who are not part of the territorial administration, or for those who have no claim to land as part of their collective rights. In other words, although they are guaranteed and protected from the point of view of their customary system, this protection does not extend to the dimension of belief, as this is covered elsewhere, such as in the 1965 PNPS Act.

Hierarchy and Discrimination

Freedom and protection of religion and belief are firmly stipulated in the 1945 constitution, in articles 28 and 29 and in article 18B on the peculiarities of indigenous communities. Nonetheless, in practice, officials show a tendency to refer to the law drafted prior to the amendment, though it has a propensity to contradict the spirit of the amendment. The 1965 PNPS Act regulates (or at least is understood to regulate) the six official religions; namely, Islam, Protestantism, Catholicism, Buddhism, Hinduism and Confucianism. In this regard, officials direct all the services and protection of religion to the abovementioned "official religions", and exclude the believers of other religious sects that do not fall under the specification of religion by the Ministry of Education.[33] This has the result of discriminating against the believers of other religions and faiths with regard to public services. Based on Law no. 24/2013 on Population Administration, for instance, believers of other faiths would not be able to have their religion entered in the "belief" column of their citizenship ID card.[34] The law requires that their religious identity be left blank or marked with a dash, while those from the six official religions have theirs written explicitly.[35] The absence of their religious identity on the ID cards leads to discrimination in services relating to other important personal identification documents, such as birth certificates, marriage certificates and wills.

Sects considered deviant in the eyes of the official religions face more problems. In many cases they cannot receive ID cards, or they receive a criminal record, such as happened to some members of Gafatar.[36] The difficulty of getting ID cards also affects some believers of the Ahmadiyah, Shia and Baha'i sects. In many cases, those from the "accepted" religions can insist that the government limits or even prohibits services to those perceived to be deviant, through Bakor Pakem's findings as a basis.[37] The government is also silent on issues of violence and expulsions of religious minorities from their homes and lands, and allows perpetrators of violence to walk free of prosecution.

Article 4 of the 1965 PNPS Act on blasphemy—subsequently incorporated into Penal Code article 156A—allows grim treatment of these religious minority sects.[38] Employing this act, the majority can proclaim a fatwa to define a particular group as deviant. During his term in office, President Susilo Bambang Yudhoyono issued three ministerial decrees on the Ahmadiyah imposing restrictions on their community. This led to discriminatory practices, not only by the central government but also by local governments and law enforcement agencies, leading to violence against these "deviant" groups.[39] For example, the local government in Pulau Bangka expelled fourteen Ahmadi families from its territory.[40]

The 1965 PNPS Act should be understood within the harsh political situation of the time. The New Order government under military rule considered some religious communities to have demonstrated sympathy towards the Communist Party of Indonesia (PKI). The victory of the New Order led to the government negatively stereotyping believers of ethnic faiths. After the amendment of the 1945 constitution, Law No. 16/2004 on the Prosecutor's Office re-enacted the role of Bakor Pakem in religious affairs. Paragraph 3 of article 30 authorizes the Public Prosecution Service in the department of social order and public safety to oversee adherents of ethnic faiths. This authority enabled Bakor Pakem's attorney to provide recommendations to the local governments about the status of believers of ethnic faiths—whether they should be monitored or even forbidden. In many cases, Bakor Pakem also determines the status of those sects considered deviant by the official religions.[41]

Twice, the Ahmadiyah community proposed to the Constitutional Court a judicial review of the 1965 PNPS Act—in 2009 and 2017—demanding removal of the phrase "religious blasphemy" and its interpretation, so as to avoid the multiple interpretations that had led to persecution and violence in society. In both cases the Constitutional Court rejected the judicial review for two main reasons. First, the court argued that the 1965 PNPS Act does not violate the constitution. The court considered the incidents of expulsions and violence to be aberrations in the application of the act and not in the content of the law itself. Second, the court is conscious of the role of the act in maintaining political stability, and elected to retain it and avoid a legal vacuum which could lead to instability. In the 2017 decision, the Constitutional Court further suggested that the Indonesian Parliament conduct a legislative process to amend the 1965 PNPS Act in order to minimize the victims of vigilantes.[42]

Thus, the government and the Constitutional Court hold on to the need to retain the law. Henceforth, the continued hierarchical status and discrimination against the believers of ethnic faiths and of minority sects is the result of the approach to the framework of social order and stability. This is not surprising, as the drafts of the Penal Code Bill and Interreligious Harmony Bill to govern religion and beliefs are in line with the security and militaristic approach, rather than one of openness that is focused on services. It is the result of entanglement of the military's point of view in the Reformasi mission.

As a result of the security approach to policies on religious beliefs, reforms have yet to touch on collective minority groups. Moreover, the increase in intolerance and radicalism has influenced the direction of change and strengthened the security ideology. Various surveys show that religious intolerance and radicalism have increased significantly in various social classes,[43] which has resulted in an increase in hate speech and in religious-based violence against minorities, such as practitioners of ethnic faiths and of minority sects, as well as atheists, communists[44] and LGBT citizens.[45] This highlights the need for the government to not ignore the aspirations of the minorities for recognition of their collective rights.

Initially, President Jokowi's government promised to respect the collective identity groups through a development initiative known as Nawacita (nine priority programmes).[46] During his Nawacita declaration, President Widodo talked of guaranteeing the protection of citizens, in particular the minorities and marginalized groups. Jokowi also distanced himself from the sectarian campaign tactics demonstrated by his political opponents.[47]

Yet, throughout Jokowi's presidency the government has not shown any significant change in the protection of collective minority identity groups. Although there have been attempts to reduce violence against or discrimination towards minorities such as the Ahmadiyahs, Shias and believers of ethnic faiths, these steps have tended to be taken in secret, behind the scenes, and there has been no follow up.[48] Therefore, the effort of setting a new direction for the government to solve human rights abuses against religious minorities seems hopeless. Opposition groups generally hold the opposite perspective to that of the Jokowi administration, embracing sectarian and discriminatory views and leveraging on religious and ethnic sentiments that hinge on populism. This puts pressure on the Jokowi government to exercise restraint in tackling problems related to discrimination.

Conclusion: Towards a Citizenship Transformation

In case no. 97/PUU-XIV/2016, the Constitutional Court issued an important decision that demonstrated a paradigm shift in the concept of citizenship from a religious perspective. In that decision, the court emphasized the equal status of the believers of the country's official religions, of the minority sects of these religions, and of the ethnic faiths, both in writing (on ID cards) and in access to services. By logical extension it should then be assumed the government would advocate equal status and provide equal services, treatment and protection to all these categories of religious adherents. By rights, the case should have provided momentum for the Jokowi government to respond by drafting laws aligned with the paradigm of citizenship and respect for collective identities. The government, however, has yet to show any such commitment, and has even complicated the follow-up process[49] to formulate a law to provide respect, services and a guarantee of collective rights for religious minorities. Cases of expulsions and violence in various regions have tended to be handled in furtive ways rather than by building patterns and rules that reflect the paradigm adapted from the verdict of the Constitutional Court.

As emphasized by Koening, the transformation of the paradigm of *bineka* (or multicultural) citizenship becomes vital to the concept of respect for a minority's collective identity. The transformation began in the era of President Abdurrahman Wahid, or Gus Dur, in relation to the separatist territorial claims made by groups in Aceh and Papua.[50] At that time, President Gus Dur had to deal with the military, with the dominant political parties, and with the established officials and politicians of the New Order establishment who were still glorifying the security approach to societal order. Gus Dur still insisted though on taking a humane and persuasive approach. He reversed the received strategy of the day, first by affording the minorities recognition and then by addressing their problems through peace talks.

Gus Dur undertook three steps to achieve long lasting peace. The first step was recognition. In this case, recognition meant not only affirming the separatist groups but also their existence as part of Aceh and Papua, represented in GAM (Gerakan Aceh Merdeka; Aceh Freedom Movement) and OPM (Organisasi Papua Merdeka; Freedom Papua Organization), all within the larger system of citizenship of the Indonesian state. This act of recognition could be seen to have an impact equivalent to that of the emancipation of the serfs in Europe in the seventeenth and eighteenth centuries, whereby by decree the social status of the serfs became equal to that of the landlords, and their civil, political and social rights became recognized. The process also resembles what Prophet Muhammad did for the slaves with the *tahrir ar-raqabah* (liberation of slaves).

The second step was to afford respect. In Indonesia, respect refers to both appreciation of customs and habits as well as permitting the freedom to speak, to gather and for security. During Gus Dur's administration the government guaranteed freedom of opinion, assembly and security to provide opportunities for the discussion of substantive and systematic aspirations. This assurance led to some groups proposing autonomy rather than seeking total independence from Indonesia. Examples include the drafting of the special autonomy bills for Aceh and Papua. Although both laws were signed into effect under the administration of President Megawati Soekarno Putri, the monitoring of the civil society movement and the debates and formulation of the bills that took place in the House of Representatives occured during Gus Dur's presidency.

The third step was the transformation of state institutions to accommodate the aspirations of the citizens. All their demands—except those for independence—have been incorporated into the special autonomy laws for Aceh and Papua, respectively. They are mechanisms for the governance, for the participation of customary lawmakers and for representation by informal leaders, to reflect the diversity of the region and to incorporate these aspects into the state system. The laws have built *bineka* citizenship into the two long-oppressed territories of Aceh and Papua.

Gus Dur had also initiated citizenship transformation pertaining to beliefs. He revoked the presidential decree on the prohibition of Confucianism, raised its status to one of the officially recognized religions, and provided protection for its adherents. Yet, this initiative failed to create a legal framework to explicitly guarantee citizens rights or to replace the 1965 PNPS Act.

With regard to the promises of the 2014 presidential campaign, especially the outlook of Nawacita, Jokowi should continue to move forward with *bineka* citizenship for believers of ethnic faiths. This is expected to have positive implications for other religious sects and minorities. The amendment to the constitution and decision by the Constitutional Court in 2017 on believers of ethnic faiths has provided a solid basis for this.

Notes

1. Jacques Bertrand, *Nationalism and Ethnic Conflict in Indonesia* (Cambridge: Cambridge University Press, 2004); Jacques Bertrand, "Ethnic Conflict in Indonesia: National Models, Critical Conjunctures, and the Timing of Violence", *Journal of East Asian Studies* 6 (2008); Jamie S. Davidson and David Henley, eds., *The Revival of Tradition in Indonesian Politics: The Deployment of Adat from Colonialism to Indigenism* (London: Routledge, 2007). See also, Thomas Reuter and Alexander Horstmann, eds., *Faith in the Future: Understanding the Revitalization of Religions and Cultural Traditions in Asia* (The Netherlands: Brill, 2012).
2. Andreas Harsono, "Indonesian Religious Minorities under Threat", https://www.hrw.org/news/2017/02/02/indonesias-religious-minorities-under-threat (accessed 24 July 2018).
3. Ahmad Suaedy, "Religious Freedom and Violence in Indonesian", in *Islam in Contention: Rethinking Islam and the State in Indonesia*, edited by Ota Atsushi, Okamoto Masaaki, and Ahmad Suaedy (Kyoto: Center for Southeast Asian Studies, Kyoto University; Jakarta: The Wahid Institute; Taipei: Center for Asia-Pacific Area Studies, Taipei University, 2010).
4. Village Law No. 6/2014.
5. Samsul Maarif, *Pasang Surut Rekognisi Agama Leluhur dalam Politik Agama di Indonesia* (Yogyakarta: CRCS-UGM, 2018).
6. Only a small number of the Indonesia Ulama Council (MUI) members have responded negatively. See http://mui.or.id/id/berita/solusi-mui-perihal-kolom-penghayat-kepercayaan/. Meanwhile, Nahdlatul Ulama accepts them. See http://www.nu.or.id/post/read/83075/hormati-dan-hargai-keputusan-mk-untuk-penghayat-kepercayaan-. Muhamidiyah also accepts some of them, but not all. See https://www.republika.co.id/berita/nasional/umum/17/11/09/oz5kig409-sikap-muhammadiyah-atas-putusan-mk-soal-aliran-kepercayaan. For this case, the Ministry of Home Affairs is still discussing the requirements, which is at odds with the decree of the Constitutional Court. See http://www.tribunnews.com/nasional/2017/11/12/penghayat-kepercayaan-perlu-miliki-organisasi-agar-bisa-diakui-pemerintah; https://nasional.tempo.co/read/1033265/organisasi-penghayat-aliran-kepercayaan-diminta-mendata-anggota. And this is despite the fact that President Jokowi has given the order for the decree of the Constitutional Court to be fully implemented. See https://www.benarnews.org/indonesian/berita/jokowi-ktp-aliran-kepercayaan-04042018151342.html (accessed 15 July 2018).
7. Such as the case of the massacre in 1965 and that of the disappearance of people during the 1998 Reformasi movement.

8. Vedi R. Hadiz, *Islamic Populism in Indonesia and the Middle East* (Cambridge: Cambridge University Press, 2016), pp. 25–28.
9. Bertrand, *Nationalism and Ethnic Conflict*, p. 5.
10. Vedi Hadiz, *Islamic Populism*.
11. Hans van Amersfoort, "'Minority' as a Sociological Concept", in *Selected Studies in International Migration and Immigrant Incorporation*, edited by Marco Martiniello and Jan Rath (Amsterdam: Amsterdam University Press, 2010).
12. UNRIC.ORG, "Individual vs. Collective Rights", https://www.unric.org/en/indigenous-people/27309-individual-vs-collective-rights (accessed 13 July 2018).
13. Ibid.
14. Robert N. Clinton, "The Rights of Indigenous People as Collective Group Rights", *Arizona Law Review* 32, no. 2 (1990): 739–47.
15. Matthias Koening, "Institutional Change in the World Polity: International Human Rights and the Construction of Collective Identities", *International Sociology* 23, no. 1 (January 2008): 95–114.
16. Benedict Anderson, *Imagined Communities: Reflection on the Origin and Spread of Nationalism*, 12th ed. (New York: Version, 2003).
17. Koening, "Institutional Change", p. 101.
18. Ibid., p. 103. See also Will Kymlicka, *Multicultural Citizenship: Liberal Theory of Minority Rights* (Oxford: Oxford University Press, 1995).
19. Ahmad Suaedy, "The Inter-Religious Harmony (KUB) Bill vs. Guaranteeing Freedom of Religion or Belief in Indonesian Public Debate", in *Religious, Law and Intolerance in Indonesia*, edited by Tim Lindsey and Helen Pausacker (London: Routledge, 2016), pp. 158–79.
20. Ibid.; Draft documents of the Penal Code Bill in the Religious Harmony Bill.
21. Koening, "Institutional Change", pp. 105–6.
22. Ahmad Suaedy, *Presiden Gus Dur, Islam Nusantara dan Kewarganegraan Bineka/President Gus Dur, Archipelago Islam and Bineka Citizenship* (Jakarta: Gramedia, in press 2018).
23. Kymlicka, *Multicultural Citizenship*.
24. Although the Law on the Elimination of Ethnic and Racial Discrimination no. 40/2008 has been effective in some capacities, it has excluded believers of ethnic faiths and religious sects.
25. Ahmad Suaedy, *President Gus Dur*.
26. Kymlicka, *Multicultural Citizenship*; Koening, "Institutional Change", pp. 102–3.
27. Renalto Rosaldo, "Cultural Citizenship in San Jose California", *PoLAR* 17, no. 2 (1994): 57–63.

28. Koening, "Institutional Change", p. 106.
29. Ibid.
30. Ibid.
31. Ibid., p. 107.
32. Ahmad Suaedy, "The Inter-Religious Harmony (KUB) Bill vs. Guaranteeing Freedom of Religion or Belief in Indonesian Public Debate". See also Constitutional Court Decree 140/PUU-VII/2009 and Institutional Court Decree on no. 56/PUU-XV/2017.
33. Human Rights Commission of the Republic of Indonesia, "The Result of the Monitoring Report: On Discrimination and Violence against Women in the Context of Freedom of Religion and Beliefs for Believers, and the Practice of Indigenous Rituals", Jakarta, 3 August 2016.
34. This regulation is also based on the 1965 PNPS Act.
35. Leaving the religious identity blank or putting a dash for believers of ethnic faiths is actually a better situation than previously. During the New Order government, believers of ethnic faiths were pushed to choose one of the official religions. They were therefore prohibited from showing their identities.
36. Freedom House, *Freedom in the World: The Annual Survey of Political Rights and Civil Liberties* (Maryland: Rowman & Littlefield, 2018), pp. 241–42.
37. "Bakor Pakem" stands for Badan Koordinasi Pengawasan Aliran dan Kepercayaan, or the Coordinating Board for Monitoring Mystical Beliefs in Society. It is a monitoring body under the Attorney-General of Indonesia to keep an eye on the believers of ethnic faiths and on those they have classified as adhering to deviant religious practices. See Ahmad Suaedy, "Religious Freedom and Violence".
38. Ahmad Suaedy, "Religious Freedom and Violence".
39. Several cases of the prohibition of particular sects have involved Bakor Pakem, the Indonesian Ulama Council and national and local governments. See Ahmad Suaedy, "Religious Freedom and Violence".
40. Human Rights Watch, "Indonesia: Jemaah Ahmadiyah Diancam", https://www.hrw.org/id/news/2016/01/17/285528.
41. Ibid.
42. *Kompas Daily*, "MK Tolak Gugatan Jamaah Ahmadiyah tentang Pasal Penodaan Agama", https://nasional.kompas.com/read/2018/07/23/13463191/mk-tolak-gugatan-jamaah-ahmadiyah-tentang-pasal-penodaan-agama (accessed 24 July 2018).
43. The results of various surveys show increasing radicalism. See https://drive.google.com/file/d/1mNy6TTISy9MSbAQ-iyfm_nJGXKNI6L88/view; https://magdalene.co/news-1734-konservatisme-agama-di-sekolah-dan-kampus-negeri-picu-intoleransi.html; https://www.cnnindonesia.com/

nasional/20170814172156-20-234701/survei-wahid-institute-11-juta-orang-mau-bertindak-radikal (accessed 24 July 2018).
44. *Tempo*, "Survei Wahid Foundation: Komunis dan LGBT Paling Tidak Disukai", https://nasional.tempo.co/read/1055349/survei-wahid-foundation-komunis-dan-lgbt-paling-tak-disukai (accessed 15 July 2018).
45. Human Rights Watch, "Indonesia Anti-LGBT Crackdown Fuels Health Crisis", https://media.hrw.org/preview/2125/indonesia-anti-lgbt-crackdown-fuels-health-crisis/eng (accessed 15 July 2018).
46. Nawacita is a developmentalist policy campaign under the administration of President Joko Widodo and Vice President Jusuf Kalla. Among the nine promises of the campaign are the following: (1) The protection of all nationals and security for all citizens through an active foreign policy, credible national security, and the development of an integrated defence of Tri Matra, based on national interests and on strengthening Indonesia's identity as a maritime country; (4) Reforming the system of law enforcement to make it free of corruption and to posses dignity and trustworthiness; and (9) Strengthening diversity and social cohesion through a policy of diversity education and creating spaces for inter-community dialogue.
47. Ahmad Suaedy, *Perubahan Karakter Gerakan Sosial di Indonesia Pilpres 2014* [Character changes in Indonesian social movements in the 2014 presidential election] (Depok: AWC-UI, 2017).
48. Human Rights Watch, "Indonesia: Silence, and Complicity on Human Rights Abuses", https://www.hrw.org/news/2017/01/12/indonesia-silence-and-complicity-human-rights-abuses (accessed 26 July 2018).
49. For example, the government is formulating illogical requirements for those who want to register officially. A minimum number of members is stipulated, yet such a requirement does not apply for other religions. So in other words, they are discriminated against with different kinds of threats or traps.
50. See the summary of peace with the Aceh and Papua separatist movements in the doctoral dissertation submitted to UIN Sunan Kalijaga Yogyakarta (May 2018): Ahmad Suaedy, *Gus Dur, Islam Nusantara dan Kewarganegraan Bineka: Penylesaian Konflik Aceh dan Papua 1999-2001/Gus Dur, Archipelago Islam and Bineka Citizenship: Solving the Aceh and Papua Conflict 1999–2001* (Jakarta: Gramedia, 2018).

12

Ahmadiyah and Islamic Revivalism in Twentieth-Century Java, Indonesia: A Neglected Contribution

Ahmad Najib Burhani

A number of scholars, such as Deliar Noer and Abdul Mukti Ali, have argued that the Ahmadiyah in Indonesia have had no significant influence on Islamic revivalism in the early twentieth century.[1] Others, such as Federspiel, perceive that the Ahmadiyah have contributed to the revival of Islam in the country to a degree disproportionate to the group's small size.[2] "[T]he Ahmadiyah groups in Indonesia remained relatively small and isolated throughout the era and probably received more attention from the modernist Muslim organizations than was warranted by their size and influence", states Federspiel.[3] Challenging the above views, Margaret Blood stated, "If Ahmadiyah is discussed simply as one organization among many Islamic based organizations in Indonesia in the early twentieth century we must conclude that its importance within the Muslim community of Indonesia is insignificant.[4] This is most true of the Qadiani branch which is primarily a sectarian organization, and as such, can be best evaluated in terms of its membership." However, Blood continues, if one evaluates the Ahmadiyah on the quality of the group's membership, then the Ahmadiyah, particularly the Lahore branch, "has of course quite a large reverberation for even those Muslims who are reluctant to associate with the sect from Pakistan".[5] Blood agrees with Justus M. van der Kroef, who believes that the Ahmadiyah have "contributed greatly to a modernistic religious quickening among younger western schooled Indonesians".[6]

These differing perceptions need to be examined by looking at the history of the arrival of the Ahmadiyah in Indonesia, the circumstances at that time, and how Muslims perceived the group. This article, therefore, intends to study the role of the Ahmadiyah in Islamic revivalism in Indonesia in the first half of the twentieth century by first looking at the circumstances in the country at that time. Second, the article aims to describe the linguistic divide among Indonesian intelligentsia—i.e., between the Arab-educated and the Dutch-educated Muslims—in accessing information and knowledge from foreign countries. Lastly, it will elaborate the appeals of the Ahmadiyah to the Muslim intelligentsia and the role of this movement in Islamic revivalism.

Receptive Attitude to the Ahmadiyah

Ahmadiyah is a transnational movement, not a home-grown Indonesian movement. The community was established by Mirza Ghulam Ahmad in British India in 1889. The group today claims that the movement is currently widespread in more than two hundred countries. There are two Ahmadiyah factions—the Qadiani Ahmadiyah and the Lahore Ahmadiyah. Previously, the former group used the name Ahmadiyah Muslim Jama'at, or Ahmadiyah Muslim Community, while the latter used the name Ahmadiyah Anjuman Isha'at Islam (AAII; Ahmadiyah Movement for the Propagation of Islam). In Indonesia, the former uses the official name, Jemaat Ahmadiyah Indonesia (JAI; Indonesian Ahmadiyah Community), while the latter is officially called the Gerakan Ahmadiyah Indonesia (GAI; Indonesian Ahmadiyah Movement). Both groups came to Indonesia in the 1920s.

There were a number of interrelated circumstances in Indonesia when the Ahmadiyah arrived. Progress had been made by Christian missions in the country, there were perceptions of impurity regarding religious beliefs and practices, there were ongoing troubles under the colonial government, the Islamic system of education was felt to be ineffective, and there was an aversion among the Muslim intelligentsia towards their religion.[7] Of these circumstances, at least two were strongly related to the receptive attitude of Indonesian Muslims to the arrival of Ahmadiyah missionaries (particularly the Lahore branch); namely, the deepening penetration of the Christian missionaries and the loss of confidence—or indifference—of the Muslim intelligentsia to their religion. Instead, the Muslim intelligentsia were more attracted to what was perceived as the modern and Western way of life.[8] Hence, it is necessary to elaborate these two circumstances here.

In 1889 the Dutch government lifted a ban on evangelical activities in regions inhabited by Muslims. The areas that were previously barred to Christian missions for political reasons—to prevent unrest and disturbances—such as Java, were opened and became target areas for them. This policy had a significant effect on the number of religious conversions to Christianity, both from local religions and from Islam.[9] In instances when a number of elite Muslims felt that their religion was being seriously threatened, they believed that the government was not neutral. Indeed, on a number of occasions, the government under L.F. Dingemans (1874–1955), the Resident of Yogyakarta (1924–27), and A.W.F. Idenburg (1861–1935), the Governor-General of the Netherlands Indies (1909–16), favoured Christianity in its policies and even supported Christian missionaries explicitly.[10] Idenburg even declared that the Dutch would not leave the colony before it was "transformed into a Christian nation".[11] In this situation, Muslim leaders certainly believed that their religion was in danger, and Idenburg's declaration was perceived as a wakeup call to stop Christian missions.

Another factor that stimulated the receptive attitude towards the Ahmadiyah was the growth of a Western-educated elite. This relates particularly to the introduction of a policy called the Ethical Policy (*Ethische Politiek*) by the Dutch administration in 1901. The policy was recommended by a Dutch socialist, C. Th. Van Deventer, and considered to be a moral responsibility, which he called "Een Ereschuld" (a debt of honour), on the part of the Dutch after having drained tremendous amounts of wealth from the East Indies. In August 1899, for instance, Van Deventer wrote an article in *De Gids* entitled "Een Ereschuld", which implied that the welfare of the Dutch was the result of the suffering of people in the East Indies. The Dutch should therefore pay their debt to Indonesians.[12] According to the policy, the welfare of Indonesians must not be completely ignored.[13] Instead, the Dutch should share the wealth received from Indonesia with Indonesians. Included in the implementation of this policy was the introduction of Dutch education to Indonesians, which resulted in the emergence of a new social class of Dutch-educated Indonesian intellectuals. However, as witnessed by Agus Salim, the system of education promoted by the Dutch tended to be secular and materialistic, and it underestimated religion.[14]

Because those who came through this educational system originated from the traditional elite, those who had never received any Islamic education, "soon they became estranged from Islam. They tended to regard Islam as an anachronism in the modern world and an obstacle to progress."[15] This became a new concern for Muslim leaders, such as those in Muhammadiyah. Some Muslim leaders then tried to show that Islam was compatible with modernity and that Islam does not contradict science. Furthermore, many Muslims of the time saw the Ethical Policy as having a strong connection to the Christian missions. The policy provided more advantages to Christianity because modernity and Western education had often been associated with that religion. In 1901, the Royal Address made at the inauguration of the policy provided strong indication of the link between the policy and the Christian mission. It was stated that, "as a Christian nation the Netherlands have a duty to improve the condition of native Christians in the archipelago, to give Christian missionary activity more aid and to inform the entire administration that the Netherlands have a moral obligation to fulfill as regards the population of those regions".[16]

These two circumstances had a significant influence on the receptive attitude of Indonesian Muslims to Ahmadiyah. As stated by R. Ng. Djojosoegito during the 13th Congress of Muhammadiyah in 1924, the Ahmadiyah were not only able to stop the Christian missions in India but were even able to spread Islam to the heart of Christianity in European countries and the United States.[17] A few people in England, for instance, have converted to Islam because of the Ahmadiyah mission to that country. The Ahmadiyah were seen not only as blocking Christian missions in Muslim countries but even as sending missionaries to the West. This is the point that attracted many Muslims in Indonesia and led them to warmly welcome the sect. The second selling point of Ahmadiyah was its ability to demonstrate that Islam is a rational and modern religion. The modern characteristics of Islam, as demonstrated by the Ahmadis, not only included adopting a Western system of education but also in countering numerous stereotypes about the backwardness of Islam. As shown in its publication, *Islamic Review*, Ahmadiyah discussed topics such as women in Islam, Islam and the sword, tolerance in Islam, peace and love, apostasy in Islam, Islam and progress, and Islam enthroning reason. In line with this modern and rational understanding of Islam, Ahmadiyah had further appeal on account of its efforts to eradicate superstitious practices and traditional admixtures, in a way similar to Muhammadiyah's project to eradicate irrational beliefs, heterodoxy and superstition.

Linguistic Divide: Arab-educated vs. Dutch-educated Scholars

The first quarter of the twentieth century was marked by the revival of Islam, as affirmed by the establishment of numerous Islamic movements, such as Sarekat Islam (SI) in 1905, Muhammadiyah in 1912, al-Irsyad al-Islamiyah in 1914, Persatuan Islam (Persis; Muslim Union) in 1923, Jong Islamieten Bond (JIB; Young Muslim Union) in 1925, and Nahdlatul Ulama (NU) in 1926. The inspiration for this revivalism came not only from the Middle East—as commonly emphasized by many studies[18]—but also from South Asia.[19] The founders and initiators of these movements were not only Arab-educated Muslims but also Dutch-educated ones. The SI and the JIB, for instance, were dominated by those who had graduated from Dutch schools, whereas organizations like Persis and NU were led mostly by those who had graduated from schools in the Middle East. In fact, these two types of scholars had different views on several matters, such as the issue of the Ahmadiyah.

As mentioned earlier, one of the selling points of Ahmadiyah for Indonesian Muslims was its modern approach to Islam. The Ahmadiyah movement published numerous books that demonstrated the religion's compatibility with modernity. Among the topics dealt with by these publications were issues commonly used by opponents of Islam to discredit it, such as the issues of women, apostasy and the spreading of Islam by the sword. This can be seen, for instance, in books written by Ahmadi leaders. Muhammad Ali, for instance, wrote on many topics, such as "Divorce in Islam", "Islam-the religion of humanity", "Jihad in Islam", and "Muhammad and Christ". Khwaja Kamal-ud-Din also wrote on similar topics, such as "Islam and Christianity", "Islam on slavery", "Women from Judaism to Islam", and "Modernism in religion". The articles that appeared in the Ahmadiyah journal *Islamic Review* also dealt with similar topics. All of these works were intended to counter and correct the distorted and misconceived images of Islam that were prevalent among many in the intelligentsia, particularly in the West.

By the turn of the twentieth century, Indonesia had been marked by a number of attacks on the fundamental beliefs of Indonesian Muslims by Christian missionaries, theosophical movements, and by secularists, atheists and materialists. As stated by Margaret Blood,[20] many young Muslims turned away from religion because these groups accused Islam of being backward and only fit for people living in the Middle Ages. The literature from the Ahmadis, therefore, went to satisfy the hunger from Indonesian Muslims for information that could create confidence in their religion, particularly in the academic or intellectual spheres. Therefore, one could say that the contribution and influence of Ahmadiyah in Indonesia at that time was primarily in disseminating modern thought and reconciling religion and science. Because most Ahmadiyah publications were written in English and Dutch, the readership for these publications was composed mainly of Dutch-educated Muslims (such as those in the SI and the JIB) who already had an attachment to Islam and who wished to study it, but who also had concerns about it and were unable to access similar types of books from the Middle East written in Arabic. As stated by Justus M. van der Kroef, the Dutch translation of Muhammad Ali's *The Holy Qur'an* "had great influence among those Westernized younger Indonesians who did not know Arabic and yet wished to study the Qur'an".[21] In short, these publications become the main sources for the Muslim intelligentsia and alternative sources of Islamic revivalism for those who could not understand Arabic.

One person who testified to the modern and rational tendencies of Ahmadiyah books was Sukarno, the first president of Indonesia.

Although he clearly declared that he did not believe in the prophethood of Mirza Ghulam Ahmad—and even did not acknowledge that Ghulam Ahmad was a *mujaddid*, or reformer, of Islam—Sukarno admitted that he had read many books written by Ahmadi scholars and acknowledged that those books had inspired him. One Ahmadiyah book that has brought many benefits to Muslims, according to Sukarno, was *Het Evangelie van den daad* (*The Gospel of Action*). This book, Sukarno said, was "brilliant, useful for all Muslims". Sukarno further stated that the Ahmadis had contributed some positive values to Indonesia. "In general, they have religious views that I agree [with]: they promote rationalism, they have broadmindedness, they promote modernism, they are very careful in accepting hadith, they prefer to use the Qur'an in the first place, and they have [a] systematic understanding of Islam."[22] Another witness to the importance of Ahmadiyah books was Oejeng Suwargana, the director of Masa Baru Publishing Co., a prominent publishing house in Bandung, as can be seen from an interview with Justus M. van der Kroef. Suwargana said that Westernized younger Indonesians liked to "buy Ahmadiyah books ... but they do not want to be considered Ahmadis".[23]

The strongest voices underlining the contribution of Ahmadiyah to Islamic revivalism in Indonesia came from H.O.S. Tjokroaminoto (1882–1934), who was the chairman of Sarekat Islam and a revolutionary leader, and H. Agus Salim (1884–1954), who was a statesman (and also a revolutionary leader). Tjokroaminoto was one of Mirza Wali Baig's students. His *Tarich agama Islam (riwajat dan pemandangan atas kehidoepan dan perdjalanan nabi Moehammad CLM* (1931), for instance, is based on Ameer Ali's *The Spirit of Islam*, as well as two Ahmadiyah books: Khwaja Kamal-ud-Din's *The Ideal Prophet* and Muhammad Ali's *The Prophet*.[24] He even attempted to translate Maulana Muhammad Ali's *The Holy Qur'an with English Translation and Commentary* into the Malay language.[25]

Besides the testimonies from the aforementioned scholars and prominent Indonesian figures, the influence of Ahmadiyah on Islamic revivalism can also be seen from its strong impact on the JIB. The members of this organization were Dutch-educated Muslims whose main sources of information about Islam were Dutch and English literature. Although they might have heard many ideas about Islamic reformism from the Middle East (for instance, ideas promoted by

Muhammad Abduh and Rashid Rida), they could not access any information transmitted in Arabic, such as *Al-Manar*, which for the most part was only available to Arab-educated Muslims. Ahmadiyah literature therefore was of great benefit for the JIB. Even though only a few JIB members joined the Ahmadiyah—like Ahmad Sarida and Soedewo—most of them were interested in Ahmadiyah books.[26] As observed by Jusuf Wibisono, a member of Muhammadiyah and an activist in the JIB, the Lahore Ahmadiyah contributed a number of monumental works. Although he himself did not join the Ahmadiyah, he participated in advertising Ahmadiyah books and encouraged people to read them. The reason for this, he said, was because Ahmadiyah books "were able to satisfy intellectual curiosity".[27]

In the early decades of the twentieth century, as noted by a number of works, such as those by Kahfi,[28] there was an aversion expressed towards Islam by the intelligentsia (Muslims and non-Muslims alike). Islam was often accused of being an inferior religion that was in contradiction with modernity.[29] To overcome this perception of inferiority, some members of Jong Java led an initiative to offer courses on Islam for Muslim members of the organization. Unfortunately, this initiative was rejected because the majority of the organization's members wanted to be neutral in regards to religious issues. This rejection prompted them to initiate a new independent organization named the JIB in 1925, whose membership was not limited to Javanese but was also open to people from other areas, as long as they were interested in Islam. They then asked some modernist Muslims, such as Agus Salim, H.O.S. Tjokroaminoto and Ahmad Dahlan, to give lectures on Islam.[30] This aversion expressed towards Islam by some members of the intelligentsia in the early decades of the twentieth century was best reflected in the motto of the JIB; namely, Sura al-Tawba 9.32: "They desire to put out the light of Allah with their mouths, but Allah will allow nothing except the perfection of His light, though the disbelievers are averse."[31] This motto has appeared on the cover of all editions of *Het Licht*, the official publication of the JIB.

The JIB was understandably very receptive towards the Ahmadis because Ahmadiyah promoted a modern and rational understanding of Islam. This can be seen, for instance, by the fact that Mirza Wali Ahmad Baig was among the teachers in the Malang and Solo branches of the JIB.[32] This appointment indicates that members of the JIB considered Baig's teachings to be congruent with their intention to create confidence in religion and counter those who attacked Islam. Besides appointing Wali Ahmad Baig as a teacher in the JIB, articles on Ahmadiyah (such as the one written by Soedewo) also appeared frequently in the JIB magazine. In fact, the name of the journal—*Het Licht* (the light)—is the same as the name of the journal published by the headquarters of the Lahore Ahmadiyah, which seems unlikely to simply be a coincidence.

It must be emphasized that the JIB was more closely associated with the Lahore branch of Ahmadiyah, not with the Qadiani branch. The JIB never had any issue towards the former. It did however on many occasions express opposition to Qadiani Ahmadiyah, including in articles published in *Het Licht*. As reported by Husni Dardiri,[33] there were long debates in *Het Licht* about Mirza Ghulam Ahmad. These involved scholars such as Ahmad Sarida, A Kamil, Mirza Wali Ahmad Baig and Djohan Mahmud Tjay. The debates were triggered by an article written by Ahmad Sarida entitled "De Wereldleraar" (the teacher of the world), and they demonstrate how the members of the JIB tended to side with the Lahore Ahmadiyah and mainstream Muslims in their conflict against the Qadiani Ahmadiyah.

Ahmadiyah Influences in Indonesia

In surveying Islamic revivalist movements of the nineteenth and twentieth centuries, Fazlur Rahman[34] classified them into four categories: (1) revivalism of the eighteenth and nineteenth century, which he calls "pre-modernist revivalism", with Wahhabism as the main example; (2) modernism or "classical modernism"; (3) neo-revivalism or "post-modernist revivalism"; and (4) neo-modernism, which he himself claims to be part of. These four categories of revivalist movements in Islam are interrelated, and "the precise lines of influence among these movements are not always easy to draw".[35]

The main characteristics of these four types of movement are the following. Pre-modernist revivalism is concerned mostly with the degeneration or decline of Muslim society. In order to restore the glory of Islam and to rescue society from degeneration, it calls Muslims to "go back" to the pristine Islam and to eradicate various accretions and superstitions attached to Islam. Different from the pre-modernist revivalism, the classical modernism promotes *ijtihād* in all spheres of life and argues for the compatibility between Islam and modernity. Proponents of classical modernism appreciate Western ideas and absorb them as inspiration for reforming Muslim society. The neo-revivalism movement is strongly influenced by classical modernism, particularly on some aspects of the modern system such as education and politics, but it also responds to it by trying to identify and distinguish Islam from the West, such as over the issue of bank interest, the status of women, and the veil. What is missing from all three of these movements is a systematic and comprehensive methodology to reform Islam. This becomes the main characteristic of Rahman's neo-modernism.

In some Muslim countries, Rahman says, efforts of the classical modernists to reform Islam have received a negative response, and they have even been regarded as the enemy of Muslim society because they seem to be "sacrificing 'Islam' to the Western social values" or because they look to be "both Westernized and Westernizers",[36] whereas the neo-revivalists have tended to become apologists in defending Islam against the West. Summarizing this, Rahman states, "just as the Classical Modernists had selected such issues as caused them to be accused of simply identifying Islam with Western mores, so now the neo-Revivalists selected certain other issues whereby they claimed to distinguish Islam from the West and set it quite apart from the latter".[37] In Rahman's view, neither the classical modernists nor the neo-revivalists could establish a comprehensive system to reform Islam, despite their claim that Islam is a total way of life. Consequently, the way they have responded to issues has tended to be on an ad hoc or piecemeal approach.

The Ahmadiyah movement may perhaps not be easily classified by a rigid system like Rahman's, since it has a number of characteristics that could be located in three different categories. Analysing the revival characteristic of the Ahmadiyah movement cannot be done in isolation from the socio-religious circumstances that surround it. As elaborated earlier, the Ahmadis came to Indonesia when Muslim society was suffering from an acute inferiority complex. Several accusations had been levelled against Islam by Muslims and non-Muslims alike. Islam was described as an irrational religion because some of its adherents were practising superstitions. It was accused of being a backward religion that was incompatible with modernity and only suited to those living in the Middle Ages. Islam was also accused of being an anachronism to science and modern civilization. Many Christians preached that Islam was inferior to Christianity, since the prophet of Islam, Muhammad, is dead whilst the prophet of Christianity is alive in heaven.

In these circumstances, many members of the Muslim intelligentsia with a commitment to Islam sought to find academic information that could be used to refute the accusations and to rescue pride in Muslim society. For those Arab-educated and *pesantren*-educated Muslims, they could find such sources in the works of reformist Muslims from the Arab world, such as Muhammad Abduh and Rashid Rida. They could also access information from various Arabic publications such as *Al-Manar*. However, for Dutch-educated Muslims lacking literacy in Arabic, their main sources were literature written in Dutch or English. At that time, most of these sources were published by the Ahmadis or were brought by Ahmadi missionaries to Indonesia.

Before Indonesian Independence in 1945, a number of Ahmadiyah books had been translated (from their original English or Urdu) into Dutch, the language of the Indonesian intelligentsia at that time. For instance, in *Di bawah bendera revolusi* (vol. 1, 1964), Sukarno mentions several Ahmadiyah books that he had found very beneficial. Among them were *Het geheim van het bestaan* (a translation of Khwaja Kamal-ud-Din's *Riddle of Life*), *De bronnen van het Christendom* (a translation of Khwaja Kamal-ud-Din's *The Sources of Christianity*), *Het evangelie van den daad* (a translation of Khwaja Kamal-ud-Din's *The Gospel of Action* or *The Secret of Existence*), *Inleiding tot de studie van den heiligen Qur'an* (a translation of Muhammad Ali's *Introduction to the Study of the Holy Quran*), and Muhammad Ali's *Moehammad de profeet* (a translation of Muhammad Ali's *Muhammad the Prophet*). Writing on 25 November 1936, Sukarno even stated that *Het evangelie van den daad* was a "brilliant book".[38] In the same article, Sukarno also admitted that the journal, *Islamic Review*, published by the Lahore branch of Ahmadiyah, had many interesting articles.

In addition to the books mentioned by Sukarno, there were many other Ahmadiyah books translated into Dutch and published in Indonesia (then the Netherlands East Indies). Among them were Muhammad Yaqub Khan's *Het nut van God* (the title of the English version is *Quest after God*),[39] Basharat Ahmad's *De geboorte van Jezus in het licht van den heiligen Qoer-an* (*Birth of Jesus in the Light of the Qur'an*) and Mirza Ghulam Ahmad's *De leerstellingen van den Islam: een oplossing van de vijf fundamenteele religieuze problemen uit Islamietisch oogpunt* (*The Teachings of Islam*).[40] Soedewo P.K. (1906–71)[41] was the translator for most of the Dutch versions of the Ahmadiyah books. The most important Ahmadiyah book was Muhammad Ali's *The Holy Qur'an with English Translation and Commentary*, which was translated by Soedewo into Dutch as *De heilige Qoer-an: vervattende den Arabischen tekst met ophelderende aanteekeningen en voorrede van Maulwi Moehammed Ali* and published in 1934. This translation of the Qur'an was received with great enthusiasm by Indonesian Muslim intellectuals at that time, particularly those who graduated from Dutch schools.[42] On many occasions, President Sukarno quoted from this translation in his speeches and writings. And according to a 1974 investigation by *Tempo*, this translation could be found in the homes of most pre-Independence Muslim intellectuals. Besides Indonesia, this translation has also been printed in Suriname and the Netherlands.

The impact of Ahmadiyah books on the Indonesian public intellectual sphere before Independence can be seen, for instance, from the works of H.O.S. Tjokroaminoto, Agus Salim and Mohammad Natsir. Tjokroaminoto's *Tarich agama Islam*[43] is based on or a reproduction of Muhammad Ali's *Muhammad the Prophet*. Agus Salim's work on Isra Mi'raj[44] is also based on Muhammad Ali's *The Holy Qur'an*, specifically his interpretation of verses that deal with Isra Mi'raj (the Prophet's spiritual journey on the night of 27 Rejab). Natsir's book on *shalat* (prayers) also refers to Muhammad Ali's books.[45] Soedewo himself, besides translating Ahmadiyah books into Dutch, also wrote a number of books inspired by Ahmadiyah literature, such as *Jesus mati di tiang salib*, *Mi'raj Nabi Muhammad Saw*, *Keesaan Ilahi*, *Islam dan ilmu pengetahuan*, and *Intisari Qur'an suci*.[46]

Ahmadiyah literature deals with two major issues. The first is Islam and its relationship with the modern world. The second is interfaith relations, particularly relations between Islam and Christianity. In dealing with these two issues, Ahmadiyah books employed two different methods. In responding to materialism, the modern world and atheism, they have tended to be "defensive" by emphasizing that Islam is compatible with modernity and modern sciences and that Islam was even a solution for the world's problems. To the second issue, Ahmadiyah books have tended to go on the "offensive" by attacking the fundamental beliefs of Christianity, such as the Resurrection of Jesus.

In analysing the way Ahmadiyah books deal with the issue of the modern world, I will look here at four books that have had the most significant influence on Indonesia: *The Teachings of Islam* by Mirza Ghulam Ahmad (translated into Dutch by Soedewo, with the title *De leerstellingen van den Islam: een oplossing van de vijf fundamenteele religieuze problemen uit Islamietisch oogpunt*),[47] *The Religion of Islam* by Muhammad Ali (translated into Dutch by Soedewo, with the title *De religie van den Islām*),[48] Muhammad Ali's *The Holy Qur'an with English Translation and Commentary* (translated into Dutch by Soedewo, with the title *De heilige Qoer-an: vervattende den Arabischen tekst met ophelderende aanteekeningen en voorrede van Maulwi Moehammed Ali*),[49] and *The Secret of Existence* or *The Gospel of Action* by Khwaja Kamal-ud-Din (translated into Dutch with the title *Het evangelie van den daad*).[50] *De heilige Qoer-an* was accepted enthusiastically by Indonesian Muslim intellectuals after it was published in 1934. As reported by *Tempo* in 1974,[51] scholars at that time were rushing to order it. It became the most precious property of many scholars, such as Roeslan Abdulgani.[52]

As already mentioned, these books were written at a time that several accusations were being made against Islam by Muslims and non-Muslims alike. Religion in general was being blamed by academics for hindering human progress and for hypnotizing people into non-productive activities. Belief in God was being severely attacked by atheists and materialists.[53] Responding to these circumstances was among the main intentions of Ahmadi writers of the period. They tried to "properly locate" the danger faced by Muslims and to "find the way out" to revive Islam.[54] Islam, according to these books, does not simply teach and hypnotize its followers to isolate themselves in caves and pray the entire day, as it was accused of, but it requires (not merely encourages) its followers to take action. In fact, Kamal-ud-Din titled his book *The Gospel of Action* because he believed that Islam is a religion of action and that it did more than teach its followers to kneel in the mosque.[55] Kamal-ud-Din wanted to use his book to refute those who claimed that Islam only taught Muslims how to "bow and raise their hands" [referring to how Muslims pray] without teaching them how to accomplish worldly achievements. "Faith and deeds were inseparably bound up in each other, so that the one could not exist without the other ... the secret of life, vitality and prosperity lies in the power of action."[56] Kamal-ud-Din's explanation is similar to that of Ghulam Ahmad's in quoting the following verse: "Give thou good tidings to those who believe and do deeds of righteousness, that for them await gardens underneath which rivers flow" (Q 2.25).

Refuting the accusation that Islam is an anachronism in the modern world and a hindrance to the advancements of science, the books explain the religion's support for invention and science. They also explain how Islam helps open the path for Muslims towards science by eradicating superstition in society. In his own words, Muhammad Ali states that "Islam gave an impetus to learning in a country which had never been a seat of learning and was sunk in the depths of superstition.... it was through Islam that the Renaissance came about in Europe."[57]

To prove that Islam is not a hindrance to modern science, Ahmadiyah books show their strong religious position in combating any elements of Muslim society that contradict reason and their eagerness to adopt Western systems and technologies, such as in education and publishing.[58] In combating elements that contradict reason, Ahmadiyah books tried to eradicate irrational understandings of Islam and attacked superstition in Muslim society. The most important effort by Ahmadiyah followers in eradicating superstition has been by translating the Qur'an into vernacular languages. This has been the main project of this movement wherever they propagate Islam. With this work of translation they have tried to stop the habit in traditional Muslim communities that projected the Qur'an merely as magic or as an amulet. In Kamal-ud-Din's statement, "We have taken good care to wrap them up in fancy coverings and given them a place of honour in our houses, but we seldom open them to find guidance therein. No doubt we do also uncover and open them at times, but only when we want to take an augury. We place it on our heads too, but simply to take an oath thereby."[59] The project to translate the Qur'an into many languages was intended to make Muslims understand their holy book and use it as their main source of guidance. Efforts by the Ahmadiyah to eradicate superstition went to the point that they tried to employ allegorical interpretations for certain verses in the Qur'an that talk about things that appear irrational, such as miracles.[60] In demonstrating an eagerness for modern development, the Ahmadiyah could be called pioneers in using technology to propagate religion. It published *Religious Review* and *Islamic Review*, among the earliest English journals from the Muslim world. For the Ahmadiyah, publishing was not only a strategy for propagating religion but it was also elevated to a religious duty. It became the implementation of the obligation to conduct peaceful *jihad*.

The Ahmadi's contribution to checking Christian missionary activity was not primarily in the form of challenging the missionaries in their efforts to convert people but rather by producing books that attacked Christianity and defended Islamic beliefs. They also challenged Christian missionaries to public debates. One such engagement took place in Wonosobo in 1932 between Muhammad Sabitun and van Dijk, a Christian missionary from a Protestant Church, *Gereja Aku Iki Pepadanging Jagad*.[61] It was largely through books however that Ahmadi efforts to slow the Christian mission bore the greatest fruit. Their approach became a model for the DDII (Dewan Dakwah Islamiyah Indonesia, or Indonesian Islamic Propagation Council), Muhammadiyah, the YAPI (Yayasan Pesantren Islam, or Islamic Boarding School Foundation) and other missionaries in Indonesia.[62] They also became a model for the study of comparative religion in Indonesia, and their writings became sources for Indonesian Muslims interested in conducting comparative studies on Christianity. Although contemporary comparative studies do not consider these books as contributing to the development of religious studies, they did create confidence among Muslims towards their religion.

The number of books produced by Ahmadis on this issue is significant. It became one of the major genres of literature issued by the Ahmadiyah. Almost all Ahmadi scholars have made an intellectual contribution to this issue by writing a book. Three books published in Indonesia before independence had a significant influence on Indonesian Muslims: Muhammad Ali's *The Holy Qur'an*, Basharat Ahmad's *Birth of Jesus in the Light of the Qur'an* (translated into Dutch by Soedewo with the title *De geboorte van Jesus in het licht van den heiligen Qoer-an*), and Khwaja Kamal-ud-Din's *The Sources of Christianity* (translated into Dutch by Soedewo with the title *De bronnen van het Christendom*).[63] These books all deal with certain fundamental doctrines of Christianity. Two of them are about the death of Jesus and his prophesized Second Coming before the End of Days.

Conclusion

Using Fazlur Rahman's categorization of Islamic revivalism, the Ahmadiyah could be included in the category of modernist movements for their strong support for modernity and rationality. It was the Ahmadi's modernist stance that appealed to Indonesian modernist movements such as Muhammadiyah. This movement even tended to be excessive in its modernist stance to the point that its leaders did not accept the literal meaning of the verses of the Qur'an that spoke about miracles. Instead of believing in miracles, they emphasized their metaphorical meanings.

Ahmadiyah's concern for irrational beliefs and superstition was an extension of the group's modernist stance.[64] This is certainly different from the pre-modernist revivalism that was concerned about purifying religion from accretions and external elements. Although they shared the same understanding that superstitions, Sufism and irrational beliefs were the main reasons for the Muslim community being trapped in a declining condition and being left behind by other communities, their efforts to eradicate superstitions were mainly motivated by their modernist stance, and only secondarily motivated by a puritan spirit.

However, only the Lahore Ahmadiyah could be classified as a modernist movement. Whilst the Qadiani Ahmadiyah were also employing modernist approaches to understanding religion, such as a way to interpret the Qur'an, they adopted certain beliefs and practices that contradicted the modern spirit, such as a belief in messianism and a reliance on "dreams" in human affairs.[65] Dreaming for the Qadiani is a method of communication between the divine and worldly realities.

From a contemporary perspective, the way modernist movements like the Ahmadiyah approach religion can be considered to be apologetic. They try to defend Islam by claiming that Islam is the most rational and modern religion, that the Qur'an contains everything needed by human beings, that any new scientific innovation has already been mentioned in the Qur'an, which was revealed 1400 years ago. The way they approach religion could also be included in the exclusive perspective. However, from the perspective of Indonesian Muslims in the early decades of the twentieth century, this approach was perhaps what they needed. Under the attack of modern materialism, atheism and Christian missionaries, they needed some form of academic device to defend Islam and to refute the various accusations.

The apologetic and polemical nature of Ahmadiyah literature meant it was filled with just such responses. And this is why Ahmadiyah (and Ahmadiyah books) attracted the Indonesian Muslim intelligentsia, who felt responsible for defending their religion, especially those who graduated from Dutch schools and those more familiar with Dutch and English literature than with the Arabic. From their education, they saw how modern and secular paradigms treated Islam, and how Christian missionaries attacked their religion. The only scholarly sources at hand they could use with a degree of credibility to defend Islam were Ahmadiyah books. Mirza Mubarak Ahmad rightly claims, "It is very true that prior to the establishment of our missions in Indonesia, literature in the Indonesian languages did not exist which could present Islam in a manner capable of meeting modern needs."[66] It is from this point, we can say, that the Ahmadis from the Indian subcontinent could be perceived as a source of Islamic revivalism in Indonesia in the early twentieth century, competing with that originating from the Middle East.

Notes

1. Deliar Noer, *The Modernist Muslim Movement in Indonesia, 1900–1942* (Singapore: Oxford University Press, 1973), p. 151n207; Abdul Mukti Ali, "The Muhammadijah Movement: A Bibliographic Introduction" (MA thesis, McGill University, 1959), p. 72.
2. Howard M. Federspiel, *Islam and Ideology in the Emerging Indonesian State: The Persatuan Islam (Persis), 1923–1957* (Leiden: Brill, 2001), p. 63.
3. Federspiel, *Islam and Ideology*, p. 63. Wilfred Cantwell Smith has drawn quite similar conclusions about the Ahmadiyah in India. He says, "The most important fact about the Ahmadiyah Movement in Indian Islam is that the Ahmadiyah Movement (though important in itself) is not important in Indian Islam". See Wilfred Cantwell Smith, *Modern Islām in India: A Social Analysis* (Lahore: Sh. Muhammad Ashraf, 1969), p. 367.
4. Margaret Blood, "The Ahmadiyah in Indonesia: Its Early History and Contribution to Islam in the Archipelago" (Honours sub-thesis, Australian National University, 1974), pp. 64–65.

5. Blood, "The Ahmadiyah", pp. 63–64. This statement resembles one by Mirza Mubarak Ahmad, the head of Ahmadiyah's Foreign Mission, who declared that "the literature of the Ahmadiyah movement has played a most remarkable role in creating confidence among Muslims in regard to the ascendency of Islam". See Mirza Mubarak Ahmad, *Ahmadiyyat in the Far East, Rabwah* (West Pakistan: Ahmadiyya Muslim Foreign Missions, 1964), p. 35.
6. Justus M. van Der Kroef, "Recent Trends in Indonesian Islam", *Muslim World* 52, no. 1 (1962): 57.
7. A number of studies have tried to classify the problems faced by Indonesian Muslims in the early twentieth century. Among them are Abdul Mukti Ali, "The Muhammadijah Movement: A Bibliographic Introduction" (MA thesis, McGill University, 1959); Alwi Shihab, "The Muhammadiyah Movement and Its Controversy with Christian Mission in Indonesia" (PhD thesis, Temple University, 1995); Fred R. Von der Mehden, *Religion and Nationalism in Southeast Asia: Burma, Indonesia, the Philippines* (Madison: University of Wisconsin Press, 1963).
8. There was actually one other factor; namely, the impurity and superstition in Indonesian religious beliefs and practices that made Islam seem to be a backward religion. However, the role of the Ahmadiyah with respect to this issue is ambiguous because the movement (particularly the Qadiani branch) adhered to strong elements of messianism and mysticism. The opposition to superstitions was more intended to clear the ground for making the claim that Ahmadiyah was the true Islam. One circumstance did not fit with the coming of the Ahmadis; namely, nationalist efforts to free Indonesia from the colonial government. Ahmadiyah teaches loyalty to any government, including a colonial one, as long as it guarantee religious freedom. This is among the reasons the Ahmadis later split from Sarekat Islam, which preferred a non-cooperation policy towards the Dutch administration. This last point, along with the excessive veneration of Ghulam Ahmad, were among the Ahmadiyah teachings that were strongly criticized by Sukarno. Soekarno, "Tidak pertjaja bahwa Mirza Gulam Ahmad adalah nabi", in *Dibawah bendera revolusi*, vol. 1 (Djakarta: Panitya Penerbit Dibawah Bender Revolusi, 1964), p. 346.
9. H. Kraemer, "A Survey of the Netherlands Indies", *Muslim World* 27, no. 1 (1937): 44–55.
10. H.B. Mansell, "Concerning Moslems in Malaya", *Muslim World* 8, no. 2 (1918): 213–16; Herman L. Beck, "The Rupture between the Muhammadiyah and the Ahmadiyah", *Bijdragen Tot De Taal-, Land- En Volkenkunde* 161, no. 2 (2005): 210.

11. Beck, "The Rupture", p. 223; Alwi Shihab, "The Muhammadiyah Movement", p. 260.
12. Noer, *The Modernist Muslim*, p. 163; Erni Haryanti Kahfi, "Haji Agus Salim: His Role in Nationalist Movements in Indonesia during the Early Twentieth Century" (MA thesis, McGill University, 1996), p. 33.
13. Noer, *The Modernist Muslim*, pp. 162–3.
14. Kahfi, "Haji Agus Salim", p. 42.
15. Blood, "The Ahmadiyah", pp. 5–6.
16. Noer, *The Modernist Muslim*, p. 165.
17. Beck, "The Rupture", p. 226.
18. Michael Francis Laffan, *Islamic Nationhood and Colonial Indonesia: The Umma below the Winds* (London: RoutledgeCurzon, 2003); Jajat Burhanuddin, "Islamic Knowledge, Authority and Political Power: The 'Ulama in Colonial Indonesia'" (PhD thesis, Universiteit Leiden, 2007); William R. Roff, *Studies on Islam and Society in Southeast Asia* (Singapore: NUS Press, 2009).
19. Blood, "The Ahmadiyah"; Michael R. Feener, "Cross-Cultural Contexts of Modern Muslim Intellectualism", *Die Welt Des Islam* 47, nos. 3–4 (2007): 264–82.
20. Blood, "The Ahmadiyah", pp. 5–6.
21. Kroef, "Recent Trends", p. 58.
22. Soekarno, "Tidak pertjaja bahwa Mirza Gulam Ahmad", p. 346.
23. Kroef, "Recent Trends", p. 58; Hasnul Arifin Melayu, "Islam and Politics in the Thought of Tjokroaminoto (1882–1934)" (MA thesis, McGill University, 2000), pp. 17–18.
24. Kevin W. Fogg, "Indonesian Islamic Socialism and its South Asian Roots", *Modern Asian Studies* (2 July 2019): 1–126, doi:10.1017/S0026749X17000646.
25. Moch Nur Ichwan, "Differing Responses to an Ahmadi Translation and Exegesis: The Holy Qur'ân in Egypt and Indonesia", *Archipel* 62 (2001): 143–61.
26. Kroef, "Recent Trends", p. 58.
27. "Ahmadiyah, sebuah titik yang dilupa", *Tempo*, 21 September 1974.
28. Kahfi, "Haji Agus Salim", p. 118.
29. Ibid., p. 118.
30. Ibid., p. 115; Yudi Latif, *Indonesian Muslim: Intelligentsia and Power* (Singapore: Institute of Southeast Asian Studies, 2008).
31. This translation follows Maulana Muhammad Ali, *English Translation of the Holy Quran with Explanatory Notes* (Wembley: Ahmadiyya Anjuman Lahore Publications, UK, 2010).

32. Dardiri Husni, "Jong Islamieten Bond: A Study of a Muslim Youth Movement in Indonesia during the Dutch Colonial Era, 1924–1942" (MA thesis, McGill University, 1998), p. 86.
33. Ibid.
34. Fazlur Rahman, "Islam: Challenges and Opportunities", in *Islam: Past Influence and Present Challenge*, edited by Alford T. Welch and Pierre Cachia, pp. 315–30 (Albany: State University of New York Press, 1979).
35. Ibid., p. 316
36. Ibid., pp. 321, 324.
37. Ibid., p. 324.
38. Soekarno, "Tidak pertjaja bahwa Mirza Gulam Ahmad", pp. 345–47.
39. Muhammad Yaqub Khan, *Het nut van God*, translated by Soedewo (Djokjakarta: Indonesische Ahmadijah Beweging, 1970).
40. Mirza Ghulam Ahmad, *De leerstellingen van den Islam: een oplossing van de vijf fundamenteele religieuze problemen uit Islamietisch oogpunt*, translated by Soedewo (Ahmadijah Beweging Indonesie, 1931).
41. His full name is Soedewo P.K. (Parto Kertodinegoro). He was born in Jember and became an active member of the JIB. See "The Late Raden Soedewo Parto Kertodinegoro: Translator into Dutch of Maulana Muhammad Ali's First Edition of the English Translation of the Holy Quran", http://www.muslim.org/activities/indonesia/soedewo.htm (accessed 20 August 2011); Soedewo, *Asas-asas dan pekerdjaan Gerakan Ahmadijah Indonesia (Centrum Lahore)*, translated into Malay by Sastrawiria (Soekaboemi: Gerakan Ahmadijah Indonesia [Centrum Lahore], 1937).
42. Moch Nur Ichwan, "Differing Responses", pp. 143–61.
43. Umar Said Tjokroaminoto, *Tarich agama Islam (riwajat dan pemandangan atas kehidoepan dan perdjalanan nabi Moehammad CLM* (Soerabaja, Abdul-Rehman Habib Patel, 1931).
44. Agus Salim, *Nabi Muhammad s.a.w.: tjeritera Isra' dan Mi'radj* (Djakarta, Tintamas, 1962).
45. Mohammad Natsir, *Marilah salat* (Djakarta: Bulan Bintang, 1960). See Zulkarnain, Iskandar, *Gerakan Ahmadiyah di Indonesia* (Yogyakarta: LKiS Yogyakarta, 2005), p. 280.
46. Zulkarnain, *Gerakan Ahmadiyah di Indonesia*, pp. 22, 233, 277.
47. Mirza Ghulam Ahmad, *De leerstellingen van den Islam*.
48. Muhammad Ali, *De religie van den Islām* (Batavia: Ahmadijah Beweging Indonesia, 1938).
49. Moehammad Ali, *De heilige Qoer-an: vervattende den Arabischen tekst met ophelderende aanteekeningen en voorrede van Maulwi Moehammed Ali*, translated by Soedewo (Batavia: Hoofdcomité Qoer-ânfonds, 1934).
50. The Dutch translation is not available to the present author.

51. "Ahmadiyah, sebuah titik yang dilupa", *Tempo*, 21 September 1974.
52. "Cak Roes, dari 'kapten' langsung...", *Tempo*, 27 December 1975.
53. Kamal-ud-Din, Khwaja, *The Sources of Christianity* (Columbus, OH: Ahmadiyya Anjuman Ishaat Islam [Lahore] USA, 1997), p. 11; Muhammad Ali, 'Preface', in *The Teachings of Islam: A Solution of Five Fundamental Religious Problems from the Muslim Point of View*, by Mirza Ghulam Ahmad (London: Luzac & Co, 1910), p. viii; Maulana Muhammad Ali, *The Holy Qur'ān: Arabic Text with English Translation and Commentary* (Columbus, OH: Ahmadiyya Anjuman Isha`at Islam Lahore Inc. USA, 2002), pp. 1–14.
54. Kamal-ud-Din, Khwaja, *The Secret of Existence* or *The Gospel of Action*, translated by Muhammad Yakub Khan (Woking: The Basheer Muslim Library, the Islamic Review Office, 1923), p. 11.
55. Ibid., p. 16.
56. Ibid., p. 17.
57. Muhammad Ali, *The Religion of Islam: A Comprehensive Discussion of the Sources, Principles and Practices of Islam* (Columbus, OH: Ahmadiyya Anjuman Ishaat Islam Lahore, 1995), p. 12.
58. Quotations of Ahmadiyah claims that Islam is compatible with modernity and reason can be found in James Thayer Addison, "The Ahmadiya Movement and Its Western Propaganda", *Harvard Theological Review* 22, no. 1 (1929): 26.
59. Khwaja Kamal-ud-Din, *The Secret of Existence*, pp. 12–13.
60. This is particularly true for the Lahore branch. For the Qadiani Ahmadiyah, this position is quite contradictory to its messianic belief and its reliance on dreams. With these kinds of beliefs it is actually difficult to categorize Qadiani Ahmadiyah as a modernist movement or as a pre-modernist revivalism movement. But if the examination on the position on messianism is directed to the Lahore Ahmadiyah, then it can be stated that Ahmadiyah is part of a modernist or revivalist movement. According to the Lahore Ahmadiyah, the messianic claim of Ghulam Ahmad was used to stop the hope and reliance of Muslims on the coming of the messiah, and to demonstrate that Jesus is not a superhuman who will descend to earth before the End of Days. As a human being, Jesus had died, and what would descend from heaven would not be Jesus in a physical sense, but rather it is meant to be understood in a metaphorical sense.
61. Zulkarnain, *Gerakan Ahmadiyah di Indonesia*, p. 245.
62. Ahmad Najib Burhani, "The Ahmadiyya and the Study of Comparative Religion in Indonesia: Controversies and Influences", *Islam and Christian-Muslim Relations* 25, no. 2 (2014): 141–58; Zulkarnain, *Gerakan Ahmadiyah di Indonesia*, pp. 278–80; "Ahmadiyah, sebuah titik yang dilupa", *Tempo*, 21 September 1974.

63. Chwadja-Kamal-Oed-Din, *De bronnen van het Christendom*, translated by Soedewo. (Djokjakarta: Ahmadijah Beweging Indonesië, 1930).
64. The Qadiani's concern with superstitious practice is mostly related to its efforts to clear the ground for their beliefs; namely, they want to restore the true and authentic teachings of Islam that were corrupted by Muslims since the beginning of Islam until the time of Mirza Ghulam Ahmad. Among the teachings corrupted by Muslims is the prophecy of the coming of Ghulam Ahmad as the Messiah.
65. They also show reverence to the grave of Mirza Ghulam Ahmad.
66. Mirza Mubarak Ahmad, *Ahmadiyyat in the Far East* (Rabwah, West Pakistan: Ahmadiyya Muslim Foreign Missions, 1964), p. 34.

Index

Note: Page numbers followed by "n" refer to endnotes

A

AAII. *See* Ahmadiyah Anjuman Isha'at Islam
Abbas Taha, Haji, 25
Abduh, Muhammad, 25, 206, 209
Abdulgani, Roeslan, 211
Abdullah Badawi, 5, 6, 119
Abou El Fadl, Khaled, 95
Aceh Freedom Movement. *See* Gerakan Aceh Merdeka (GAM)
Administration of Islamic Law, 168
Administration of Muslim Law Act (AMLA), 41, 56
Ahmad Abdullah, Syeikh, 25
Ahmad, Dzulfefly, 132
Ahmadiyah, 190, 191
   Arab-educated *vs.* Dutch-educated scholars, 203–7
   influences in Indonesia, 199–200, 207–13
   Islamic revivalism, 199, 215
   Lahore branch, 200
   receptive attitude towards in Indonesia, 200–203
Ahmadiyah Anjuman Isha'at Islam (AAII), 200
Ahmad, Kassim, 76
Ahmad, Mahmud, 70
Ahmad, Mirza Mubarak, 215
Ahmad, Muhammad Ariff, 70, 74, 75
Ahmad, Shahnon, 76
Ahmad, Zainal Abidin Bin, 73
ajaran sesat (deviant teachings), 41
Akyol, Mustafa, 127
al-Afghani, Jamal al-Din, 25, 98
Alatas, Syed Farid, 127
Alatas, Syed Hussein, 26, 77, 90, 102, 121
Al-Attas, Syed Muhammad Naquib, 5
Al-Azmeh, Aziz, 89
al-Banjari, Muhammad Arsyad, 161
Albar, Syed Hamid, 165
alcohol consumption, by Muslim youth, 24
al-Hadi, Syed Sheikh, 70, 71, 72
Ali, Abdul Mukti, 199
Aliran Kebatinan, 184
Aliran Kepercayaan, 184
Alisjahbana, Sutan Takdir, 73
al-Kalali, Sheikh Muhammad Salim, 25
al-Minangkabawi Khatib, Sheikh Ahmad, 24–25
Al-Qaradawi, Yusof, 129

American Muslim communities, 96
Aminurashid, Harun, 70
AMLA. *See* Administration of Muslim Law Act (AMLA)
Ampera, Kapitra, 145, 146
Amrullah, Sheikh Abdul Karim, 25
Anak Panglima Awang (1961), 73
An'Naim, Abdullahi, 29, 95
Anwar, Chairil, 73
Anwar, Zainah, 29, 126, 127
Arab-educated *vs.* Dutch-educated scholars, 203–7
Arabism, in Singapore, 59
arabization, 6, 118
Asha'arism, 156–57
Asnawi, Ahmadi, 160
Association of Women Lawyers (AWL), 125
atheism, 39, 148, 210, 215
Awang, Usman, 72, 76
AWL. *See* Association of Women Lawyers (AWL)
Ayub, Nisha, 132

B
Babu Sahid, Moulavi M.H., 26
Badawi, Abdullah Ahmad, 131, 179n46
Bakor Pakem, 191, 197n37
Bangsa Melayu Singapura Dalam Transformasi Budayanya (Suratman Markasan), 26
Barisan Nasional government, 12, 119
Barton, Greg, 13
Berger, Peter L., 17
bineka (diversity) citizenship, 187, 194
Birth of Jesus in the Light of the Qur'an (Basharat Ahmad), 210
Bisri, Mustofa, 141
Boff, Leonardo, 95

Buang, Saedah, 80
Buehler, Michael, 143
Bush, George W., 6

C
CASIS. *See* Centre for Advanced Studies on Islam, Science, and Civilisation (CASIS)
'Catholic' Islam, 111
Centre for Advanced Studies on Islam, Science, and Civilisation (CASIS), 5
CEP. *See* Council of Eminent Persons (CEP)
Chopp, Rebecca S., 95
Christianity, 209, 210–11
civilizational Islam, 120
civil law, 56, 57
civil society organizations (CSOs), 12, 147
    IKRAM Foundation, 12–13
    Kairos Dialogue Network, 13–15
    Projek Dialog, 11–12
Committee for Islamic Institutional Reforms, 159
Communist Party of Indonesia (PKI), 191
conservatism, 11, 15, 40, 118, 142–46, 149–51
Constitutional Court, 184, 186, 187, 191, 192
Council of Eminent Persons (CEP), 159
Crescent Star Party, 146
customary law, 186, 189

D
Dahlan, Kyai Hj Ahmad, 25

DDII. *See* Dewan Dakwah Islamiyah Indonesia (DDII)

Decline of Liberalism as an Ideology, The (Hallowell), 93
Defending Islam Act, 139
Department of Islamic Development Malaysia (JAKIM), 118, 119, 122, 126
Dewan Dakwah Islamiyah Indonesia (DDII), 213
Dingemans, L.F., 201
divorce in Islam, 204
Djojosoegito, R. Ng., 202

E
Eck, Diana L., 17
"Een Ereschuld" (debt of honour), 201
Embong, Ghazali, 163
Engineer, Asghar Ali, 29
Ethical Policy, 201, 202
European Muslims, 18

F
Faisal Tehrani, 6
Faruqi, Ismail, 5
Faruqi, Shad Saleem, 121, 159
Fealy, Greg, 140, 141
Federal Constitution, 160
Federal Territories Religious Department (JAWI), 127
Freedom Papua Organization. *See* Organisasi Papua Merdeka (OPM)
Fromm, Erich, 67

G
Gabungan Bertindak Malaysia (GBM), 13
GAI. *See* Gerakan Ahmadiyah Indonesia (GAI)
Gandhi, Indira, 167, 171
Gerakan Aceh Merdeka (GAM), 193
Gerakan Ahmadiyah Indonesia (GAI), 200
Ghulam Ahmad, Mirza, 200, 205, 210, 211
Golkar Party, 21
Gospel of Action, The (Kamal-ud-Din), 205, 211
Gul, Abdullah, 127
Gutiérrez, Gustavo, 95

H
halal, 4–5, 19, 34, 57
Halida, Rizka, 144
Halil, Rasiah, 70, 80
Hallowell, John H., 93
Hamid, A. Ghani, 78
Hamzah, Amir, 73
haram, 19, 160
Harmony Bill, 191
Hashemi, Nader, 95
Hassan, Ibrahim Azmi, 162
Hassan, Ustaz Ahmad, 26
Het Licht (journal), 207
hibah ruqbah (rukbah-gift), 46
Himpunan Mahasiswa Indonesia (HMI), 40
HINDRAF. *See* Hindu Rights Action Force (HINDRAF)
Hindu Rights Action Force (HINDRAF), 6
Hisyam, Usama, 145
Hizbut Tahrir Indonesia (HTI), 146–47
HMI. *See* Himpunan Mahasiswa Indonesia (HMI)
Holy Qur'an, The (Muhammad Ali), 210
humanism, 76–81
Human Rights Commission of Malaysia (SUHAKAM), 164
human rights issues in Indonesia

hierarchy and discrimination, 189–92
political identity and populism, 184–87
Hussin, Zaleha, 163

I
Ibn 'Abd al-Wahhab, Muhammad, 111
Ibn Khaldun's socio-historical method, 103
ICCR. *See* International Covenant on Civil and Political Rights (ICCR)
ICERD. *See* International Convention on the Elimination of All Forms of Racial Discrimination (ICERD)
Idenburg, A.W.F., 201
IFSO. *See* International Federation of Students Organisations (IFSO)
IIUM. *See* International Islamic University of Malaysia (IIUM)
ijtihad (reasoning), 26
IKRAM (IKRAM Foundation Malaysia), 12–13
Indonesia
  Ahmadiyah Community, 200
  changing religious-political landscape, 140–42
  civil society organizations, 147
  conservatism, 142, 150
  democracy and conservatism, 149–52
  elections and intolerance, 143–46
  Hizbut Tahrir Indonesia, 146–47
  Indonesian Ulama Council, 139, 145
  Jakarta gubernatorial election (2017), 143
  literary scene, 73
  Muhammadiyah, 141
  Nahdlatul Ulama, 141
  National Awakening Party, 141
  non-Muslims, 144
  Nusantara Islam, 59
  Pancasila *vs.* Islamists, 146–49
  Perppu Ormas, 147
  pornography bill, 148
  post-1998 democratization, 140
  presidential election of 2019, 140
  religious education, 151
  religious intolerance, 144
  212 movement, 145–47
  Yudhoyono, Susilo Bambang, 143
Indonesian Democratic Party of Struggle, 145
Indonesian Islamic Propagation Council, 213
Indonesian Muslim organizations, 142
Indonesian Ulama Council (MUI), 139, 145
Institute of the Malay World and Civilization (ATMA), 124
Institutional Reforms Committee (IRC), 159
Intellectuals in Developing Societies, 92
International Convention on the Elimination of All Forms of Racial Discrimination (ICERD), 7, 12, 131
International Covenant on Civil and Political Rights (ICCR), 169, 188
International Federation of Students Organisations (IFSO), 40
International Institute of Islamic Thought and Civilization (ISTAC), 5
International Islamic University of Malaysia (IIUM), 126
inter-religious marriage, 39, 142
Iranian revolution of 1979, 4, 40, 161

Index

IRC. *See* Institutional Reforms Committee (IRC)
IRF. *See* Islamic Renaissance Front (IRF)
ISIS. *See* Islamic State in Iraq and Syria (ISIS)
Islam Berkemajuan (Modern Islam), 120
Islam Hadhari (Civilizational Islam), 5, 120
Islam Nusantara (Archipelagic Islam), 120
Islam Wasatiyyah (Moderate Islam), 120
Islamic Boarding School Foundation, 213
Islamic discourse in Malaysia, 119–27
  "arabization", 118
  foreign speakers, 127–29
  Islamic institutions, 122–23
  Islamic NGOs, 118
  Pakatan Harapan government, 119
  reforms, 129–33
  religious bureaucracy, 118, 133
  universities, 133
Islamic education, 42
Islamic Institute of Thought and Civilisation (ISTAC), 126
Islamic law, 49, 93, 98, 103
Islamic Party of Malaysia (PAS), 130
"Islamic Protestantism", 112
Islamic reform, 24, 72
Islamic religious literature, 24
Islamic Renaissance Front (IRF), 11, 119, 124
Islamic Resurgence in Malaysia (Chandra Muzaffar), 3
Islamic revivalism
  early twentieth century, 199

  Fazlur Rahman's categorization of, 214
  in Indonesia, 200, 204–5, 215
1979 Islamic Revolution, 157, 158
Islamic State in Iraq and Syria (ISIS), 120
Islamism, 4, 111, 145
Islamization, 28, 42
"Islam on slavery", 204
Islams and Modernities (Al-Azmeh), 89
Islam, Songkok dan Bahasa (Maarof Salleh), 26
Ismail, A. Samad, 72
Ismail, Hamed, 70
ISTAC. *See* Islamic Institute of Thought and Civilisation (ISTAC)

J

Jaafariyyahs, 160, 163, 165
JAI. *See* Jemaat Ahmadiyah Indonesia (JAI)
Jakarta Charter, 35
Jakarta gubernatorial election (2017), 143
JAKIM (Department of Islamic Development Malaysia), 5, 7
Jalaluddin, Sheikh Tahir, 25, 70–72
Jamaluddin al-Afghani, 25
Jaringan Islam Liberal (JIL), 128
Jemaah Islamiah (JI), 120
Jemaat Ahmadiyah Indonesia (JAI), 200
JIB. *See* Jong Islamieten Bond (JIB)
"Jihad in Islam", 204
JIL. *See* Jaringan Islam Liberal (JIL)
Joko Widodo (Jokowi), 145, 146, 147, 150, 184, 193
Jomo, Kwame Sundaram, 159

Jong Islamieten Bond (JIB), 203, 206, 207

K
Kairos Dialogue Network (KDN), 13–15
Kamali, M. Hashim, 95, 121
Kamal-ud-Din, Khwaja, 209, 211
Kamaluddin, Mohd Zuki, 164
Kamari, Isa, 70, 80
KDN. *See* Kairos Dialogue Network (KDN)
Khan, Muqtader, 95
Khomeini, Ayatollah, 130
Koening, Matthias, 186, 188, 192

L
Latiff-Mohamed, Mohamed, 70, 78
LGBT issues, 132
Lukacs, George, 68
Lutfi, Ahmad, 26, 70, 71

M
Maaruf, Shaharuddin, 35, 37, 77
Madjid, Nurcholis, 59
madrasah education, 34, 42, 43–44, 44, 45
Mahathir Mohamad, 3, 5, 6, 15, 119
Mahendra, Yuzril Ihza, 146
Majid, Nurcholish, 95
Malay Muslim community, 28, 83, 85
Malay/Muslim religious discourse in Singapore, 22
  predominance of religious traditionalists, 23–24
  religious reforms in history, 24–27
  revivalists' criticism, 27–29
Malaysia
  Arabization, 6
  Chinese minority in, 41
  Christian-Muslim relations in, 14
  civil society organizations, 12
  halal certification, 5
  IMAN, 10
  Islamic institutions, 4
  Islamization of modern sciences, 5
  non-Muslim groups, 7
  politics of islamic discourse in, 3–8
  population, 9
  post-Islamic revivalism, 4
  poverty in, 9
  radicalization, 6
  religiosity in, 3, 11
  security threats, 6
  state responses to Islamization, 5–8
  women in, 10
Malaysian Federal constitution, 34
Malaysian Islamic universities, 5
Malaysian Muslim Solidarity (ISMA), 12
Malaysian United Indigenous Party, 131
Malik, Maszlee, 132
Mannheim, Karl, 94
Markasan, Suratman, 26, 70, 74, 78
marriage laws, 40
Mas, Keris, 72, 76
Masuri S.N., 70, 74, 78
matrimonial property, 46, 56, 57
Maznah, Sharifah, 77, 80
Menk, Mufti, 51
Merdeka Centre, 10
Mietzner, Marcus, 143, 144
Mihardja, Achdiat, 73
Minah Joget Moden (1968), 73
Moderate Islam, 120
"Moderation in the Quran" (forum), 128–29
Moosa, Ebrahim, 103
Moussalli, Ahmad, 95
Mufti Menk, 52
Muhammad Haniff, Hassan, 95

Muhammadiyah, 25, 26, 141, 203, 214
Muhammad the Prophet (Muhammad Ali), 209
Muhtadi, Burhanuddin, 143, 144
Muis, 29, 43–46, 53, 54, 56
Musa, Faizal, 119
Musa, Mohd Farouk, 126
Muslim law, 45, 50, 56
Muslims
    Administration of Muslim Law Act, 41
    Christian-Muslim relations, 14
    European, 18
    Fellowship of Muslim Students Association, 28
    Indian Muslim community, 26
    Islamophobia—anti-Muslim sentiments, 17
    matrimonial issues, 56–57
    modern education, 42
    and non-Muslims, 7, 15, 34, 49, 50, 51
    reformism, 25, 28
    religious resurgence, 18
    sanctity of *hudud*, 47
    "tauhidic (monotheistic) worldview", 42–43
    World Assembly of Muslim Youth, 40
Muzaffar, Chandra, 3, 29, 121, 127
Myth of the Lazy Native, The (Syed Hussein Alatas), 94

N
Nahdlatul Ulama (NU), 141, 203
Naik, Zakir, 15, 51, 129
Najib Razak government, 6, 7, 119, 123
Nashir, Haedar, 141
Nasir, Bachtiar, 146

National Awakening Party (PKB), 141
National Fatwa Committee, 124, 164, 165
National Fatwa Council (NFC), 160
National Trust Party, 131
National University of Malaysia (UKM), 124
Natsir, Mohammad, 210
NFC. *See* National Fatwa Council (NFC)
Ngabalin, Ali Mochtar, 146
9/11 attacks, 5, 33, 51
Noer, Deliar, 199
non-Muslims, 15, 49, 51
NU. *See* Nahdlatul Ulama (NU)
Nusantara Islam, 59

O
Office of the United Nations High Commissioner for Human Rights (OHCHR), 170
On Politics (Ibn Khaldun), 110
Organisasi Papua Merdeka (OPM), 193
Othman, Abdul Hamid, 165

P
Pakatan Harapan government, 15, 119, 173
Pak Lah. *See* Abdullah Badawi
Pancasila *vs.* Islamists, 146–49
Panglima Awang (1958), 73
Penghulu yang Hilang Segala-galanya (1998), 75
Persatuan Islam, 203
Pertubuhan Jamaah Islah Malaysia (JIM), 12
Pesta Filem KITA 2, 12
Pesta Puisi Kota, 12
PNPS Act of 1965, 186, 189–91, 194
Prabowo Subianto, 143

Primary School Leaving
    Examinations (PSLE), 43
Progressive Islam
    anti-Milton-Friedman pleas, 106
    articulation of, 95–96
    asabiya, 104
    badawi-hadari dichotomy, 104–5
    business and trade, 109
    captive mind, 100–101
    "circle of justice", 110
    civilizational and religious
        traditions, 112
    *Decline of Liberalism as an Ideology,
        The* (Hallowell), 93
    description, 91, 94–95, 97
    exoteric-esoteric continuum,
        99–100
    feudal values, 102
    freedom-coercion continuum, 100
    Ibn Khaldun's socio-historical
        method, 103
    inclusive-exclusive continuum, 99
    Intellectuals in Developing Societies
        (Syed Hussein Alatas), 92
    internal-external continuum, 99
    Islamic humanism, 95
    Islamic law, 93–94
    Islams and Modernities (Al-Azmeh),
        89
    knowledge-practice continuum, 98
    "the middle way", 97
    Myth of the Lazy Native, The, 94
    nationalist-imperialist continuum,
        100
    nativism-orientalism continuum,
        98
    nomadic and sedentary social
        organization, 104
    non-rational-rational continuum,
        100
    private investment, 105–6

"Regeneration of Islamic Societies,
    The", 91
social justice, 95
socio-historical context, 101, 102
tradition-modernity continuity, 99
and Western traditions, 94
worldly-otherworldly continuum,
    100
Projek Dialog, 11–12
PSLE. *See* Primary School Leaving
    Examinations (PSLE)
Putri, Megawati Soekarno, 194

Q
Qaradhawi, 48, 52
Quraysh (tribe), 103

R
Rafaat Hamzah, 80
Rafaat, Othman Effendi, 26
Rahmat, Hadijah, 76, 80
Rais, Hishamuddin, 133
Ramadan, Tariq, 18, 29
Rasmin, Zaytun, 146
Rawa, Mujahid, 132
Razak, Najib Abdul, 123, 131, 165–67
"Regeneration of Islamic Societies,
    The" (editorial), 91
religious consciousness, in Indonesia,
    17, 18
    civilizational orientation, 21
    economic orientation, 19–20
    ideological orientation, 20
    political orientation, 18–19
Religious Harmony Bill, 183
riba (usury), 19
Rida, Rashid, 206, 209
*Risalah Penting pada Mas'alah Jilatan
    Anjing di atas Empat-empat
    Madzhab* (Abbas), 25–26

Index

S
Sabu, Mohamad, 132
Sachedina, Abdulaziz, 95
Salafism, 20, 35, 59, 118, 129
Salim, H. Agus, 205, 210
Salleh Abas, 167
Salleh, Maarof, 26
Samad, Khalid, 132
Secret of Existence, The, 209, 211
secularism, 36, 37, 42, 49
Sedition and Public Order Act, 164
Sekolah Diniyyah al-Islamiyyah, 25
Sharia Criminal Offences Act, 168
Sharom, Azmi, 127
Shihab, Rizieq, 149
Siddiqui, Maulana Abdul Aleem, 26
Singapore
    antagonism against Shias, 55
    Arabism in, 59
    freedom of religion, 49
    Indian Muslim community, 26
    inhibited reformist voices in, 22
    Islamic religious literature, 24
    madrasah education, 42, 44
    multiculturalism in, 54
    reformist Islamic ideas, 23, 24
    resurgence discourse, 35
    socio-economic conditions, 38
    as transit centre for pilgrimage to Mecca, 24
Singapore Islamic Scholars and Religious Teachers Association (PERGAS), 41, 53, 56, 64n36
Singapore Malay literary scene, 67–85
    academic setting, 73
    articulations, 69–70
    challenges, 67
    cultural planning and vision, 82–83
    ethno-chauvinists, 72
    humanism, 76–81
    indigenous history, 73
    Islamic reformist ideas, 72
    Lutfi's vocal criticism, 71
    Malay teaching fraternities, 73
    post-separation literary development, 74–76
    poverty and social disruption, 74
    progressive ideas, 69, 85
    prominent writers, 70
    reformists, 71
    religious traditionalism and obscurantism, 68
Singapore Shariah Board of Appeal, 48
Siradj, Said Aqil, 141
Sirry, Munim, 119, 128
Sisters in Islam (SIS), 11, 119, 123, 124
Soedewo P.K., 210
Sources of Christianity, The, 209, 213
Southeast Asian Network of Civil Society Organisations (SEAN-CSO), 13
Special Autonomy Law, 184, 189
Sukarti, Ahmad, 24
Sunnah, 39, 47
Sunni-Shia reconciliation, 156–59
    after GE14, 159–61
    characteristic of rebelliousness, 158
    fear towards Shias in 1996, 161–65
    Islamic Revolution in Iran of 1979, 157
    Ottoman Empire, 158–59
    Pakatan Harapan government, 173
    remedies and challenges, 167–72
    Shias under Najib Razak, 166–67
Suratman's literary repertoire, 75
Syed Sheikh al-Hady, 25, 26

T
Taha, Haji Abbas, 70
Tahir, Sheikh Muhammad, 25
Tak Ada Jalan Keluar (1962), 74

Tambak Minda: Mengamat Perkembangan Islam Semasa (Maarif Salleh), 26
taqlid (absolute imitation), 26
Teachings of Islam, The, 210, 211
Tehrani, Faizal, 124
Teik, Pang Khee, 132
Tengku Maimun Tuan Mat, 160
Thohari, Hajriyanto, 21
Tjokroaminoto, H.O.S., 205, 210
Toer, Pramoedya Ananta, 73
Trump, Donald, 184
Tukimin, Djamal, 78
212 movement, 145–47

U
Ulama Council of Indonesia (MUI), 19
Ulil Abshar-Abdallah, 29, 95, 119
UN General Assembly, 188
Unitary State of the Republic of Indonesia Based on Sharia, The, 149
University Sains Islam Malaysia (USIM), 133
Uthman El Muhammady, 126

V
van Bruinessen, Martin, 141, 151
van der Kroef, Justus M., 204, 205
Van Deventer, C. Th., 201

W
Wahhabism, 35, 59, 118, 129
Wahid, Abdurrahman, 59
WAMY. *See* World Assembly of Muslim Youth (WAMY)
Westernization, 42
Westminster-style parliamentary system, 9
Wibisono, Jusuf, 206
Wicktorowicz, Quintan, 20
Wilders, Geertz, 17
"Women from Judaism to Islam", 204
World Assembly of Muslim Youth (WAMY), 40

Y
Yang di-Pertuan Agong, 122, 131, 181n62
YAPI. *See* Yayasan Pesantren Islam (YAPI)
Yapp, Eugene, 14
Yaqub Khan, Muhammad, 209
Yayasan Pesantren Islam (YAPI), 213
Yudhoyono, Susilo Bambang, 143, 144, 183, 190
　　accommodation of Islamic conservatives, 144, 150
　　anti-pornography bill, 145
Yusof, Zaleha, 160

Z
Zaidiyyahs, 156, 160, 163, 165